HOW TO

SELL *Your*
HOME
Fast
in ANY MARKET

For the Most Money Possible

**6 Reasons Why Your Home Isn't Selling…
And What You Can Do To Fix Them**

Loren K. Keim

Gideon Publications

First Edition: 2019

Published by Gideon Publications
2299 Brodhead Road Suite J
Bethlehem PA 18020

This publication is designed to provide accurate and authoritative information in regard to the subject matter covered. It is sold with the understanding that the publisher is not engaged in rendering legal, accounting, or other professional service. If legal advice or other expert assistance is required, the services of a competent professional person shall be sought.

This product is not a substitute for legal advice.

ISBN 978-0-578-54870-8

To my wife Theresa, always

Acknowledgements

I would like to acknowledge my wife, Theresa, and our children, Bridgett, Caitlin, Logan, and Kourtney, for putting up with my twelve-hour workdays and my hectic writing schedule.

I also acknowledge my parents, Loren and Geri Keim, for everything they have done for me over the years. Without their support, nothing I've done would be possible.

I would also like to thank my team and staff at CENTURY 21 Keim Realtors for helping to create a great and fun environment to work in, and my co-workers at Lehigh University's Goodman Center for Real Estate for their continued support and invaluable advice.

Contents

Introduction to Selling Your Home

Even in the best markets where homes are selling in just days or hours, some homes just do not sell. Any good psychologist will tell you that the stages of grief begin with denial. Many homeowners go into a state of denial if their home doesn't sell as quickly as their expectations: *Of course, my home will sell. My neighbor's home sold last year in only two days, and he had three offers, and his home certainly isn't as nice as mine! I had extra insulation installed and included hose bibs on both sides of my house!*

The next stage of grief is anger: *It's that Realtor's fault my home isn't selling. She couldn't advertise her way out of a paper bag! And what was she thinking with those shoes?*

When the initial version of this book was first published, the country had just experienced a huge run-up in homes prices from 2005 through 2007 followed by a dramatic slowdown that drove many home prices across the country into freefall. Some areas of the country experienced a real estate marketplace where fewer than half the homes on the market sold during their initial listing period. Homeowners hired staging companies, made price reductions, and even buried statues of Saint Joseph in their yards to improve their odds of selling.

While the market is humming in many parts of the country today, there are still homes that are not selling, and there is no guarantee of when the market cycle will once again make that shift that we all dread.

If you're in the market to sell a home today, whether the market is strong or soft, you must carefully position your home for the market in which you are trying to sell.

If your home is not selling, you need to get past the denial and anger stages and move toward acceptance of the steps you need to take to sell your home and get the most money in your required time frame.

This book will provide you with the steps necessary to deal with the sale of your home in any market. We will examine the primary reasons homes do not sell and how you can overcome them. Then we will examine parts of the home sale process step by step and show you where you might be able to improve your odds of selling more quickly and obtaining a higher sales price. The last sections of this book are dedicated to desperation measures for those trying to sell their homes in significant recessionary real estate markets. These methods include auctions, lease options, second mortgages, and other similar measures.

In every market in the country, there are specific reasons homes do not sell. Even when an area is experiencing a major economic downturn, or when competition is fierce for the buyers in the marketplace, there are still homes selling. You want to make sure that yours is not one of the unlucky ones, and you want to get it sold for the most money possible in a reasonable period of time.

Even in the worst markets in the worst economic times, homes *do* sell. In almost every market there are people who need to buy or sell. These people face job transfers, relocations, divorces, deaths, and moves from apartments into first homes. Our goal is to tap into the available pool of buyers and get your house sold.

In most markets, there are three primary components to selling a house, and none of them are "location, location, location." Even in the poorest locations, homes sell. The three components are *pricing, marketing*, and *staging*. In the worst location in town, if a property is offered for sale for a dollar, someone will buy it very quickly. The question we must ask is: *What is the maximum price you can receive for your home in the time frame that you need to receive it?*

My team has spent over twenty-five years studying sales patterns and marketing techniques. We have determined that there are six major reasons a home does not sell:

1. poor staging;

2. incorrect pricing;

3. improper marketing;

4. location-challenged properties;

5. functionally obsolete properties;

6. "no one is buying in the area!"

Reason #1: Poor Staging

Staging a home correctly may be the critical difference between selling and not selling in any real estate market. The most interesting dynamic I have found in working with home sellers for a quarter century is that very few home sellers are willing to do anything to the home they are selling in order to achieve top dollar for the property. When someone sells a car, on the other hand, he or she typically vacuums, washes, and waxes it, and may even tune it up, change the oil, or clean the engine. He or she does this in order to get the highest price when he or she sells the car. A home may be the owner's most valuable asset and is certainly more valuable than an automobile, yet most homeowners do not want to take the time and effort to maximize the return on their investment. A real estate trainer once told me that a gallon of paint may cost thirty dollars, but when applied correctly, it is worth $2,000 in the price of the home.

Over the years, we have worked with many investors who would *fix and flip* properties. Basically, they would buy a home that was outdated, spray the interior white, put in cheap wall-to-wall carpeting, replace some light fixtures, and maybe replace or reface the kitchen cabinets, and they would earn a return on their investment ranging from 10% to 50%.

As a home seller, you may also be competing directly against new construction. Many builders of new homes understand that buyers purchase what looks pretty, while sellers of previously built homes may say, *"They don't build homes like mine anymore. New construction is junk. I have real plaster walls!"* Unfortunately, very few buyers understand quality, and very few buyers want to do any work on a property they buy.

Reason #2: Incorrect Pricing

Pricing a property too high or too low can keep the home from selling. In a world of Internet searches, pricing can be a critical component in obtaining the showings that are necessary to sell your home. You are also likely to be competing against other homes for sale in the market and possibly even new construction, which is preferred by many buyers. You need to price your home correctly to position or leverage it against the competition.

Real estate agents can assist you with pricing your property, but these same experts may also be a detriment in determining the best listing price. Realtors® have learned, from years of experience, that home sellers typically hire the agent that provides them the highest suggested list price. This is most unfortunate. Home sellers tend to price their homes emotionally, and some Realtors® understand this and play on it in order to obtain the listing. Why do they do this? Because the more signs an agent puts up, the more buyer calls they receive and the more homes they sell. Additionally, if an agent can lock you into a listing contract, they hope that you will eventually agree to come down in price over time to a point where the home will sell. Other agents may be unrealistically optimistic, and others are simply inexperienced. Not all agents inflate prices in order to list homes, but too many successful ones do.

Pricing must be objective: *I put $3,000 into that landscaping, put in brand-new stainless-steel appliances in the kitchen, and had to replace the furnace last year, so I expect to get that back in my sales price.* Buyers, on the other hand, compare homes based on their current location and amenities. What you spent to purchase and improve the house has no bearing on what a buyer is willing to pay for it. If a home is overpriced from the beginning of the listing term, it may become stigmatized and avoided by buyers and Realtors®.

Reason #3: Improper Marketing

There are benefits to a homeowner marketing a home him- or herself, and there are benefits to hiring a professional real estate firm to market the home. Real estate brokers and agents have more tools in their tool belts to target and market a home to prospective buyers. However, too many brokers and agents list a property without putting any serious effort into marketing it. The agent will enter the home into the *multiple listing system* (MLS) and go on to the next listing. In a slow market, putting a sign on the property, entering it into the MLS, and entering the listing on Zillow and other online services may not be enough to attract the highest price for the property.

As the owner of the property, with or without an agent, you need to take charge and design a full marketing program to attract those ready, willing, and able buyers to your door. Any area has groups of likely buyers. A good marketing program includes directly targeting the most likely buyer of a product, so any marketing program to sell your home should include a way to identify and target those likely prospects.

Reason #4: Location-Challenged Properties

Some properties do have specific location issues, such as being at the end of an airport runway, backing up to a major highway, or having train tracks running through the backyard. A unique property will often require a unique buyer.

While some properties appeal to a large percentage of home buyers, others do not. A typical two-story colonial home with four bedrooms, two and a half baths, and a two-car garage will fit the dream home description of most families. A home next to the community sewage treatment plant with no yard but plenty of flies does not. There is hope, however.

Just like any other property, most location-challenged homes need to be staged correctly, marketed to the most likely target audiences, and priced appropriately *for the location*. An investor may see the potential in buying a location-challenged property and renting it to obtain a return. Some savvy real estate agents and home sellers find ways to make the property useful to the neighboring properties and sell to a neighbor. A local quarry may pay for a neighboring property in order to house their offices. This type of sale takes research, skilled marketing, and the proper presentation.

Reason #5: Functionally Obsolete Properties

Over the past twenty years, my team has actually sold two properties that *still* did not have indoor plumbing. The owners had lived in the properties for many years and saw no need to invest in indoor plumbing when they had a well and an outhouse that worked just fine, and seriously we sell real estate ninety minutes outside Manhattan. As with location-challenged properties, functionally obsolete properties have a much narrower market appeal. Challenge properties include one-bedroom homes, uninsulated homes, homes with indoor streams, tiny homes under six hundred square feet, homes with undersized lots, or homes with cisterns or cesspools.

Despite these challenges, the home's highest and best use may be found by tearing the home down and starting over, adding onto the house, or changing the use of the property to something more appropriate to fit the dwelling or the property. However, few home buyers are willing to put the time or effort into adapting a property to their needs.

To realize the highest return on the property, the home seller may need to adapt, rebuild, or add onto the property prior to selling. The home seller may not have the means or the fortitude to accomplish these tasks and may need to either obtain backing from a partner or sell to an investor who will make the appropriate changes.

Reason #6: "No one is buying in the area!"

While this is rarely the case, there are areas where a very small number of properties sell each year. Slow sales in these areas are generally due to a lack of job opportunities. As I write this book, our team recently listed a home in central Pennsylvania, only two-and-a-half hours from New York City. The home is a single, detached home with three bedrooms, one-and-a-half baths, a fenced yard, and a two-car garage, and it is priced at $44,900. No, I'm not kidding. It's really priced at $44,900. Some of you from metropolitan areas are flipping back to the beginning of this book to check the publication date.

In Pennsylvania's coal mining towns, whole cities declined as the primary source of work in the area closed. Similar situations can be found across the country. Even in these locations, some homes do sell. Investors may buy homes in hopes that a resurgence in the area will happen at a future date. Residents remain working in service positions, such as the local grocery store, gas station, or bank. Some retired couples move back to the town of their roots, and others find the towns quaint and telecommute to work in a bigger city.

When a home is located in a significantly declining area, you may have to turn to aggressive marketing methods, such as auctions, lease options, and seller-held second mortgages in order to get the property sold. These methods and examples will be discussed in Chapter 6.

The Steps to a Successful Sale

We are a society of immediate gratification. The typical homeowner decides he or she wants to sell, and immediately calls a real estate agent or puts a sign in the yard. Sometimes a homeowner looks at move-up homes for sale first, makes an offer on one, and then decides to sell his or her home quickly. After all, the home will sell with no problem because homes in his or her particular neighborhood always sell quickly, right?

Selling a home in a reasonable time frame, without leaving thousands of dollars on the table when you sell, requires planning. First determine if you truly want to sell and move. What is your motivation? Do you need to move right now, or is it a whim? This information will affect the pricing of your home and the time at which you put it on the market for sale. When do you want to move by? How long does it take to sell the average home in your area? What is the average time from the sale of a home to closing in your area? Timing can be very important to understand in order to keep your stress level at a minimum. Moving is one of the most stressful events in your life, ranking close to death and divorce. If you do not plan for a typical marketing period, you will find yourself frustrated and not thinking clearly. We will discuss timing in Chapter 3.

Once you have decided that you want or need to move, before calling a Realtor® or hammering a sign in your front yard you will need to consider the appeal of your home. Look at your home from a buyer's perspective and enhance the appeal so that you are not just selling a 30-year-old home, but a buyer's dream of lifestyle. You need to differentiate your home from others that are competing for buyers in the same marketplace. That requires home staging that we will outline in Chapter 1.

As you are contemplating what needs to be touched up, modernized, or neutralized in your home, you can begin investigating property values. That doesn't mean basing your decision on a Zestimate®! I highly recommend getting assistance from professionals like a Realtor® and possibly an appraiser. I also recommend that you take the time to view the other homes that are currently for sale and competing with yours. Keep an eye out for open houses and view the homes as objectively as possible. Determine what kind of cash you need to get out of the home in order to make your move. We will go through property pricing in detail in Chapter 3.

Only after you have carefully carried out your home staging and contemplated the likely sales price and cash you will receive in selling should you seriously interview Realtors® for the position of marketing your home. View each Realtor® critically and ask questions about their marketing plans, servicing of their clients, commission rates, and track record. Remember that you should never select an agent based on the list price they suggest. Sample questions to ask a real estate agent can be found in Chapter 4.

After you select a Realtor®, work with him or her to determine the best marketing programs available to get your home in front of the maximum number of potential buyers. Ask for his or her suggestions for any additional home staging and showing techniques.

Next you will either be overwhelmed and frustrated by the number of potential buyers walking through your house, opening your closets, and looking at your stuff, or you will be frustrated because you are not getting much activity on the home. Ask your agent for complete feedback on the showings and reassess where you are in the process. Find out what buyers liked about your home, what they did not like, what they would suggest changing for a quicker sale, and what they think of the price. You may have to make adjustments to the staging or the price, depending on the response.

When you receive an offer on your home, use the Purchase Agreement Analyzer in Chapter 9 to determine the pros and cons of the offer. What are the conditions, inspections, or contingencies of the offer? Then use our tips and techniques to prepare a counteroffer for the buyers and, with the help of your agent, negotiate to obtain the best contract possible.

Once the agreement is signed, homeowners begin to relax, their stress subsiding; however, there are plenty of issues that can crop up while under contract. Whatever can go wrong *will* go wrong. Be aware of the possible problems and be prepared to negotiate or find solutions to fix them. We will outline several such possible situations in Chapter 8.

Whether you are reading this book to prepare your home for the market, or you have had your home on the market and you are trying to determine why it is not selling, you are concerned about selling your home for a reasonable price in a reasonable amount of time. Following this step-by-step guide will help you avoid the common pitfalls of a real estate transaction.

chapter one:

Staging Your Home for Top Dollar

A few years ago, a client came into my office with a problem. His home had been on the market for almost two years without selling. He had tried four different real estate companies and a variety of marketing programs and nothing was working. His prior Realtors® kept trying to get him to lower his price, believing that was the only solution to selling the home, but he owed too much to bring the home down to the level his most recent Realtor® had suggested. His job transfer was only weeks away, and he was desperate for help.

Before I went to the property, I looked over the listing information and it appeared to be a very nice home that was priced correctly based on the current real estate market— it had over four thousand square feet of living space on two acres of land with an in-ground pool. It was actually quite a package for the price compared to other similar properties in the area. When I arrived at the home, I determined the problem was not the asking price, but rather the staging of the home.

The home was intentionally hidden by huge trees in front to obscure the home from the road. While this accomplished the owner's goal of having privacy and seclusion from curious eyes, it did not fit with most buyers' desire to have a sharp curb appeal.

Walking into the home felt like walking back in time. Although this was an extremely well-constructed home, it was built in 1969 and the decorating was original. While buyers will overlook some things and are usually willing to do some redecorating to their tastes—in terms of the paint color on the walls or the color of the carpets—almost no buyer will purchase a home he or she feels needs to be completely remodeled unless he or she gets a true premium on the price.

Upon first entering the home, a potential buyer would walk into an enormous living room with narrow yellow pine floors and white walls—a very 1970s look. To further exacerbate the problem, the front door was at the far corner of the living room, and the ceilings in the room were lower than normal—under eight feet. The room appeared awkward and rather than giving the appearance of a spacious living room, it appeared to be a long, generic room.

As buyers turned toward the kitchen, they found green oak cabinets that were probably very expensive in the 1970s. However, thirty years later, this was probably where the sellers were losing most of the buyers. Every buyer who came through the house for the first two years it was on the market would say there is too much work to be done because the first two rooms they looked at both needed updates.

The bright side of the home was that it had spacious bedrooms with hardwood floors, a walk-out lower level, a beautiful private backyard, and plenty of closet space. Unfortunately, the initial impression the potential buyers had entering the home impacted their view of the rest of the property.

We solved the problem for less than $500 and sold the home in six weeks for full price, without reducing it like the prior Realtor® wanted to. First, in order to change the initial impression buyers had when walking into the home, we asked the owner to place a mauve-colored area rug, a simple inexpensive carpet remnant, in the middle of the living room, leaving hardwood exposed around the edge, yet updating the colors. Then we had the owner wrap the room in a black and mauve wallpaper border which took only twenty minutes for the owner to install and yet made a big difference in the appearance of the room. The border helped to pull the mauve out of the carpeting. The final touches in the living room were mere furniture rearrangements. When I had first viewed the home, I did not realize that there was a pair of windows directly across from the front door. These windows looked out over the backyard, a highlight of the property. The owner, however, had chosen to place large furniture in front of the windows, obscuring them from the view of potential buyers. By removing the furniture, a buyer entering the home immediately looks across the room at the expanse of yard behind the home.

Other changes we made included asking the owner to remove and cut back some of the trees in front of the house and to place flowers and color in the kitchen. A new country tablecloth with reds in it helped to compliment the green cabinets. Matching hand towels were hung from two cabinets. Bright flowers and table settings helped the buyer's eyes to focus in a different direction than directly at the cabinets, and they brightened the room. The last addition was some decorative towels in the bathrooms. A few hours work and a few hundred dollars probably saved that home seller ten thousand dollars or more.

Competing with New Construction

In many marketplaces, your primary competition for buyers is *new construction*. Buyers gravitate toward new homes for several reasons. The home can be built to the buyer's specifications. Everything in the home is new, so buyers don't have to worry that the roof may start leaking in three years or the furnace may explode. Just like buying a new car, there is also that new house smell of fresh paint, new carpeting, and even the lumber to entice the buyer into a new model.

Some builders are masters at staging their model homes and others hire professional decorating or staging companies to assist them in making their models stand out. Some of the tricks of the trade include lighting, colors, decorative accents, and undersized furniture. The goal of the builder is to make the home appear crisp, new, and very spacious, with plenty of room for all of the buyer's belongings.

Lighting

Lighting plays a crucial part in making a home appear larger, newer, and more inviting. Bright rooms can fool the eye into believing the space is larger than a similar darker room. Builders will typically turn on all lights and open curtains to let in outside light before the model is open.

Color

Although some builders choose to paint with contemporary or trendy colors, most choose very light and neutral colors with white trim. Light colors reflect the most light, making rooms brighter and appear cleaner and larger. White or off-white walls are also more likely to match with a buyer's furniture.

Decorative Accents

Because builders tend to use very light colors to neutralize the property and enhance the perceived size, they need to place drops of color throughout the home to catch a buyer's eye. In many smaller homes, such as townhomes and condos, builders will successfully use large mirrors to accentuate the space and continue to give the illusion of larger rooms. Colorful flower arrangements, dish towels, sconces, vases, potted plants, and similar items help to create a picture in the buyer's mind of inviting over family and friends to show off his or her new home.

Undersized Furniture

One of the sneakier things done by some builders staging a home is to purchase undersized furniture. There is a cottage industry making tables, chairs, and sofas at 85% of the normal size of those items. This again creates the illusion that the room is larger. The easiest way to test this is to sit down at the dining room or kitchen tables and see if the chairs are just a wee bit snug. This tends to be one of the reasons that builders have their offices in the garage rather than the home. Another technique is to put glass-top tables in the kitchen or breakfast areas because light filters through and helps the room to appear larger.

One of my strong recommendations to homeowners competing against new homes is to have the homeowner go out and visit several different builder models in the area. Check out what these builders do to attract the attention of buyers through their decorating and use that knowledge to improve your own home for sale.

Staging a Home: Step by Step

Unfortunately, most clients argue with me when I begin talking about staging a home. What they fail to realize is that they may be leaving thousands of dollars on the table when they sell the property if it doesn't appear in its best condition. Clients religiously watch HGTV and house flipping shows on television and marvel at how some paint, carpeting, and repairs improve the value of the home, but refuse to work on their own home.

One of my relatives sells a lot of children's clothes on eBay. Before selling the clothes, she cleans and presses them, so they look new. She receives a better price and a faster sale on the items because of their appearance. If you use the steps outlined in this chapter to increase the appeal of your home, you may not only sell it faster, but also sell it for more money. Homes that appear larger, cleaner, and well cared for will be attractive to more buyers, and

QUICK TIP:
Color Harmony

Interior decorators tell us that color harmony brings rooms to life. Neutral colors tend to work best in the marketing and sale of a home because they tend to match the largest percentage of buyers' tastes, ideals and furnishings. Also, light colors tend to reflect light, giving the room an illusion of being larger.

Dark colors tend to make the room appear smaller or closer in around the person viewing the room. One reason to paint ceilings white is to give the illusion of the ceiling being at a greater distance. Bold colors, in contrast, may induce a strong reaction from buyers hopping for homes. Color choices are very subjective, and therefore any bold choice of colors may stimulate a very positive or negative reaction depending on the individual. Neutral colors have a wider appeal.

(cont)

buyers will be less hesitant to spend more money to acquire the home.

White colors tend to make people think the room is clean and fresh.

Trim molding, chair rail, crown molding, pillars, and other architectural details can either be highlighted or blended into the background with color choices. If the molding is painted the same color as the walls, it will tend to blend into the background. If these same details are painted a contrasting or accenting color, they will stand out against the walls and may frame other details of the room. For example, a contrasting color on the trim around a window accents the window and draw the viewers eye to the window

To make a room really pop, you may use one of three major color harmonizing techniques used by interior decorating experts.

1. The first technique is to use a complementary color scheme. The key is to use opposite colors from the color wheel. The contrast can be very dramatic. Examples of contrasting colors include black and white, red and green, and blue and orange.

2. The second harmonizing technique is to use two or three colors from the same color

Every real estate guru has their own set of steps for staging a property for sale. Our time-tested method follows a five-step process.

1. decluttering & repair stage;

2. enlarging stage;

3. deep cleaning stage;

4. neutralizing stage;

5. setting the home apart stage

Decluttering and Repair Stage

First is our decluttering and *repair stage*. Let's face it— you have too much stuff in your house and it makes the home look small and unkempt. You don't need all that stuff out on the counters, and the kids can put away some of their toys. During the decluttering stage, you should realize that you are planning a move. Try to get rid of anything that you don't need or that is taking up space. Try to throw out or sell what you don't need or don't plan to move with you. If you still find that you have too much stuff, rent a storage bin, pack up your extra belongings, and store them away from your house.

Repairs should be done to anything that you know is an issue in your home. You will have to provide the buyer with a seller's property disclosure that outlines everything that is wrong with your home. Buyers will be concerned about any issues that remain unresolved. Keep in mind that with any potential repairs, the buyer will overestimate the cost to repair and then take off more than the overestimation for the trouble of having to do the repairs! Take a little time and do all the little things that you've been avoiding the last few years. Fix the drippy faucet, caulk the bathtub, and patch that hole in the drywall outside your son's bedroom door.

color family. Navy blue, sky blue, and ocean blue are all in the same color family. For neutral rooms, bright white, ceiling white, and egg-shell are all from the same color family.

3. The third harmonizing technique is to use a monochromatic color scheme by varying intensities of the same color.

Software packages, such as Color Wheel Expert by Abitom Software, can assist a home owner with selecting contrasting or complimentary colors.

Enlarging Stage

The second phase we call the *enlarging stage*. Dark colors and an excess of furniture crammed into a room tend to make a house appear smaller than it actually is. Buyers don't feel they can fit their furniture in the space, or they feel cramped when they walk through. *National Home Builders* are masters of displaying space in homes. They will put very limited amounts of small furniture in rooms, paint all the walls off-white, and use mirrors to successfully give the illusion of more space than exists. You can use the same techniques fairly easily by painting your rooms an off-white color, removing extra, unnecessary furniture that you have piled up in each room, and replacing some of your pictures on the wall with a mirror or two.

Deep Cleaning Stage

The third stage of enhancing the appeal of your home is to perform a *deep cleaning* of the home. You will not only make the house appear more attractive; you will eliminate people's fear that the home was not well maintained. One of our best tips is to wash all the dust off the furnace. Even a furnace that is only a year old appears older because of the dust settling on it. You can eliminate worry by simply cleaning it off. You may be competing against newer homes that appear fresh and shiny. Clean the fingerprints off the light switch plates, dust off the molding on the walls, and make sure to spray any mildew in the basement. Also, make sure that your stovetop is clean—replace the stovetop burner drip pans if necessary—and clean your bathrooms.

QUICK TIP:

Pet Odors

Dog and cat people often do not notice the odors in their own homes. Have friends or relatives be brutally honest with you about whether or not you have pet odors. Even if you have very limited odors, many buyers are completely turned off by homes that have pet odors.

If you have dogs, cats, or other pets, have your flooring professionally cleaned to try to minimize the odors. During showings, try to remove the pets from your home. Be continually conscious of pet hair and vacuum regularly. Finally, try giving your home a pleasant odor by burning candles or baking.

Neutralizing Stage

Stage four is *neutralizing*. You may not believe this, but some people actually select one home over another because one home has carpeting that goes better with their furniture. You don't need to run out and replace all the carpeting in your house, but you should try to neutralize your home as much as possible. Off-white or light colored walls appear brighter, make a room look larger, and fit with most buyer's furniture and decorations. In the event your home truly needs updating, replacing carpeting, or even laying neutral area carpeting over top of your current floor covers, will go a long way to getting your home sold for top dollar. In a slow market, this may be the difference between selling and not selling.

Setting Your Home Apart Stage

The last stage is *setting your home apart*. Add warmth and character to your home. This will help your buyers to discover an emotional connection to the home. Lighting a fire in the fireplace, burning lightly scented candles, and setting up a nice chess set on the coffee table are all staging techniques to set your home apart. You are giving the buyer a picture in his or her mind of how he or she might want to use your home. They can better imagine friends and relatives visiting and sitting around the fireplace.

Over the next several sections, we will apply these five steps to the major areas of your home to help you see how staging can positively and effectively impact potential buyers. This impact will hopefully lead to more offers and higher offers than you would receive if your home stays in its current condition.

Curb Appeal

Have you ever had the experience as a young adult of gazing across the room at the perfect woman (or the perfect man if you're female)? You think to yourself that this may be a person you would like to date or maybe spend the rest of your life with. She looks back at you and smiles, but not the kind of smile you were hoping for and walks away. For better or worse, people make snap decisions or judgments about each other based on their clothes, their appearance, and so forth.

People also make snap decisions about homes. Everyone has heard the line that you never get a second chance to make a good first impression. If a potential buyer doesn't get a good feeling from the outside of the home, he or she is unlikely to even walk through the inside.

A few years ago, I was working with a well-known Academy Award nominated actor who had been in a few dozen movies. We'll call him Bob. Bob was looking at very expensive homes in Eastern Pennsylvania as a place to get away from New York City when he wasn't performing on Broadway. He wanted his home to create the right impression for his friends. Out of the twelve homes we selected to view, Bob only looked at the interior of three of them. As we pulled up to a home that did not look perfect from the outside, he would ask me to make apologies and head for the next home. Did he have the means to make any changes or alterations to make the homes conform to his expectations? Certainly, he did. Very few buyers, however, *want* to make changes to the home they purchase. The majority of buyers look for the perfect home where they can move their families and furniture in with a minimal amount of effort.

How is your lawn? Are there bare spots? Are your shrubs overgrown? Do they obscure a potential buyer's view of the home? I realize that you are a very busy person with a lot on your plate and plenty of fires to put out, and you just didn't get the time to put fertilizer on the lawn this year or cut back those shrubs. Unkempt front landscaping and poorly maintained lawns, however, evoke an emotional response from buyers. If your lawn isn't well maintained, the buyers may feel that the interior isn't maintained either.

Some homes are completely hidden by their own landscaping. Buyers view this as heavy maintenance. Although some individuals love privacy, most would prefer a clean and unobstructed look for the front of the home.

Curb Appeal Checklist

Decluttering and Repair Stage

- [ ] Remove any children's toys from sight.
- [ ] Remove any garbage bags or other discarded items from against the side of the home.
- [ ] Replace any burned out lightbulbs located in the front of your house.
- [ ] Repair any tears in your screen door.

Enlarging Stage

- [ ] Move cars parked in front of the house because cars block the view of your house from the street.
- [ ] Cut back any large trees or bushes that may hide parts of the house.

Deep Cleaning Stage

- [ ] Mow and trim the lawn, bushes and trees.
- [ ] Weed the yard and garden.
- [ ] Sweep and clean the sidewalks.
- [ ] Clean the exterior of the home with a power washer or hose.
- [ ] Clean the driveway with a power washer or reseal if necessary.
- [ ] Paint any chipping exterior areas.

Neutralizing Stage

- [ ] Remove lawn ornaments unless they fit in with a very neutral appearance.
- [ ] If the exterior is an unusual color, you may need to repaint with a neutral shade.

Setting the Home Apart Stage

- [ ] Plant lots of flowers—it adds color to the landscape.
- [ ] Add fresh mulch to the flower beds.

There are plenty of homes on the market, and contrary to popular belief, most buyers do not want to see every home available. They want to drive by and narrow the field to less than a dozen. If your house does not have good curb appeal, your home is probably getting crossed off people's lists as they drive by your house.

Take a drive around your neighborhood and look at the other homes for sale. Drive by the homes as if you were a buyer looking at how well kept the lawn, landscaping, and home may be from the exterior. How do they compare with your home? Is the front door freshly painted? Are there toys laying in the yard, or bags of garbage setting next to the home? Next, drive back to your own home and take an objective look at your own curb appeal. What will make the property look more warm and inviting to potential buyers so that your home is the *one* home they have to see?

A clean, unobstructed view of the front of the home always attracts more showings than a home that is hidden behind dense landscaping. Landscaping should accent the home.

Entrance Foyer or Entry Hallway

In most homes, the front door opens to either a living room or an entrance foyer or entry hallway. The entryway or entrance foyer is one of the key components to creating the initial positive reaction you want from a buyer. The home should feel warm and inviting, updated, and well maintained. The entrance should be a focal point of your staging efforts.

Entry hallways tend to be the place where handprints and scuff marks collect. Kids take off boots coming into the home in the winter, leaning against the wall. Small children run their hands along the wall. If there are scuff marks, dings, or dents in the entry hallway, the area needs to be repainted. You do not want a potential buyer's initial reaction to be "Gee, I'd have to paint here. I wonder what other work I'll have to do if I buy this house." The value of the home in the buyer's mind declines with each issue discovered.

Again, the wall colors should be neutral, and the trim should be bright white. The floor must be in good condition in this area. If you have torn vinyl or worn carpeting, replace it. The foyer should be tile, hardwood, or another rich material. If you are short on cash to hire someone to replace the floor, and are unable to lay tile yourself, try laminate wood flooring. Pergo or Mohawk floors are relatively easy to install in a small area and can dramatically change the appearance.

The entrance hallway should be clear of obstructions and allow an open view into the home. Decorating this area should be kep to a minimum and family photos should be removed from the area.

Decorating in the entrance foyer should set the tone for the house. Take down any family portraits and hang up a nice framed piece of artwork or a mirror. A single hall table may be in this area with a decorative accent piece or a potted plant on top. A large plant in the corner may also accent the entrance way, as long as it does not impede movement through the entrance into the home.

Entry Checklist

Decluttering and Repair Stage
- ☐ Remove any personal or family photos.
- ☐ Remove umbrella stands, shoe racks, and anything else that detracts from the entry look.
- ☐ Put away your keys and cell phone chargers.

Enlarging Stage
- ☐ Remove all furniture with the exception of a hall table or potted plant.

Deep Cleaning Stage
- ☐ Wipe down all walls and trim thoroughly.
- ☐ Scrub the floors (if they are salvageable)

Neutralizing Stage
- ☐ Repaint walls with a neutral color and bright white trim.

Setting the Home Apart Stage
- ☐ Place one decorative item or a potted plant on the hall table.
- ☐ Hang a framed piece of artwork or a decorative mirror.

The Living Room

The living room is generally adjacent to the entrance hall in most homes, or in some homes the front door opens directly into the living room. In either case, this room is one of the first seen by any prospective buyer viewing the home. Like an entrance hallway, this room should be crisp, clean, and neutral. The walls should be free of marks or chipped paint. The floor coverings should be in good condition. The room should be decorated with a minimum amount of furniture and a few decorative items.

If the walls need to be repainted, this is an area that you should absolutely take the time to repaint or call a local contractor and get it done before putting your home on the market. As with the entry foyer or hallway, I generally recommend light colors. Light colors make rooms appear larger and brighter.

There is a second school of thought, however, on living area colors. Some staging experts believe that modern or popular colors will make the home stand out against the competition. It is true that color can make a room or a whole house really pop. I have actually had experience with buyers that were excited while walking through homes with deep mauve walls, forest green kitchens and other rich colors. They commented how well these homes show against those "plain white" homes. However, I still believe that light colors match more buyers' furniture and make rooms appear brighter and larger. If you choose to go with a popular color, you should take some time with home decorators to determine the best color scheme possible.

If the carpeting or floor covering in the living room can be professionally cleaned, have it done. If the floor covering is worn to the point where cleaning won't help, consider replacing it. A carpet remnant for one room can often be purchased inexpensively and new carpeting will change the entire appearance of the room. You want the buyers thinking how new the room looks as they enter the home. Their subconscious will tell them that the home has been well cared for and doesn't need money put into it to make it livable.

When considering replacing a floor covering, research what is most popular in the area. In many parts of the country, hardwood flooring or laminate flooring that resembles hardwood is most popular. While new, neutral-colored carpeting will make the room stand out, a laminate floor with a hardwood appearance may really make the room pop. Additionally, laminate hardwood flooring can often be installed by a handy homeowner on his or her own in a matter of hours.

Neutralizing the room to fit the maximum number of potential buyers is critical as well. One of our clients for several successful transactions was John H. John is an avid hunter and sportsman, and he is very proud of his collection of animals, including several very large bears he killed in the wilderness of Washington State. When we placed his most recent home on the market, he had "staged" the home so that when a visitor entered his living room, they would be greeted by an eight-foot-tall stuffed bear. To make matters worse, the focal point of the living room was a huge glass coffee table containing a stuffed red fox stalking a stuffed bird.

Some buyers may be turned off by mounted or stuffed animals

Although this was a hunter's dream home, it greatly narrowed the appeal of the house because too many buyers were turned off by the dead animals. Many of those who were not turned off by the decor found themselves spending time looking at the carefully crafted animals and ignoring the actual home. He finally moved the majority of his collection into storage, and the home sold within days.

Proper lighting also plays an important role in obtaining the highest sales price. As with new construction, you should open the drapes and curtains during daytime showings. If the living room doesn't have a ceiling light fixture, turn on the lamps. If you still don't have enough light, pick up a free-standing LED lamp or two. These generate a lot of light.

Small living rooms appear even smaller when too much furniture is crammed into the room. Our suggestion, in this case, was to remove the loveseat and the chair. We also suggested that the owner replace the coffee table in the middle of the room with an end table to make the room appear larger.

A comparable size living room looks much larger with only one sofa and two chairs. There is no coffee table to cover the center of the room, and most of the furniture is against the walls to give the appearance of greater space. You will also notice that the end tables are free of knickknacks, personal photos, and other items, giving the room a clean appearance.

Finish with a minimal amount of furniture. Too much furniture makes a room look small. If your living room is somewhere between ten feet by ten feet and sixteen feet by ten feet, you probably should have no more than one sofa, one love seat, and a few end tables in the room.

If your living room is larger, you may want to include a matching chair and a coffee table. Leave plenty of floor space or the room will look cramped.   Be careful to balance the furniture in the room. If you do not have an eye for balancing the size and amount of furniture, seek the help or someone who does.

Your final phase of staging the living room is to set it apart from the competition. If the room has a fireplace, light it for showings. You may even light it during the summer, because you are attempting to create that emotional picture of curling up in front of the fire with a good book. Set a chess set out on the coffee table, or some splayed coffee table books. Turn on some soft, light music, like jazz or classical.

Living Room Checklist

Decluttering and Repair Stage

☐ Remove all unnecessary items from tables and other surfaces.

☐ Put away extra pillows, blankets, and unnecessary items from sofas and chairs.

Enlarging Stage

☐ Paint walls a light and neutral color.

☐ Open all shades and curtains and turn on all lights, including closet lights, during showings, even during the daytime.

☐ Arrange the furniture close to walls, away from the center of the room. If you have too much furniture, remove some and place it in a storage facility. If you must keep the excess furniture in the house, move it to your basement.

Deep Cleaning Stage

☐ Shampoo or steam clean all carpets, and scrub all tile, vinyl, and wood floors and all woodwork. Remember to clean the furniture you are leaving in the room, too.

☐ Deodorize pet areas.

☐ If the carpets have stains that cannot be removed, you should consider replacing the pieces that are stained. Remember that you are probably competing with model homes with brand new

> **QUICK TIP:**
>
> ### Using Window Treatments
>
> Drapes, curtains, or other window treatments are often the quickest, least expensive, and simplest method of changing the look of a room. A plain white room can be transformed by draping a casual swag over a curtain rod, or mounting curtains against the ceiling to give the room depth.
>
> Window treatment colors and patterns may match or compliment the furniture in the room, pulling the room together. Curtains can also frame a window, pulling the buyer's eye toward the yard or landscaping outside.

carpeting throughout. Carpet remnants can often be found at wholesale carpet outlets at very low cost.

Neutralizing Stage

☐ Remember to use light, neutral colors when you repaint this area.

☐ Remove any ornate furniture or items. Make certain this area is decorated well but very neutrally.

☐ Remove pictures of children or family photos. Buyers have a hard time mentally moving in when they think of the home as yours.

☐ Remove any dated light switch plates and outlet covers. Replace them with neutral covers or give the room a rich appearance by replacing them with brushed nickel or brass, depending on your location and the style of home.

☐ Remove any couch covers. If you're truly concerned about soiling your furniture, have it sprayed with a stain protectant.

Setting the Home Apart Stage

☐ If the home has a wood-burning fireplace, arrange logs in it. Many home sellers build fires to stage their homes, even in the summer. The smell adds to the "homey" feeling a buyer will get from your home and the lit fire will help the buyer imagine what it must be like to live in the house on cold winter nights.

☐ Set up a chess set or game on the coffee table.

☐ Play soft easy-listening music and turn off the television.

The Kitchen

Let's talk frankly. Kitchens sell homes. The kitchen is the focal point of a home and often the most important room to buyers. Remember that buyers are not purchasing a commodity, but rather a dream or a lifestyle. Many buyers imagine having their whole families over for Thanksgiving dinner or sitting with friends at the center island or breakfast table, talking over a cup of coffee or tea.

Your staging should help them paint the picture of the lifestyle they want to create by purchasing your home.

Decluttering this area includes clearing out unnecessary items on the counters, in the cabinets, and even in the pantry. Clear, sparkling counters let the buyer know that there is plenty of room to prepare even their biggest meals. Remove all of your counter appliances like toasters, toaster ovens, automatic can openers, and coffee makers. If you use them regularly, put them in a cabinet before showings. Maximize the space on your counters.

Make room in your cabinets and pantry, as well. You want to show potential buyers that there is plenty of space for everything they bring with them. Let's face it—there are many pots, pans, and electric devices somewhere in your kitchen that you are simply not using on a regular basis. Pack them away and get them ready for your move.

Clean out the sink, scrub it down, and remove any stains. If the sink faucet is dripping, make sure to replace the washer inside or repair it. Check for any slow dripping under the sink because your buyers will. Wash and wax the floors. Carefully clean under the cabinets. Open the curtains to let in the sunlight.

Take a step back and look at the top of your cabinets. This is generally where knickknacks collect. Although they may be your prized possessions, they are generally distracting and detract from the clean look of the kitchen, so put them away when buyers come through. Wipe down the cabinets thoroughly, and if they're wood, try wiping down the cabinet doors with Murphy's oil to make them look clean and shiny. If there are chips on the front of any cabinets, try touching them up with a wood-tone touchup stick from the hardware store.

In addition to decluttering, you should also depersonalize this area. The kitchen refrigerator is often a family history lesson with dozens of photos, awards, shopping lists, and refrigerator magnets. In order to neutralize the kitchen, you need to remove everything from the front of your refrigerator. You want the buyer to mentally move into the home. Your family photos and souvenir magnets are a distraction from that goal.

If the kitchen is an eat-in kitchen or has an adjacent breakfast area, you can make the space appear larger by removing a leaf from your table.

The Most Commonly Asked Kitchen Questions

What If the Kitchen Countertops are Chipped or in Poor Condition?

If you have laminate countertops, such as Formica, that are in poor condition, consider replacing them. Replacing the laminate may be an inexpensive upgrade that alters the look of your kitchen entirely. If your counters are tile, it can be a very large job to replace them. Instead, scrub the tile thoroughly and attempt to scrape off the top of the grout. Then, re-grout the tile. You'll have a whole new look!

If your counters are Corian, granite, or marble, it is unlikely that there is anything wrong with them that a good scrubbing wouldn't take care of. If you do have damaged Corian, you can sand off the upper layer. If you have cracked granite or marble, though, there is a good chance that you will need to replace it. This can be a costly and time-consuming job, but damaged counters in the kitchen seriously impede the sale of homes because potential buyers see the work they need to put into the house before they can live their comfortably. In a slower home market, you do not want to give potential buyers any excuse to not buy your property.

What If the Cabinets are Very Old?

Upgrading a kitchen by either refacing the cabinets or replacing them is one area that a homeowner often receives his or her money back for when the house sells. In many cases, entire nice-looking oak-front or raised panel white kitchen cabinets can be installed for less than $4,000. If your kitchen cabinets are in good condition, though, and it is just the cabinet doors that look old and warn, consider replacing the doors and drawer fronts instead of replacing the entire cabinet. Install classy hardware that attracts the eye. Be sure to compare the cost of re-facing your cabinet doors with the cost of replacing your cabinets entirely. Sometimes replacing the cabinets is actually less expensive.

If the kitchen has a hodge-podge of different cabinets, you should seriously consider replacing them. Likewise, if the kitchen has older metal cabinets, consider an upgrade. If the cabinets are a 1970's style wood, you may want to repaint them white and add new hardware on the front. This update is relatively inexpensive and can change the entire appearance of a kitchen.

An old adage is that you pay for upgrades to your home when you own it, or you pay for them when you sell it. An upgraded kitchen, done correctly, will pay you back as much or more than you put into the kitchen. If done correctly, you can install a kitchen for significantly less than a buyer believes the cost to be. Consequently, if you do not update, reface, or replace an old kitchen, the buyer will want a discount on the price or a credit equal to what he or she believes the cost of replacement to be, and will want an additional discount because of the headache of doing the work.

Another important consideration is that homes with newer kitchens generally sell more quickly than homes with older kitchens.

What If the Appliances are Old?

I'm hoping you don't still have gold-colored appliances in the kitchen, but any older appliances also impact a buyer in a negative way. Keep in mind that this may be the most important room in the home to a buyer. Appliances can be very expensive, but even a low-end new range looks new. Shop around to find moderately priced appliances that will have the sparkle of brand new. You will get the cost back in the sales price of the home.

What if I Just Offer a Credit?

Again, buyers will believe the cost to replace the kitchen to be substantially higher than it will cost you to do yourself. You are trying to appeal to the buyer's emotional need to show off his or her new home to their family and friends. Most buyers want no part of repairing or upgrading a home and are turned off by dated kitchens.

This kitchen has snacks lined up along the back of the counter. The refrigerator is covered with photographs of children and artwork, baskets are on top of the cabinets, and the buyer's eye is drawn to the clutter instead of the overall kitchen.

A staged kitchen has nearly empty countertops, nothing on top of the cabinets, nothing tacked on the refrigerator, and no appliances sitting out on the counter. Now potential buyers can see the kitchen instead of the clutter.

If you cannot afford to update the kitchen, try to get a credit card from a home improvement store that will give you a large discount on your purchase along with a low interest rate, and pay off the appliances and cabinets once you sell your home. Yes, it's that important.

Kitchen/Breakfast Area Checklist

Decluttering and Repair Stage

- ☐ Clear everything off the countertops and the tops of any other surfaces. Hide your dish drying rack under the sink.
- ☐ Remove extra appliances and accessories from view.
- ☐ Take knickknacks off the top of kitchen cabinets.

Enlarging Stage

- ☐ Remove and pack extra dishes and items from the cabinets to make them appear to have plenty of room.
- ☐ Remove a leaf from your kitchen table to make the room look larger.
- ☐ Turn on all the lights for showings. Open all the curtains. You may even want to turn on the lights over the sink and over the stove for added effect.

Deep Cleaning Stage

- ☐ Wipe down all walls and trim thoroughly.
- ☐ Scrub the countertops. If the countertops are tile and dirty, remove the top layer of grout and re-grout to give a fresh, clean look to the counter.
- ☐ Scrub out the sink and remove any stains.
- ☐ Scrub the floors.
- ☐ Clean the inside and outside of all appliances.
- ☐ Deodorize any pet areas near or around the kitchen.

Neutralizing Stage

- ☐ Remove personal photos, menus, notes, and magnets from the refrigerator.
- ☐ Repaint the walls with a neutral color and the trim bright white.
- ☐ Touch up any scratches on the cabinets with wood-tone touch-up sticks.

Setting the Home Apart Stage

☐   Wipe down the kitchen cabinet fronts with Murphy's Oil.

☐   Bake cookies or bread for showings or light a vanilla scented candle.

☐   Upgrade, reface, or replace your kitchen countertops or cabinets if necessary.

The Dining Room

The dining room may also be very important to certain types of buyers. Couples who have large extended families or entertain regularly may make a large formal dining room a requirement of any home they purchase. Potential buyers have a picture in their minds what it would be like to have family and friends sitting around a table in your dining room. You need to help paint that picture for them.

The biggest detraction from dining rooms is the size of the room. This is complicated by the fact that many families purchase large buffets, china cabinets, hutches, or dry sinks to accent their dining rooms or to display all their prized dishware. These large pieces of furniture can make a room look small. Try to look at your dining room from an objective perspective. If it looks small, try to remove the buffet or china cabinet and store it until you move. This takes a great deal of effort, but it may be worth it in the price you receive for your home.

Next, should stage the room as if you were having an upscale dinner party. Set out place settings with linens and your best china. Put a tasteful centerpiece on the table. The formal dining room is often the most fun to stage. Most families eat in the kitchen, so you may be able to stage the dining room and leave it staged until the home sells.

In many cases. Homeowners use the dining room for other purposes. If the home was lacking an office, the dining room may have become a home office or den. The dining room may also be used as an exercise room for the adults or a playroom or craft room for the kids. In one instance, a homeowner was using the dining room as a pool table room. When he had guests for a big event, he would simply lay a plywood board over the pool table, cover it with a tablecloth, and serve dinner.

If you are planning to sell a home for top dollar, you should appeal to the maximum number of potential buyers. Although some buyers may desire an office or playroom, the vast majority want to see a traditional dining room for entertaining. Women make the home buying decision far more often than men, and surveys indicate this room is one of the four most important rooms in the home to female buyers.

QUICK TIP:
Homes without Dining Rooms

If your home doesn't have a formal dining room, but has a large living room, consider creating the illusion of a dining room in the open space. Carefully arrange your furniture in one side of the living room around a central focus point You might have a sofa and two chairs facing each other with a small rug or table in the center.

Next, add a small dining table at the other end of the room to create a formal dining area. A small round table with four chairs, decorated as if you're planning a small dinner party, will set the stage for two completely separate uses in a single room.

The dining room is often a place where homeowners store various knickknacks for display. A lot of furniture and items on display make a room feel crowded and small. Buyers have difficulty imagining their own furniture in the room or having enough room for an extended family.

An uncluttered dining room of roughly the same size has a much more open feel. Remove all excess furniture and display items when you are staging this room.

Dining Room Checklist

Decluttering Stage

☐ Remove any large plants or extraneous furniture.

Enlarging Stage

☐ Remove hutches, buffets, or china cabinets if they make the room appear small.

☐ If the room still appears small, remove a leaf from the table and possibly two of the dining chairs.

Deep Cleaning Stage

☐ Wipe down any furniture pieces in the room.

☐ Wash the floors or have the carpets or rugs cleaned.

Neutralizing Stage

☐ Repaint walls with a neutral color and the trim bright white, if necessary.

Setting the Home Apart Stage

☐ Set out place settings with fine china and linens.

☐ Hang a framed piece of artwork or a decorative mirror on the wall. The artwork or mirror should be carefully sized to fit the room

☐ In an early American home, hang sconces on the wall.

☐ In a more traditional home, you might hang a wreath with a floral arrangement.

☐ In a contemporary home, display crystal or glass.

QUICK TIP:

Dining Room Light Fixtures

According to Yvonne Root, the President of the Staging Northern Arizona Professional Association, one common mistake made by homeowners is to hang their light fixtures too high above the dining room table. A general rule of thumb is to hang the light twenty-six inches above the tabletop.

Additionally, depending on the location of the home and the style of the home, brass fixtures may need to be updated with a more contemporary metallic look such as brushed nickel or painted to look like brushed steel.

Bathrooms

Bathrooms are also a focal point of the modern buyer. Bathrooms can be a turn on or a turn off for the average buyer. Bathrooms that appear mildewed, used, and cluttered are always a negative for the buyer. If the same room is sparkling clean, with clear counters, designer towels, a flower arrangement, a framed painting and the scent of lavender, berries, or vanilla, your buyer will linger in the room and have a more positive feeling toward the home.

Unfortunately, bathrooms tend to collect a lot of stuff. Counters are often full of hairbrushes, toothpaste, hair spray, contact solution, and everything else we use on a daily basis. All these items need to be hidden away. Go through the medicine cabinet and get rid of anything that is not absolutely necessary. Use this space for the toothbrushes and hair spray so they're off the counter. While you're in this area, thoroughly clean the mirror, and check under the sink to make sure there's no water dripping. Clean out under the sink, as well, if possible, since people looking at houses will open up any cupboards or storage areas you have to see what they are like.

Next, go over the tub and shower enclosure. If the shower curtain is showing some age, replace it. This is an inexpensive change that can really improve the look of the bathroom. Try to find an accent color for the curtain. The tub and shower should sparkle. Scrub the area completely. If there is caulking between the tub and the tub surround, peel it out and re-caulk the area. There are few more serious turnoffs than blackish caulk in a bathtub.

After cleaning the floors, you're ready to stage the area. Try to remove all the regular bath towels you're using and hide them. In their place, hang a few matching, plush towels. Color coordinate the towels with a flower arrangement or the shower curtain. Add some decorative scented soaps. If possible, hang a framed print on the wall.

Bathrooms should be sparkling clean. The countertops and bathtubs should be free from most personal bath items. A candle or decorative soap basket works well and creates an image in the buyer's mind of taking a luxurious bath. A single decorative item on the wall completes the picture.

Bathroom Checklist

Decluttering and Repair Stage

- ☐ Clean off the countertops. Put away toothpaste, hairbrushes, and sprays.
- ☐ Minimize what is in the tub or shower, e.g., the eight different shampoo containers.

Enlarging Stage

- ☐ Clean out the medicine cabinets. Show all the available room in them Minimize the number of towels hanging in the bathroom.

Deep Cleaning Stage

- ☐ Check for any mildew and clean it up.
- ☐ Scrub the tubs, sinks, and floor thoroughly.
- ☐ Check for dripping under the sink and repair as necessary.
- ☐ Caulk the tub. Remove the old, dirty caulk and replace it with new fresh white caulk.

Neutralizing Stage
- ☐ Replace existing shower curtain with a neutral one, or one that will accent the bathroom.
- ☐ Paint walls with neutral colors if necessary.
- ☐ Change the hardware on bathroom cabinets or vanities to more updated hardware.

Setting the Home Apart Stage
- ☐ Add scented soaps or potpourri.
- ☐ Purchase or borrow display towels for hanging on towel racks and to set on the back of the toilet.
- ☐ Include a framed print on the wall.

Bedrooms

Bedrooms are often considered secondary rooms to buyers. However, properly staging these areas can seal the deal. Remember that you're selling a lifestyle, not a home. Carefully positioning the right pieces in the master bedroom, for example, can evoke an emotional response from the buyers.

First, of course, the rooms must be perfectly clean. Cleaning includes the floor coverings, the bureaus or dressers, and even the closet. The closet is an important area because couples are often concerned about storage. Remove out-of-season clothing or clothing that doesn't quite fit anymore. If you are planning to save it, box it and store it. Re-hang the clothes you are keeping in the closet on one type of hanger. Appearing organized not only increases your credibility with the buyer but will make your closets look larger, which is a big selling point.

As you begin setting your bedrooms apart from other homes, make your beds every day and be sure you use nice bedspreads. Pillows add to the ambiance of the room. A combination of several different size or color pillows that complement each other focuses the eye on that area. Teddy bears also work well in kids' rooms. Flower arrangements on the dresser that complement the bedspread or pillows can also make the colors of the room pop.

Even a very small bedroom can be staged. In this case, extra dressers were removed to display some wall space and a nice comforter was placed on the bed with decorative pillows and a pair of teddy bears. For effect, a small flower vase was placed on the floor in the corner.

One of our top agents stages the master bedroom for a little romance. She asks her homeowners to place a coffee tray or bed tray on the bedspread before showings. A pair of coffee cups, silk napkins in napkin holders, and maybe a candle or a single rose completes the picture. This is truly showcasing a lifestyle rather than simply a home.

Bedroom Checklist

Decluttering Stage

- ☐ Clean off dressers, bureaus, night stands, and other furniture.
- ☐ Place hampers in closets to keep out of view.
- ☐ Remove jewelry boxes or items of value from sight.

Enlarging Stage

- ☐ Remove any large furniture that makes the room look small.
- ☐ Clean out the closet of any unnecessary clothing.

☐ Remove exercise equipment and furniture that doesn't belong in a bedroom (unless you have a separate sitting area in the master bedroom that you can stage).

Deep Cleaning Stage

☐ Vacuum and thoroughly clean the room.

☐ Dust the dressers and check for dust daily.

☐ Clean ceiling fans or light fixtures.

Neutralizing Stage

☐ Remove family photos and personal items from dressers.

☐ In children's bedrooms, remove posters from walls and excessive toys.

Setting the Home Apart Stage

☐ Add decorative pillows and a nice bedspread, or a teddy bear in the kid's rooms.

☐ Place a coffee tray on the bed with silk napkins, a pair of mugs, and a rose.

☐ Place flower arrangements on the dresser.

☐ Place a basket with a few books on the nightstand or a diary and pen.

☐ Inexpensive curtains that match the bedspread or wallpaper borders that match the bedspread can often pull the room together.

☐ Open the curtains or drapes during showings to let in additional light.

Backyard

The yard is a place for reading, relaxation, kids playing, and picnics. Since your goal is to appeal to the emotional needs of the potential buyer and deliver a vision of a lifestyle, you'll need to stage the yard as well.

First things first. There should not be a lot of bare spots and brown grass in the yard. If you have yard issues, make sure you fertilize and water, water, water. If you don't have time to wait for your lawn to grow back, consider investing in some sod. Cut back any overgrown shrubs so the buyers don't immediately think of how much work it will take to maintain the yard. Pull any weeds in any gardens you have. Remove any debris, like the junk sitting next to the shed that you had intended to remove at some point in the past but never got around to.

Once you have the yard in passable condition, you can begin setting the stage for the emotional appeal. If you're selling in a warmer season or climate, add colorful flowers to your garden, or place flowerpots near the back doors or at the sides of the patio or deck. If you have patio furniture, try to stage it prior to showings as if you were preparing for outdoor cooking.

A favorite technique of mine is to find the perfect place to create a reading nook. Gather a pair of chairs and a small high round table. If the weather is right before a showing, set a book open on the table, and a tall glass of lemonade next to it. Paint a picture for the buyer to trigger that emotional response.

Adding a birdfeeder to the landscaping or something else for the buyer's eye to focus on helps to set the stage for the buyer's imagination. You're trying to paint a picture of peace and quiet.

Use any lawn, patio or deck furniture you have to create a scene for the buyer. Show them what possibilities exist in outside entertaining, relaxing, or playing with the kids.

Another possible addition would be to consider adding a fountain or a bird bath as a focal point of part of the yard. Add some flowers around the base of the fountain for color.

Backyard Checklist

Decluttering Stage
- ☐ Remove any debris from the yard.
- ☐ Put away any children's toys you have scattered throughout the yard.
- ☐ Pull the weeds and lay mulch in the flower beds.

Enlarging Stage
- ☐ Cut back any shrubs that are getting out of hand.
- ☐ Trim the edges of the lawn around patio and garden areas.

Deep Cleaning Stage
- ☐ Keep the lawn trimmed. Reseed any bare spots or lay sod, and water regularly.

Neutralizing Stage
- ☐ Although buyers with children love to know there are children in the area, store away children's colorful slides, trampolines, and playhouses.

Setting the Home Apart Stage

☐ Stage the patio table before showings.

☐ Create a reading place or nook in the yard with a couple chairs and a small table with a book.

☐ Add a fountain or bird feeder.

☐ Place potted flowers around the patio or deck, and add color.

Garage

Although this is a secondary area, it is also important to keep clean. New homes have freshly painted garages that are empty and appear to have all the room in the world. Your garage may be so filled with boxes, tools, bicycles, and lawn equipment that you may not be able to wedge a car into it. The walls may be scuffed and dirty.

When you are decluttering your home, boxes tend to accumulate in the basement and garage. Consider renting a storage unit in order to store your belongings because buyers looking at mounds of boxes in the garage get the impression that the home doesn't have enough storage room inside for all of the stuff they plan to bring with them.

Put up vinyl or PVC shelving to hold anything that remains in your garage. Hang bicycles from hooks on the wall if possible and put the tools into toolboxes on the shelves. If the walls are badly scuffed, consider painting them.

Although I get a lot of arguing when I suggest this, if you are using your garage as a workshop instead of a garage, consider dismantling the workbench and storing it to allow room for cars. More home buyers want a place for their cars rather than a place for a workshop. If you absolutely must keep your workbench or table where your car belongs, then at least clean it up, carefully store or stack the tools, and neaten the entire work area.

Garage Checklist

Decluttering Stage
- ☐ Put up PVC or vinyl shelving and make sure everything fits on the shelves.

Enlarging Stage
- ☐ Remove boxes and take to storage.
- ☐ Hang bicycles from the ceiling.

Deep Cleaning Stage
- ☐ Completely sweep out the garage.

Neutralizing Stage
- ☐ Remove workbenches and return the garage to its original purpose.

Setting the Home Apart Stage
- ☐ Paint the interior off-white.

Basement

Before retiring, my father was a superintendent of a moderate-sized school district. On the side, he was a real estate broker and sold real estate with our local office. His most recognized saying was, "For every pot, there's a lid." His belief

QUICK TIP:
Parking Cars

Home staging experts appear to be split on whether or not to park cars in the garage during showings. Those who believe cars *should* be parked in the garage believe that cars parked on the driveway detract from the exterior of the home, and parking the car in the garage shows that the garage has sufficient space.

Stagers who believe the car should stay out of the garage believe that parking the car makes the garage less accessible to view and can make the garage appear smaller. If you, as the owner, are not home for showings, the car isn't in either the garage or the driveway

If you are selling the home yourself or if you're going to be home for showings, you may consider parking your car down the street and walking back to the home. This gives the buyer the best view of the home from the exterior and keeps the garage open.

was that homes may fit a buyer's needs if they look at the home a little differently.

He was showing a home close to the top of a small mountain in the Allentown area. As his buyers walked down the basement steps, they heard a gushing. The home was over 200 years old and had been built lower than an adjacent spring. Water seeped through the basement wall and cascaded down the interior basement wall into a French drain.

My father looked across at the flowing water in the damp dingy basement and said "Wow. Isn't that just beautiful." The potential buyers looked up at him in surprise. "Picture this. The basement ceiling is high enough to finish. Build a semicircular planter or half brick wall around the water that's coming in. Focus some blue lights from the ceiling and create your own indoor waterfall. You'll be the talk of the area." The buyers purchased the home and finished the basement. He was able to turn a negative into a positive.

Most home sellers can't rely on someone else coming up with the answer to their problems, and most home buyers don't want to do any work on the home they buy. If you have issues with the home, including dampness in the basement, you should try to resolve them before selling the home. Water issues turn off buyers and reduce the ultimate selling price for your home.

Clean up as much of the basement as possible. If the basement is unfinished, put everything on shelves against the wall. Leave the center of the basement as open as possible so buyers can imagine finishing the area. You may help to stage this area by placing an area rug in the center of the room.

If the basement is finished into a family room, playroom, or living space, declutter, repair, neutralize, deep clean, and stage as you would any other room. Basement living space is particularly important to keep clean for showings. Unless the basement is a walk-out, it will probably lack full-size windows, so brighten the room with additional lighting.

If the basement is damp, buy, lease or borrow a dehumidifier. Any mildew on walls should be sprayed. If there are any signs of mold, have them inspected by a certified mold inspection company. Remember, all mold issues must be disclosed to any potential buyer.

An inexpensive tip is to clean off the entire furnace. Even a furnace that is only a year old appears older because of the dust that settles on it. You can eliminate worry by simply cleaning it off. It will appear shiny and new.

If your home is built on a crawl space, you will want to check that area before putting your home on the market. Buyers will want to examine every part of the home, and crawl spaces may also attract water. Damp areas with mildew can affect the rooms directly above and can give the buyers cause for concern. Remedy any problems prior to selling the home.

Basement Checklist

Decluttering Stage
☐ Put up PVC or vinyl shelving and make sure everything fits on the shelves.

Enlarging Stage
☐ Remove boxes and take to storage.

☐ Move everything to the outside walls in order to maximize the visible space.

Deep Cleaning Stage
☐ Completely sweep out and clean the basement.

☐ Spray any mildew and wash walls where necessary.

☐ Clean off the furnace and make it sparkle.

☐ Install a dehumidifier if the basement is damp.

Neutralizing Stage
☐ If the basement is unfinished, white-wash the walls. If the basement is finished, select a neutral and soft color for painting.

Setting the Home Apart Stage
☐ Place an area rug in the center of the basement to show it can be finished.

What to Do if Your Home is Vacant

The most common question I am asked is "Will my home show worse if it's empty?" The honest answer is, "Yes." Vacant homes sit on the market longer, typically sell for slightly less than occupied homes, and often strain the finances of the owner who is carrying two mortgages.

Example:

Ted and Alice were a couple who relocated to the Lehigh Valley in Pennsylvania from Texas. They looked at two-story colonials in a moderate-priced neighborhood that they fell in love with. The first home we showed them was a beautiful 3-year-old colonial that had been vacated by the prior owners. The hardwood floors were refinished, the carpeting was professionally cleaned, and the owners had touched up the paint prior to leaving. Alice remarked to Ted, while they were walking through the home, "This just feels too cramped."

The second home was occupied by an older couple without any children. The furnishings were very nice, but sparse and the decorating was impeccable. Alice turned to Ted and said "Can't you just feel it? It's so much more spacious than the one we just looked at." They purchased the second home. Both homes they looked at were identical models. Every room size was exactly the same.

A positive initial impact in a vacant home is challenging. Part of the challenge is that a person's mind makes a judgment about size. The mind tries to fill the empty space with furniture and fools the person into believing the furniture proportions are different than they are. Furniture actually helps to define the space so a buyer can position their own furniture in place of what is already in the home. Some buyers have great visualization skills and can see what the vacant home could be, but unfortunately most do not.

The other part of the challenge is that vacant homes are empty. There isn't the same emotional reaction as there is with homes that are staged properly. Finally, vacant homes don't have furniture or artwork hiding the flaws. Any defect or imperfection in the floor coverings, walls, cabinets, and the like are visible to any potential buyer who walks into the home.

Rooms in vacant homes fool the eye into believing they are smaller than they actually are. Someone viewing the home will often unconsciously overestimate the size of furniture in comparison with the available wall space.

If nothing else, when selling a vacant home, make sure it is properly maintained. A lawn service should be contracted to keep the lawn and flower beds in good condition. Have the interior professionally cleaned and have a cleaning crew stop by every ten days to keep it clean. Dirt will follow buyers and their Realtors® into your home. Dust balls seem to appear out of nowhere and flies just seem to materialize in the home. Also ask the cleaning crew to double check the lights and replace any burned-out bulbs.

Keep the utilities on. It is very difficult to show a home in its best light during the fall when there's no electricity in the home. A cold home in the winter or a very hot home in the summer turn buyers off as well.

Another option is to have a staging company lease furniture to you so that you can leave it in the home. While this is certainly a costly investment, consider the impact of taking an additional sixty to ninety days to sell your home. If you have a $250,000 home with a mortgage payment including taxes and insurance of around $2,200 a month, you could lose $6,600 in just three extra months of being on the market. Some staging companies also have house sitters, or representatives who stop by and check on homes on a regular basis.

General Staging Issues

Recently, I met an owner who wanted to sell a circa-1900 farmhouse. I love historic homes and was excited to take a look. Walking into the home, my shoulders fell. The owner had paneled just about everything in sight. He dropped the ceilings in the living room, and the bedrooms. Worse, he was very proud of his accomplishments.

"I bet you don't find many like this, do you? It's already done. In most farmhouses, you have to break through walls to run wiring, cable, phones and such. With these drop ceilings, you can get at all the wiring easily. And don't worry about chipping or flaking plaster walls. I've covered this baby with strong paneling. It's not the cheap stuff, either. It's real wood paneling, a ¼-inch thick. That means no maintenance. I'm expecting to get a pretty good price after all the work I've put into this house."

Unfortunately, I've heard this speech several times. You may be one of those home sellers who are very proud of the work you did to your home in 1978. Unfortunately, this isn't 1978. Paneling is *way* out of date in virtually every part of the country. If you are planning to sell your house for top dollar, you have three choices.

1. You can remove the paneling and fix the walls.

2. You can drywall right over top of the paneling.

3. You can paint the paneling to try to hide it.

Drywall will certainly look the best, but it can be expensive, very time consuming, and makes quite a mess in the rest of the house with drywall dust.

Painting paneling can be difficult as well because wood tends to soak in the paint, leaving you putting one coat after another on it. Before painting wood paneling, make sure you use some sort of oil base first or a strong primer to seal the paneling. Then finish with a coat of a thick latex paint. Buyers, of course, will still be able to see the lines of the paneling, but the room will be transformed. Paneling is very dark, which makes rooms look small. A light color will brighten and visually enlarge the room.

Drop ceilings are more of a problem because they often hide something above them. In most cases, you cannot simply remove a drop ceiling and paint. Either the ceiling is damaged and needs repair or wiring was run over top of the drop ceiling requiring extensive work to put it into the real ceiling. In some cases, you can paint old drop ceilings. Take down the tiles and paint them with a primer to seal them before finish coating them. Paint the tracks with something that will adhere to the metal or plastic.

Drop ceilings are more common in a basement or a family room below grade, so they won't have to be replaced. If you have them on your main living level, though, you should consider how best to replace or mask them.

The Keys to Staging

Although some believe staging to be an art form, the simple techniques listed in this chapter, when applied correctly, can greatly enhance the appeal of your home. Homes with great appeal will sell more quickly and often for more money than other homes you are competing for buyers with. These simple tried and tested methods begin with decluttering and enlarging your home and removing anything that is unnecessary, so your home doesn't look cramped to buyers. Repair any small items that may detract from potential showings. Thoroughly clean every area of the inside and outside of the home.

   Neutralizing will allow the home to appeal to a wider group of buyers. Light colors match more buyers' furniture and decor and also add to the brightness and warmth of a home. Finally, set the home apart from the rest with the addition of staging the home to evoke an emotional response from the buyers. Light a fire in the fireplace, put a coffee tray and decorative pillows on the master bed, put place settings at the dining room table, and set up a reading nook in the back yard with a glass of lemonade.

chapter two:
Pricing Your Home Properly

Real estate training superstar Floyd Wickman jokes that nearly every client tells him that his or her home is better than others in the neighborhood because their home used the heavy-duty nails instead of the regular nails. The sad truth is that we all have an emotional attachment to our homes, and many of us view our home as if it's worth more than the reality of the marketplace dictates.

The most often heard line by real estate agents is "I don't want to give my house away." I know you don't want to hear this, but houses are a commodity. The prices are set by the marketplace, based on what other homes are selling for. If you are planning to sell a fifteen year old Ford sedan with one hundred thousand miles on it, and you know of ten others just like it for sale, and they're all listed around $5,000, you will not get $8,000 no matter how well you advertise your car or polish and wax it. It doesn't matter that you upgraded the stereo six years ago.

I accompanied one of our associate brokers, Tim Mahon, on a listing appointment a few years ago to a townhome in Allentown. The pricing of the townhome was relatively easy because several had sold in the neighborhood recently, and the unit directly next to this one had sold within a few weeks. The homes were identical. We met the owner, Randy, at the front door and walked through the home, noting that it was fairly typical of the townhomes in the neighborhood.

We sat down at the kitchen table, and Tim proceeded to outline pricing and explain that Randy's home would likely sell very close in price to the next-door neighbors. Randy leaped to his feet, offended that we would even compare his home with his neighbors. "My home is worth at least $25,000 more than his. Do you realize that the neighbor's home still has all the rooms painted white? Mine has color! And the neighbor has regular closet bars. I had Creative Closets put in double racks in PVC. Also, I had a hose bib put on both the front and back of my home. The neighbor only had a hose bib put on the back. Plus, I'm planning to throw in the twenty-five-foot garden hose." Tim actually lost it. I had never seen him so hysterical. "The garden hose is included? Wow." He said as he laughed. "That's got to be worth $5,000 to $10,000 in price. Why don't we make this house $40,000 higher than the neighbors if you're throwing in the garden hose!" Needless to say, we didn't get the listing.

Certainly, you don't want to underprice your home and give away money to the buyer. You want to maximize the return you get out of your investment in the home. On the other hand, you don't want to overprice your home either. Overpriced homes can sit on the market, generate a negative feeling in the real estate community, and ultimately sell for less money than if they had been priced correctly initially.

"I understand my home is only worth $225,000, but I'd like to try to start it at $350,000. After all, I can always come down in price, but I can never go up!" This type of thinking is a killer in the real estate industry. A slowing market is not the time to test the waters of pricing. Even in a stable or good real estate market, the most attention a home receives is in the first two to six weeks the home is for sale. An initial listing in the MLS and on the Internet is seen by far more people than homes that have been on the market for any significant period of time. Real estate auto search programs sift and sort new listings and email them to prospective buyers. The home is listed near the top instead of three pages down on major sites like Zillow. Buyers searching for deals seek out the most recent listings. The *for sale sign* generates word of mouth in the neighborhood and with people driving by.

As a home sits on the market unsold, neighbors begin to talk about something being wrong with the house. Buyers searching on the Internet overlook homes that have been for sale for a significant period because they think that there must be something wrong with them. Even as you reduce your price, the pool of buyers who may have interest in your home dwindles. Realtors® who showed the house when it was overpriced still have a negative connotation in their mind about the property, even if the price has been reduced.

Determining price means investigating homes that are for sale or currently in competition with yours, similar homes that have sold recently, and homes that failed to sell. You may want to talk to several Realtors® to collect their opinions of value, and you may want to have an independent appraisal done to obtain an unbiased professional opinion.

The Realtor's Competitive Market Analysis

Also known as a *Broker's Market Analysis* or a *Broker Price Opinion*, a *Competitive Market Analysis* is a comparison by a real estate broker or agent of your home against other homes currently for sale, recently sold, and homes that *expired* or didn't sell during the initial listing term.

Home sellers immediately glom onto the currently available homes as the best comparison with their own property. The truth, however, is that the recently sold properties are a better indication of a property's likely sales price. Sold properties show what buyers in the marketplace are willing to pay for a home like yours. Even when home prices are skyrocketing at 1% or more per month in hot markets, the best evaluation is to review sold properties and add a little for appreciation. In a slowing market, it is crucial to the sale to price the property perfectly.

Available properties are your home's competition. Keep in mind that some of the homes currently for sale in your marketplace will not sell. Even in a hot market, where homes are selling in days or hours, some homes will not sell. Often these homes are overpriced, so you should not use them as an indication of your own sales price.

Unfortunately, people hear what they want to hear. I am consistently surprised by home sellers who only hear part of what I tell them about competing properties.

"Well, Mr. and Mrs. Grenada, there are currently six homes for sale in your neighborhood that are identical to yours. The first two are both priced at $219,900. The third home is priced at $221,900. The fourth and fifth homes are both priced at $224,900, but both have brand new kitchens with granite counter tops, which is an upgrade from your home. The last one is priced, and you won't believe this, at $289,900."

The response is almost always the same. "Yes, we saw that one. It's on Frankfurter Street. We've been comparing our home to that one, and ours is much nicer. We have better landscaping and we dry-walled the garage. That one still had an open studded garage."

You may laugh, but the truth is that it is far easier to view another person's situation objectively than to view your own objectively. Everyone wants to believe the best possible scenario, and some neighbor has probably told you that he knows something about value and your home is worth at least $50,000 more than it really is.

Of course, you also need to price your home competitively with other similar homes in the marketplace. This is hard because you must be completely objective. If you are pricing your property above the most similar homes, it is very unlikely to sell. Buyers viewing the property may have a positive feeling. They may even like your home the best out of the dozen or fifteen homes they view. However, they will most often make an offer on the home they feel is the best value. This is critical in any market and extremely critical in a slowing market. Fewer homes are selling, so you need to make every showing count. If only one in two homes being put on the market is selling, you will need to make sure your home shows better than your neighbor's and is priced competitively. Overpricing your home leads to your neighbor's home being sold at your expense.

The form included below is a typical *Realtor's Competitive Market Analysis* (CMA) *form*. When reviewing one with an agent, pay close attention to the homes that have sold recently in the area and their sales prices. These indicate what buyers in the marketplace are willing to pay for homes like yours. Also, when your home eventually sells, a buyer will be likely to take out a mortgage. The mortgage company will hire an appraiser to verify their investment in loaning money to the buyer. The appraiser will look at the same sold comparable properties and determine what your home is worth based on these comparables. If the appraiser feels the buyer overpaid for the home, the bank will not fully fund the loan on your home.

Competitive Market Analysis

	Style	Size	Beds/ Baths	Lot Size	List Price	Sales Price	Sales Date
Available							
153 Juniper Street	2 Sty Colonial	2850 sf	4/2.5	33 Acres	$359,000		
1416 Court Lane	2 Sty Colonial	2778 ft	4/2.5	32 acres	$349,900		
255 Caitlin Way	2 Sty Colonial	2825 sf	4/2.5	28 Acres	$354,900		
1215 Bridge Street		2695 sf	4/2.5	35 Acres	$365,000		
Recently Sold							
867 Ravens-wood Drive	2 Sty Colonial	2885 sf	4/2.5	34 Acres	$359,000	$345,000	11/1/07

1428 Logan Avenue	2 Sty Colonial	2790 sf	3/2.5	36 Acres	$349,900	$341,000	2/1/19
875 Six Flags Lane	Bi-level	2880 sf	4/2.5	29 Acres	$329,000	$328,000	2/12/19
233 Orange Grove Avenue	2 Sty Colonial	2650 sf	4/2.5	42 Acres	$345,000	$339,000	1/15/19
Expired							
192 Addison Way	2 Sty Colonial	2650 sf	4/2.5	29 Acres	$359,000		
210 Jupiter Street	Bi-level	2770	4/2.5	33 Acres	$362,500		
1915 Parlay Court	2 Sty Colonial	2890	3/2.5	35 Acres	$369,000		

The second group to pay attention to on a CMA form is the *available* or *active listings*. These are homes for sale now that are similar to yours. Remember that you are competing with these homes for the same buyers. If the market is hot, you may have to wait for or hope for other homes to sell if they are priced more aggressively. You may find, however, that there are always more homes coming on the market as competition. If the market has slowed down, you will need to be one of the best homes on the market in order to attract the buyers.

The last group is the *expired listings*, or homes that had been on the market but were unsuccessful in selling. These may have failed to sell because of marketing or staging, but they may also have been overpriced for the current market. View these as an upper limit to a price range that may not be selling for your type of home.

The Dirty Little Secret of Realtor® Pricing

As I explained in our introductory chapter, one of the problems with relying solely on Realtors® to provide you with an evaluation of your price is that some Realtors® artificially inflate their numbers in order to obtain a listing. While most Realtors® are of honest and have a great amount of integrity, there are others who are not.

Unfortunately, however, home sellers tend to select the agent who gives them the highest price. That agent typically smiles, gets excited about the home and tells the seller that she is absolutely certain she can have the house sold in a few weeks. Other Realtors® have found themselves losing over and over to these artificially inflated prices, and they begin exaggerating prices as well. It's a vicious cycle.

Example

A few weeks ago, I found myself at the home of James and Lisa, home sellers who were competing against new construction. The model of their home was the exact same model as the builder's model, which was for sale across the street. The builder's model was professionally decorated, absolutely beautiful, and priced at $424,900. I was the fourth Realtor® to meet with James and Lisa.

"At what price would you sell the home?" Lisa asked me.

"I don't price homes, Lisa." I replied calmly, "The market prices them. I simply interpret what the market is currently doing."

"I don't understand." She said.

"Let me ask you a question. What price do you want for the home?"

"I'm looking for you to give me a price. You're the professional."

"I understand that. Then let me ask what the other Realtors® you met with told you."

"Well," James chimed in. "The first one told us $450,000 easily. We had Pergo floors put in two of the bedrooms. The second said he really thought we could get closer to $500,000. The last one agreed with the second and said $500,000 would be no problem."

"Did any of them mention that the home across the street is only $424,900?"

"Well, sure, but they said that home wasn't selling because it wasn't being marketed properly." James explained.

"And the last agent said they could get higher prices because they had connections in New Jersey, and New Jersey buyers pay more than Pennsylvania buyers." Lisa added.

"Wow. Do you honestly believe that a buyer would drive an hour to save on taxes and buy a less expensive home than they could buy in New Jersey, only to look at just one home without viewing the exact same model that's for sale across the street with a big sign and banners on it?" I asked.

"I'm not sure." She replied. "Maybe."

Sadly, this kind of treatment of clients by some agents is what gives some agents a bad name. Another agent might have told them "$500,000? I have connections in New York and can probably get you $525,000!" With a good story, and the hope of getting more money, too many sellers fall into the trap of over listing. Sellers find their own version of irrational exuberance. The agent then spends the next six months beating up the client to reduce the price or avoiding the client altogether, while they take client calls on the sign in front of the client's home and switch them to more reasonably-priced properties. Worse, some agents may use the property to show first, and then take buyers to a second, lower-priced home, in order to show the value in the second home.

Luckily, finding a good Realtor® is not difficult. Ask your friends, relatives, coworkers, and neighbors for recommendations of whom they've used and who worked hard. Then consider the pricing objectively and base your decision of which Realtor® to hire on the strength of their marketing and servicing programs, not because they tell you a number you want to hear.

One way to price your home is to take matters into your own hands and visit all the local open houses, drive by homes for sale, and ask an agent to show you any competing homes that are vacant. Buyers learn about the pricing of homes by viewing homes for sale.

You can do the same thing in order to position your home correctly in the marketplace.

If you are still having difficulty determining an accurate price range for your home, or if you have a truly unique property, try hiring an appraiser. An appraiser will give you an independent, objective professional opinion of the value of your property.

Appraised Value

In order to understand proper pricing, it is necessary to review the methods used to determine value. Appraisers are considered the last word on a property's value. An appraisal is supposed to reflect the likely price at which a property will sell during a normal marketing period. This is known as the *fair market value* of the property. The appraiser should have no interest in the value of the house, and therefore is an objective professional.

Typically, an appraisal is based on an inspection and evaluation of the home. The evaluation is laid out on a standard form known as a *Uniform Residential Appraisal Report* (URAR). The report allows the appraiser to use three methods of evaluating the property's value and assigning each method a different weight in the final analysis.

QUICK TIP:
Price vs. Timing

Timing has a lot to do with garnering the highest sale price. If you are in a desperate position to sell quickly, you may have to price your home under the market value in order to have a quick sale. Each year we receive calls from several prospective clients who ask for help forty-five to sixty days before a sheriff's sale, at which time their lender will foreclose and take back the home.

Most of these clients honestly believe they have time to shop for the highest price from a buyer. If the average home sale, however, takes forty five days from the time a buyer makes an offer until he or she settles on the home, and the average home in your marketplace takes forty five days to sell, that home seller needed to have the home on the market a month or two ago. In order to attract buyers quickly, the homeowner should price the property at a wholesale number, approximately 10% to 15% below market value.

If a prospective buyer requires a mortgage, the bank or lender will generally require an appraisal by a licensed real estate appraiser. An appraisal is required by the lender in order to ensure the lender that the home contains sufficient equity and value and that the property could be resold to pay off the debt, should the buyer default on the loan.

The appraiser typically makes his or her determination of value by using several methods of comparison with other recently sold homes in the same general area and of the same type as the property being sold. In the appraiser's final report to the lender, he or she will reconcile the three different approaches and give different weights to each. The primary three methods of comparison are:

- *the market data approach or sales comparison approach;*

- *the reconstruction cost less depreciation approach; and,*

- *the income method approach.*

Market Data Approach or Sales Comparison Approach

The *market data approach* or *sales comparison approach* to appraising property is a comparison of the property to other properties of similar size and condition in the same area. Evaluating the property entails adjusting the value of the home by adding and subtracting for size, location, amenities, and condition in comparison to other recently sold properties in the market. Typical appraisals will only use comparable homes that were sold within six months of the date of the appraisal. The market data approach is widely accepted as the most accurate method of comparison for residential real estate. One of the difficulties in analyzing unique properties is that there are limited options for comparing properties, as you will see in the sample appraisal provided.

Reconstruction Cost Less Depreciation Approach

The *reconstruction cost less depreciation approach* determines value by determining the value of the land under the home, and then adding the cost to rebuild the dwelling at current market prices. The appraiser then subtracts the *physical depreciation* (wear, tear, and age) and any *functional obsolescence* (new homes have features that older homes do not). This is often a useful comparison if the home being purchased is relatively new.

Income Method Approach

The *income method approach* is still based on similar properties in the same area, but the comparison is strictly of the income generated by the property if the property were leased in comparison to the income generated by other similar properties recently sold in the market.

While an appraiser should have no interest in the ultimate fair market value of a house, some appraisers may be swayed by the mortgage company that assigns them appraisals. Mortgage brokers are not paid commissions unless they close a loan. The loan is partially predicated on the home appraising for the full sales price. So mortgage officers may apply pressure to their appraisers, holding out the carrot of more paid appraisals. This is an unethical practice.

Despite this, when you are attempting to determine your home's most likely sales price, appraisal by a certified appraiser is one way to obtain an unbiased professional opinion of value.

Sample Appraisal with Sales Comparison Approach:

Valuation Section

File No. 00000135

COST APPROACH		
ESTIMATED SITE VALUE .... = $		Comments on Cost Approach (such as, source of cost estimate, site value, square foot calculation and for HUD, VA and FmHA, the estimated remaining economic life of the property):
ESTIMATED REPRODUCTION COST-NEW-OF IMPROVEMENTS.		
Dwelling _____ Sq. Ft. @ _____ = $ _____		
_____ Sq. Ft. @ _____ = _____		
Garage/Carport ___ ___ Sq. Ft. @ _____ = _____		
Total Estimated Cost New .... = $ _____		
Physical Functional External		
Less Depreciation _____ = $ _____		
Depreciated Value of Improvements .... = $ _____		
"As-is" Value of Site Improvements .... = $ _____		
INDICATED VALUE BY COST APPROACH .... = $		

ITEM	SUBJECT	COMPARABLE NO. 1	COMPARABLE NO. 2	COMPARABLE NO. 3
Address	170 Crestview Drive	248 Windy Hill Road	30 Valley Lane	513 Fox Drive
	Center Valley, PA 18032	Coopersburg PA 18036	Center Valley, PA 18032	Coopersburg, PA 18036
Proximity to Subject		0.27 MI NNE	3.4 MI WSW	0.44 MI NW
Sales Price	$ 425,000	$ 429,500	$ 420,500	$ 425,000
Price/Gross Liv. Area	$ 129.73	$ 116.90	$ 131.41	$ 121.43
Data and/or Verification Source	Personal Inspection	MLS/PUBLIC RECORDS	MLS/PUBLIC RECORDS	MLS/PUBLIC RECORDS

VALUE ADJUSTMENTS	DESCRIPTION	DESCRIPTION	+(-)$ Adjustment	DESCRIPTION	+(-)$ Adjustment	DESCRIPTION	+(-)$ Adjustment
Sales or Financing		CONVENTIONA		CONVENTIONA		CONVENTIONA	
Concessions		CONCESSIONS	-1,500	CONCESSIONS	0	CONCESSIONS	0
Date of Sale/Time	8/1/2008	5/20/2008 CL	0	2/01/2008 CL	0	7/16/2008 CL	0
Location	AVERAGE	AVERAGE	0	AVERAGE	0	AVERAGE	0
Leasehold/Fee Simple	FEE SIMPLE	FEE SIMPLE	0	FEE SIMPLE	0	FEE SIMPLE	0
Site	0.93 ACRES	1.07 ACRES	0	1.07 ACRES	0	1.03 ACRES	0
View	AVERAGE	AVERAGE	0	AVERAGE	0	AVERAGE	0
Design and Appeal	COLONIAL	COLONIAL	0	COLONIAL	0	COLONIAL	0
Quality of Construction	AVERAGE	AVERAGE	0	AVERAGE	0	AVERAGE	0
Age	30+ YRS	33 + YRS	0	31 + YRS	0	22 + YRS	0
Condition	AVERAGE	AVERAGE	0	AVERAGE	0	AVERAGE	0
Above Grade Room Count	Total 10 / Bdrms 5 / Baths 2.0	Total 10 / Bdrms 5 / Baths 2.1	-3,000	Total 9 / Bdrms 5 / Baths 2.1	-3,000	Total 8 / Bdrms 4 / Baths 2.1	0
Gross Living Area	3,276 Sq. Ft.	3,674 Sq. Ft.	0	3,200 Sq. Ft.	0	3,500 Sq. Ft.	0
Basement & Finished	FULL	FULL	0	FULL		FULL	
Rooms Below Grade	FINISHED	FINISHED		FINISHED	6,000	FINISHED	0
Functional Utility							
Heating/Cooling							
Energy Efficient Item							
Garage/Carport	2 CAR GARAGE	2 CAR GARAGE	0	2 CAR GARAGE	0	2 CAR GARAGE	0
Porch, Patio, Deck,							
Fireplace(s), etc.							
Fence, Pool, etc.							
Air Conditioning	OBB-CENTRAL	OHW/CENTRAL	0	OBB-CENTRAL	0	EHA/CENTRAL	0
Net Adj. (total)		+ X - $	-4,500	X + - $	3,000	+ - $	0
Adjusted Sales Price of Comparable		-1.05 % Net / 1.05 % Grs	$ 425,000	0.71 % Net / 2.14 % Grs	$ 423,500	0 % Net / 0 % Grs	$ 425,000

Comments on Sales Comparison (including the subject property's compatibility to the neighborhood, etc.) _____

ITEM	SUBJECT	COMPARABLE NO. 1	COMPARABLE NO. 2	COMPARABLE NO. 3
Date, Price, and Data Source, for prior sales within year of appraisal	04/11-1998 268,000	NONE IN LAST 3 YRS	NONE IN LAST 3 YRS	NONE IN LAST 3 YRS

Analysis of any current agreement of sale, option, or listing of the subject property and analysis of any prior sales of subject and comparables within one year of the date of appraisal: SUBJECT PROPERTY HAS NOT BEEN SOLD OR LISTED WITHIN THE PAST 36 MONTHS EXCEPT AS AFOREMENTIONED.

INDICATED VALUE BY SALES COMPARISON APPROACH .... $ 425,000
INDICATED VALUE BY INCOME APPROACH (If Applicable) Estimated Market Rent ___ 3,000/Mo. x Gross Rent Multiplier ___ 140 = $ 420,000

This appraisal is made X "as is" ☐ subject to repairs, alterations, inspections or conditions listed below ☐ subject to completion per plans and specifications
Conditions of Appraisal: _____

Final Reconciliation: _____

The purpose of this appraisal is to estimate the market value of the real property that is the subject of this report, based on the above conditions and the certification, contingent and limiting conditions, and market value definition that are stated in the attached Freddie Mac Form 439/Fannie Mae Form 1004B (Revised _____).
I (WE) ESTIMATE THE MARKET VALUE, AS DEFINED, OF THE REAL PROPERTY THAT IS THE SUBJECT OF THIS REPORT, AS OF _____ (WHICH IS THE DATE OF INSPECTION AND THE EFFECTIVE DATE OF THIS REPORT) TO BE $ _____ 425,000

APPRAISER:	SUPERVISORY APPRAISER (ONLY IF REQUIRED):	
Signature	Signature	☐ Did ☐ Did Not
Name	Name	Inspect Property
Date Report Signed	Date Report Signed	
State Certification # _____ State	State Certification # _____ State	
Or State License # _____ State	Or State License # _____ State	

Freddie Mac Form 70 6-93   PAGE 2 OF 2   Fannie Mae Form 1004 6-93

Understanding Price Positioning and Price Points

Whether you are selling your home on your own or you choose a Realtor® to market the home, you have to understand how pricing may affect your number of showings. Buyers searching on the Internet and Realtors® searching on the MLS both search by price range. On most major real estate portals on the Internet, there are drop down boxes that allow a user to limit the search by price range. The top two restrictions that buyers put on Internet home searches are number of bedrooms and price range.

In low and moderate price ranges, buyers tend to search in increments of $10,000. A buyer looking for a townhome in Memphis may search Century 21's real estate pages for homes priced between $150,000 and $180,000. In higher price ranges, buyers tend to search in $25,000 ranges. Luxury home buyers often search in increments of $100,000.

If, for example, you have a twenty-four hundred square foot detached home in the suburbs of Chicago and wish to sell it for $450,000, you may decide to price the home at $459,900 to give yourself some room to negotiate. While this may sound like a good idea on the surface, you may be eliminating many potential buyers from even knowing your home is for sale.

Recently, we had a home listed for sale just about $300,000. The home seller really needed to sell at $300,000 in order to make his move. In nearly four months on the market, the home did not receive a single offer, because the owner was slightly above the range for this type of home. Reducing the price to $299,900 and re-entering the home into the MLS and Internet sites as if it were a new listing repositioned the home to buyers. Even in a buyer's market, we were able to generate three offers in less than a week and sell the home for full price.

Net Proceeds

While the sales price is important, the most important number you will need to know is the amount of net proceeds from your sale.

You may have an outstanding mortgage on the property and an equity loan for those new windows you put in last year or for the pool out back. You will also have closing costs to pay in order to sell a home.

First, determine what is currently owed on your mortgage. If you receive monthly mortgage statements, your principle balance should be printed on it. The principle balance is a close approximation of your current mortgage payoff. Your mortgage, however, is paid in arrears. This means that if you settle on the house halfway through a month, you can owe part of the next month's payment when you settle. A safe calculation is to include an extra month's mortgage payment on top of the balance printed on your statement. If your lender does not send you a monthly statement, you may need to call to find out your payoff amount.

Next, determine if you have any other loans that may have been placed against the home. Home equity loans are liens against the property and must be paid off when you settle the home. If you purchased new windows, siding, or other upgrades to the home that were financed through the home improvement company, these liens were also placed against your home. I have had many homeowners argue that the window company told them it was a personal loan, only to find that they had a lien placed on the home for the money owed for the improvement.

If you owe any money to any municipal authority, such as water or sewer bills, these are often placed against the home as liens and will need to be paid off in order to transfer clear title to the buyers. The Internal Revenue Service (IRS) may also place liens against the property if you are behind on paying your income taxes. If you are concerned about any potential liens being held against the property, you may want to ask a local title company or attorney to run a lien search or title search on the property. Additionally, states are passing laws that require any overdue child support payments to be paid in full prior to the transfer of any property.

Finally, you will need to determine how much you have to pay in typical *closing costs* in your area. Closing costs paid by the seller may include realtor fees, recording fees, notary fees, transfer taxes, and even title searches in some parts of the country. As of the writing of this books, thirty-seven states and Washington D.C. have all imposed taxes on the sale of real estate. The taxes range from .01% of the sales price in Colorado to over 4% in some locations. Additional transfer taxes have been imposed by counties or municipalities that increase transfer taxes in some areas to 5% of the sales price of the home. To determine your area's common closing costs, consult a Realtor®, title agent, or attorney. The following formula and example show how you would calculate your net proceeds from the sale of the home:

Calculating Net Proceeds

Projected Sales Price:

Closing Costs:

    Realtor Fees: _____

    Transfer Taxes: _____

    Notary Fees/Filing Fees: _____

    Deed/Document Preparation: _____

    Title Insurance Fees: _____

Net Proceeds Before Liens:

    Less First Mortgage: _____

    Less Second Mortgage: _____

    Less Other Liens: _____

Net Proceeds After Liens: _____

Example:
    A home seller sells a $200,000 home with a Realtor® who charges 5% commission. The local transfer tax is 1%, and other fees add up to approximately $120. The seller owes $102,080 on his first mortgage and a balance of $5,000 on new windows.

Calculating Net Proceeds

Projected Sales Price: $200,000

Closing Costs:

> Realtor Fees: (5%) $10,000
> Transfer Taxes: (1%) $2,000
> Notary Fees/Filing Fees: $120
> Deed/Document Preparation: $0
> Title Insurance Fees: $0

Net Proceeds Before Liens:

> Less First Mortgage: $187,880
> Less Second Mortgage: $0
> Less Other Liens: $5,000

Net Proceeds After Liens: $80,800

chapter three:

Market Timing

Market Timing—Is Now the Time to Sell?

When is the best time to sell a property? If the market is declining, should you wait until the decline is over and the market starts uphill again? If you need to sell this year, should you wait for the spring market, or is it okay to list the property for sale on January 2? Will you get more for your home if you sell it in June instead of April? These are all questions asked regularly by home sellers attempting to sell for top dollar.

Is Any Season Really Any Better Than Any Other Season?

The honest answer is usually no. In most parts of the country, sales are at their highest levels in the spring. The warmth and sunlight bring out spring fever in buyers. Lawns begin turning green and flowers erupt in yards everywhere. Potential buyers begin getting tax refunds and they consider using the refund as part of a down payment.

This does not necessarily mean that you will sell your home for more money in the spring than any other time of year. There are certainly more buyers in the marketplace looking at homes, but there are also more homes on the market for sale. Ask local Realtors® or check local news articles to determine your own market's hot months for selling.

If you're timing your home sale by the peak season, be careful to analyze the bar graph depictions in news articles that describe when houses sell. Many of the graphs are based on the date that the property deed transfers. The deed, however, transfers after settlement, and in most cases, settlement occurs thirty to sixty days after the home is placed under agreement. Make sure any graphical representation of the market is based on the sale's contract date, not the settlement date or transfer date.

Next, find out from the local Association of Realtors® how long the average home in your market is for sale before selling. Your local association can be found under the "Directories" tab on www.Realtor.org. This average time on the market is often called *days on market* by Realtors®. If you plan to sell a home during the peak sales season in your area, determine what that sales season is, and count back by the average days on market. If a large portion of the homes sold each year sell between April 15 and June 15, and the average days on market is forty-five days, you may want to list on March 1, which should be forty-five days prior to the market taking off in your area.

1Homes sell in every season, although they may not show their best in the dead of winter.

Despite the fact that fewer home sales occur in the winter nationally, some real estate pros swear by winter marketing. They explain that many homeowners remove their homes from the market in November and December for the holidays, to avoid showings during that period. A significant percentage of home sellers keep their homes off the market for the winter because they believe there will be little activity and they don't want the aggravation of buyers tramping snow or mud through their homes.

Additionally, home sellers argue that homes in colder climates tend to show their worst in the winter months. The yard is brown. The flowers are dead. Daylight is significantly shortened, leaving a home appear darker in the winter. Windows are constantly closed, making some homes appear stuffy.

However, even in the dead of winter in Maine and Nebraska, there are people who want or need to purchase a home. Leases are ending for tenants. Companies are relocating employees who want to purchase rather than lease, and other potential buyers simply get an itch to purchase. A shortage of inventory may ultimately help a seller to realize a higher sales price from a serious buyer in the winter market.

Example:

A few years ago, one of my clients had to make the decision whether or not to keep her home on the market through the winter. Caitlyn's husband had already been transferred out of the area and was working on the other side of the country. She and their children had stayed behind until the home sold, and she was worried that she would get even less in the winter than during the spring. The decision was whether to hold the home off the market for a few months and try again, or to keep marketing straight through the holidays.

She elected to keep the home on the market, in hopes of reuniting with her husband more quickly. She decorated every part of the home, and even ran Christmas lights to the For Sale sign in the lawn. We put the finishing touch of a red bow on the sign. A relative of one of the neighbors was visiting for the holidays and saw the home with all its decorations. She called to see the home, fell in love with it, and decided to relocate close to her relatives. The seller negotiated by throwing in all the appliances and the lawn tractor and was able to sell the home at full asking price.

If you decide to market your home during winter months, there are a few recommendations to keep in mind. First, make sure to keep your walkways clear of ice and snow and lay down salt or sand on areas that tend to get slippery. You do not want the liability of someone falling while visiting your home. Second, put the warmth of your home on display by making certain the heat is set a little high. You can even keep any fireplace on for showings. Finally, take some time and decorate festively for whatever holiday you might celebrate. A festive home at a holiday time of year really stands out from the crowd.

Is it a Seller's Market or a Buyer's Market?

Like a rollercoaster, the number of homes that are sold in the country, or in any local market, go up and down from year to year. There are three types of markets: a seller's market, a buyer's market, and a normalized market. Recognizing which market you're in can help you to maximize your sales price. If the market is declining, for example, you may want to price your home slightly lower than competing homes in order to sell the property before prices decline further. If the market is improving, you may be able to price the home slightly high, if you have the time, and wait for the market to catch up with your price.

A *seller's market* is defined as a market where there are more buyers searching for homes than there are homes for sale. The price of homes tends to rise because the demand of buyers exceeds the supply of homes for sale. In very strong seller's markets, demand pushes prices up very quickly as buyers bid against each other to purchase a home. Homes sell quickly and close to asking price or higher.

A *buyer's market* is a market where there are more homes on the market than buyers in the marketplace. In a buyer's market, home prices tend to fall as sellers compete for offers from the buyers.

Sellers offer more incentives to buyers, and buyers have far more choice in their purchase. Homes sell more slowly in a buyer's market.

A *normalized market* occurs when the market is in balance. There are roughly as many home buyers as there are home sellers. Prices tend to stabilize and may slowly rise or fall.

Your local news will be likely to report whether your local market is a booming seller's market or declining buyer's market. It's trickier to watch for a change of direction. Markets can change very quickly, and even experts are fooled into believing a market is going one way when it's actually begun a slide in the other direction.

One way to keep track of the market is to check the statistics kept by your local Association of Realtors® . When the average home begins taking longer to sell, the market is likely to be slowing into a buyer's market. When the average home starts selling more quickly, the market is likely to be accelerating into a seller's market.

The Market is Declining. Should I Wait until it Recovers?

Whether or not to sell a home in a slowing market depends on several factors. Are you planning to purchase another home? Must you sell in order to purchase that other home or to complete a job transfer? Must you move this year, or do you have the luxury of selling at your own pace? Can you possibly purchase another home without first selling your current home?

If you're planning to move up to another home in the same marketplace and need the equity from your home in order to purchase, then it doesn't matter if you sell in an improving or declining market. This is a concept that many homeowners have difficulty wrapping their brains around. The local real estate market is what's moving up and down, not the individual value just of *your* home.

If the market depreciates by 5% and you're selling a $200,000 home in order to purchase a $400,000 home, you may have lost $10,000 in equity by selling at the bottom of the market rather than at the peak. However, the home you're purchasing as a replacement may have been reduced by 5% also, which is $20,000 on a $400,000 home. In this case, a declining market may actually work in your favor when trading up.

> ## QUICK TIP:
> ### Researching Your Market
>
> There are several ways to research your local real estate market. The best statistics may be found by calling your local Association of Realtors. You can find your local association by going to www.Realtor.com and clicking on "Directories." Many associations have their research online in easy-to-understand formats.
>
> A Second source is your local newspaper website. Search through the business or real estate section over the past few months for numbers or statistics about the marketplace. Newspapers keep a wealth of information online. Although you may have to pay a small fee for access to their database, the information is usually worth the price. Additionally, you may be able to find physical copies of newspapers from the last several months at the local library.
>
> Other good sources of information are local real estate blogs, state and local economic development offices, and local realtors and appraisers

The only other factor where you may lose money trading up in a local marketplace is if you purchase a home when interest rates are rising. If you are holding a 4% fixed rate mortgage on your current home, and the current interest rates are 6.75%, you may consider that a loss as well, because the cost to borrow the same $200,000 you owe on your home is now higher. The home you purchase will cost significantly more per month. Keep in mind, however, that the interest rates in the early 1980s were around 15% to 17%. The historical averages tend to be close to 9%. You may never see that 4% interest rate again in your lifetime. If you are waiting for 4% to come around again, you may be in for a rude awakening if rates go back to 9%.

If, alternately, you're planning a move from your home to another area of the country, you'll have to determine if the market you are moving to is a strong seller's market or a weak market. If you're moving from a depressed market in Detroit to a stable market in St. Louis or a strong market in Honolulu, you're going to have some hard decisions to make.

Should you sell the home, taking a loss, or should you attempt to rent out the home and hold onto it until the market improves? There are a few key elements to consider when making your decision.

First, many property owners find it difficult to manage rental properties when they live in the same town as the rental properties. It is extremely difficult to manage a property across the state or the country.

Second, real estate cycles tend to be long cycles. Some last ten years or more. The market will fall and then stabilize for a few years before it picks up again. If your intention is to rent out the house until the market improves, you may be in for a very long wait.

Third, there are tax consequences of holding onto a property once you vacate it. If you move out of your primary residence and lease it for a few years, the IRS will consider it an investment property and nail you with capital gains taxes, which may eat up most or all of the gain you make from the rise in the market.

Finally, if you are considering holding onto your property as an investment until prices rise, look objectively at other investments. Keep in mind that by holding onto the property, you are considering it to be a hard asset or an investment. Whatever money you would get out of the property today is your investment in that property. What kind of return would you get if you invested that same amount of cash into another investment vehicle like a mutual fund or money market?

For example, if you owe $100,000 on a property currently valued at $150,000, you have some equity. You may pay $10,000 in closing costs when you sell the property, but that still leaves you $40,000. The reason you do not want to sell now is that your home *had* been valued at $160,000 a couple years ago at the peak of the market and you do not want to "give your house away." You should expect to hold onto the home for at least the next three or four years to get back to that $160,000.

If, instead, you took that $40,000 and placed it in a certificate of deposit or money market for the next four years, would you make more money, or a better return, than you would by leaving the money in the home, hoping for home prices to rise? While this is a question for you to discuss with your Realtor® or your accountant, in many cases, you are better off using the money for something else.

chapter four:

Figuring Out
the Best Way to Sell

Every year I speak with a few dozen home sellers who tell me that they don't understand why anybody would pay a realtor 5–6% of their hard-earned equity for simply putting a sign in the ground and listing the property on Realtor.com and Zillow. After all, there are plenty of books on the market about selling a home by yourself, and no one knows the home like the owner.

Trying to sell your home on your own is not as easy as many homeowners believe. It's a complicated process of financing, legal paperwork, skilled negotiating, and marketing. Further, only a small percentage of owners trying to sell by themselves actually complete a transaction. Different studies have placed the number between 7% and 20% of those who initially try to sell on their own do. If you can save the commission on a home sale, though, you might be able to save a lot of money. If the market is very hot, you may want to try selling your home for a few weeks by yourself.

If you do attempt to sell on your own, there are several issues to be conscious of. First, you must be concerned with safety. Houses that are for sale by owners can be the target of thieves casing the property, so you should try doing some basic prequalification of a potential buyer over the phone to determine his or her sincerity and qualifications before you let him or her into your house. Some thieves look though a home in order to determine what they will come back to take later. Other thieves work in pairs, where one partner talks to the owner and the other attempts to look through the home and take small items such as jewelry, money, or other small items of value.

Second, you should be concerned about any buyer's ability to finance your home. I cannot tell you the number of times a home seller has called me and said they had their home under agreement "by owner" for several months, only to find that the buyer really did not qualify for the mortgage. The buyer had initially provided the seller with some form of a prequalification letter from some Internet lender, and had strung the seller along, hoping to find a way to finance the home. Sellers lose valuable marketing time waiting for buyers like these to close, only to find they never really qualified to purchase a home.

There are many benefits to hiring a Realtor® in addition to the safety factor and the fact that agents prequalify buyers prior to entering into a contract. Several National Association of Realtors® surveys have shown that Realtors®, on average, sell homes for significantly more than 'For Sale By Owners.'

There are two primary reasons that Realtors® typically sell homes for more than owners. First, Realtors® have greater access to buyers. According to the National Association of Realtors® study, most buyers find their home through either the Multiple Listing System or through major Real Estate websites and portals. Owners who market their own homes do not have access to the MLS, and Realtors® have access to the top real estate web sites such as **Realtor.com, Century21.com, Remax.com** and other sites that are not open to homeowners selling their properties privately. Most buyers search on the Internet prior to calling on any advertisement.

Other home marketing websites, like Zillow and Trulia, allow owners to advertise their own homes, but then redirect leads on the homes back to real estate agents. This is done because Zillow is a marketing company that makes money by selling leads. A FSBO listing becomes a product by which Zillow can collect potential buyer information and sell it to agents.   Although you may be marketing independently, the buyer is more likely to come to the home represented by an agent.

Buyers elect to work with Realtors® in order to have access to the most listings possible and because they want someone to guide them through the purchasing process including mortgage application, real estate contracts, negotiations and even title insurance. All this service cost buyers absolutely nothing when working with a Realtor®, assuming the agent isn't charging an additional fee.

In a hot market where buyers are scrounging around looking for properties for sale, a sign and an ad can often be enough to sell a home by owner. In a slow market, though, signs and ads are seldom enough. Realtors® simply have a larger pool of potential buyers, and that can often lead to a higher price.

The second reason that Realtors® tend to sell homes for more money than owners is that Realtors® are negotiating as third parties. They do not have the emotion wrapped up in a sale that can often lead to the seller or buyer arguing or taking a hard stand that costs a seller the transaction. Realtors® also don't give away as much information while negotiating with the buyer as sellers tend to.

One of the major reasons some buyers choose to shop for sale by owners is that they think they will have an easier time negotiating a good deal for themselves. These buyers actually feel that you are saving the 6% commission so you should be able to drop at least 6% off the average price in the area for them to purchase your home. The primary reason homeowners attempt to sell homes on their own is to save that fee, not to reduce their asking price by that amount.

Selling For Sale By Owner

Example:
Carol is a successful attorney in Pennsylvania who tried marketing her stone-front townhome *for sale by owner*. She had experience in successfully completing negotiations and

transactions for other clients, and handled settlements at her office, so she saw no need to pay a salesperson 6% of her home's value.

A client of mine noticed her for sale sign while we were previewing another home across the street. I called Carol and asked if she would mind if I showed her home to my client, and she agreed. The home showed a bit nicer than the one across the street, but still appeared to be overpriced by about $5,000 when compared with recent sales in the neighborhood. The buyer decided to make an offer of $8,000 less than Carol's asking price, because the buyer knew the market had recently been very slow. I scheduled an appointment and sat down with Carol and her husband to review the offer. She looked at me as if I were a Martian. "I am not willing to even consider such a ridiculous offer," she informed me.

"Would you consider countering the offer? The market has been slow for several months and very few homes are selling. There are three other homes within a block of yours that are for sale, and your home is currently the highest price on the market."

"And mine is also the nicest," she countered. "Those homes are priced low because they have to sell. I do not and let me explain something. Perhaps I should have told you this earlier. I'm having an open house this

QUICK TIP:

Selling on Your Own

When deciding whether or not to sell a home on your own, you should consider the primary four components of a successful home seller and determine if you can fill those roles, or if you and your spouse can fill them together.

1. Marketing. The best home sellers, whether they are realtors or homeowners, understand the power of positioning the home correctly and attracting potential buyers through their marketing efforts. Advertising and marketing pieces should be carefully constructed to catch the attention of the most likely target buyers of a property like yours.
2. Sales. Good salespeople smile and are friendly to everyone around them. When buyers view your home, you can turn them off from making a purchase offer if you are

.(cont)

weekend. We have a large ad in the newspaper, directional signs, balloons, the works. I expect when buyers come to my home this weekend, we will have a multiple offer situation and then we'll consider your paltry offer once we've reviewed the other offers we receive."

I left. Carol called me six weeks later to ask if the buyer still had interest in the property.

Too often, homeowners cannot see the value in hiring a professional Realtor® to market their home. Worse, it's far too easy to become licensed in the real estate industry, leading to unqualified agents who give others a bad name. Everyone has an Uncle Bill or Aunt Ethel who tried out real estate for a while and left the business. That vision of unqualified Realtors® is what tends to cloud homeowners' minds to the real value of hiring a professional.

Full Service versus Discount Brokers

Another option is to hire a discount broker who charges a flat fee as the commission or a broker who sells services on an a la carte basis. Discount brokers can be advantageous in a hot market, as long as they provide the home seller with access to the multiple listing services and the major Internet sites that home sellers do not usually have access to. Of course, in a hot

grouchy or condescending. Make buyers feel welcome in your home, and chat with the buyers to determine their level of interest in the home

3. Negotiation. To obtain the highest sales price or best terms on the sale of your property, you should understand negotiating techniques and have some skill in keeping buyers interested while getting them to improve their initial offer

4. Organizing the details. Once you accept an offer, you will need to carefully lay out the steps to get to a successful closing. The sales process will be outlined later in this book, but you'll need to be certain you receive deposits on your home in a timely fashion, have inspections done promptly, follow up with the lender to make certain everything is moving smoothly, hire the moving company, and schedule title insurance and settlement. A good detail-oriented person should be able to follow the

market a trained monkey may be able to sell your home as well. In a slow or declining market, I believe that most discount brokers don't have the advertising resources to attract the greatest groups of potential buyers to your home.

The hidden secret of the discount broker, though, is that you may have to pay a traditional commission split or close to a traditional commission split once a buyer is located. Many discount real estate firms make the phones ring by advertising full service for a discounted flat fee. A homeowner interviews the agent because he or she believes he or she will be paying $3,000, $5,000, 1%, or some other reduced fee.

My experience with several discount brokerages has been that once the discount agent is in the house, they explain several options. Option one is to take the $3,500 flat fee commission. This commission often does not include the multiple listing system. If you would like MLS access, then the agent up-sells you to something closer to a traditional commission structure. Worse, under some flat fee options, if an agent outside the discount brokerage brings you a buyer, the agent charges a standard buyer's agent side commission on top of their flat fee. Let me explain it a different way. In your marketplace, there may be 2,500 Realtors®, of which ten to twenty might be part of the discount firm. If the discount firm's agents sell the property, you pay a reduced fee. If, on the other hand, any of the other 2,490 agents sell the home, you might pay an additional 3%. Since most buyers do not come directly through the listing agent, the likelihood is that you will pay the additional fee.

Under the second option, where an MLS service is included, you will be likely to pay closer to a traditional commission program. You may believe you're saving 1% or 2%, but honestly a good Realtor® can make that difference up in negotiating skill. Although there are some very skilled agents at some discount brokers, my experience has been that the majority are very new to the business and not necessarily well-trained. If the company is receiving a discounted fee, it may not be spending as much to train its agents. If the agent is receiving a discounted fee, he or she tends to go to a traditional brokerage with higher commission splits when he or she becomes skilled. This is not always the case, but it has been my experience that it is often true.

There are also a la carte real estate brokers in many markets across the country. These brokers offer a flat fee to place a property on the MLS with little or no service above the MLS access. These are forbidden in several states that have minimum Realtor® requirements of service. When you simply have the advertising tool of the MLS, you will have access to more showings, but you are again showing the property on your own, and now, rather than negotiating with the buyers directly, you're negotiating with the skilled buyer's agents for your price.

If you are attempting to sell your home for top dollar in a declining or slow market, I highly recommend using a professional. Seek out an agent who is skilled, has a strong marketing program and hopefully one that has been referred to you.

Interviewing Realtors®

In any field, there are those who are good at their chosen career. There are those who are not very good, and there are a few who are excellent. What you should look for is an agent who knows the market, understands your goals and needs, has the time to devote to marketing your property, has a good marketing and servicing program, and has the skill to properly represent you.

You should carefully research potential candidates to be your agent. Ask friends, relatives, and coworkers about good or bad experiences they have had with agents. If someone you know highly recommends a particular agent, add that person to your interview list. You can also find agents by searching for homes like yours online. Carefully review the way each agent markets properties. Do they write good advertising copy and take multiple photos of their listings? Do they offer any guarantees of their services? Many have their qualifications and experience listed on their individual websites.

Another method is to drive around the neighborhood and look for agent signs that may be repeated on multiple homes. If you know the neighbors, call and ask them how they like the agent they've chosen. Is the agent maintaining consistent contact with them? Is the agent regularly advertising the property and providing copies of ads and feedback to them?

Select three or four agents to interview. In the case of hiring a real estate professional, remember that you are the employer, interviewing prospective candidates for the position of selling your property. Just as if you were interviewing someone for a full-time job, you should check the agent's background, experience, ethics, and ask questions that will help you determine which agent is best for your situation. A sample list of questions is included in this text. Some of the most important questions to ask include the following:

- **Are you a full-time agent?** Although there are many great agents who work with our firm that started part-time and grew into our top agents, if you are looking to sell your property in a slowing market or for the most money possible, you need to hire a dedicated, full-time professional.

- **What kind of real estate experience do you have?** This is a tricky question, because I have met many agents and brokers with twenty years in the real estate industry, but who still don't know what they're doing. Ask an open-ended question and find out what kind of experience they have actually had. It's important to find out how experienced the agent is, but the next question may be more important.

- **How many properties have you sold in the last year, or in your career?** I have met a number of Realtors® who advertise they are number one producers who in reality sell very few homes each year. A successful agent sells more than two homes per month or at least twenty-four per year. If the agent is selling sixty or more homes per year, find out how many homes they list for sale. There are agents who are listing machines that prospect to find home sellers, list them, and never communicate with the seller again. You want an agent who sells a significant number of homes, but also take the time to service his or her clients.

- **What is your average list price to sales price ratio?** This question often stumps agents. Your objective is not to torture the agent while you are interviewing him or her. Your goal is to determine if the agent is successfully selling homes at or near list price. If they are, then they may be skilled at both marketing and pricing.

- **Have you sold other homes in my neighborhood or area?** This is not always necessary. A good Realtor® can sell homes anywhere in his or her market area regardless of whether or not he or she has ever sold there before. However, it is a good idea to get a feel for his or her knowledge of the marketplace.

- **Do you have any assistants or support staff?** Assistants are not necessary for an agent to be a good fit for you in marketing and selling your property. However, if the agent is selling more than thirty properties a year and does not have someone assisting them, you should be concerned that the agent will not be able to find adequate time to assist you in truly marketing your home.

- **Do you have any references?** The best agents either carry references or can provide some within a day. You are interviewing this person for the position of marketing your home. Just like any employee, you want to be able to verify the quality of their past work history.

- **Can you provide me samples of marketing you have done on other properties?** Some real estate agents can talk a good game, but don't have follow through. You want to verify that they've done the job in the past.

- **How often will you be in contact with me during the term of the listing?** A good agent should be communicating with you on a weekly basis. Any less than that, and they are clearly not focused on selling your property.

- **Do you offer any guarantees?** You are not looking for someone to guarantee that he or she will buy your home if he or she cannot sell it. Those programs are often not worth the paper they are written on. You want to know if the agent will call you regularly, try to find feedback on showings, and guarantee that they will release you from the listing if you are unhappy with the service.

- **Am I locked into this listing for six months?** Agents who are certain of their excellent service will often offer a cancellation clause in their listings. If you, as the seller, are unhappy with their service, they will release you from the listing.

- **Will you send me copies of all advertising?** What gets verified gets done. You want an agent to be willing to send you copies of all their marketing efforts so you can have input into the marketing.

- **What do you believe sets your marketing and service apart from other Realtors®?** This question may be the clincher for finding the best agent. The agent you are looking for should have integrity and should have a well thought out marketing and servicing plan.

- **At what point in time would we need to sit back down and re-evaluate the marketing?** How long will the agent work on the listing before he or she finds that you need to change direction. There is no right or wrong answer, but it gives you insight into the thought process the agent goes through when marketing a property.

The Listing Process

Once you have selected an agent, you will need to complete and sign several documents in order to list your home for sale. Most states require a consumer notice that explains how an agent works for you, a seller's property disclosure statement, a closing cost estimate, and a listing contract. Some states or municipalities require more paperwork or less.

Consumer Notices

Required consumer notices vary from state to state, but they generally spell out the real estate agent's duties and responsibilities to you as their client. When listing a property, the Realtor® generally represents your best interests in the transaction. If a buyer calls on your property or comes to an open house, the agent has a fiduciary responsibility to represent you. If the buyer tells the agent that he or she want to offer $190,000, but will pay $200,000, the Realtor® has a responsibility to repeat that because the Realtor® represents you.

A conflict can occur if your agent meets a buyer, signs a buyer agency contract with that buyer, and then introduces them to your home. The agent is now representing both sides of the transaction. At times, it may be hard to avoid this conflict. For example, if you sign a listing agreement with Realtor® Bob Smith, and Bob also has a home for sale two miles away on Cottonwood Lane, he is representing both parties. If you decide you want to purchase the house on Cottonwood Lane, then Bob would have a conflict.

These conflicts are resolved different ways in different states. In some areas, the agent may represent both parties as a *dual agent* or *limited dual agent*, being careful what information to disclose and what information not to disclose. In other areas, the agent must refer one of the clients to another agent to represent them. Discuss these options with your agent when reviewing the state's consumer notice.

Seller Property Disclosure Statements

As the name suggests, these documents are designed to disclose any known material defects to the buyer. These are important to fill out carefully so you do not unintentionally forget something that may have occurred in the past. If there has been some water penetration in the home in the past and you had it corrected, disclose the problem. The last thing you want is the buyer to move into the home, hear about the problem from a neighbor, and attempt legal action against you for fraudulent misrepresentation.

The Listing Contract

The *listing contract* is probably the most important document to review thoroughly. There are three primary types of listing representations, which are described as follows.

Exclusive Right to Sell Listing. The most common type of listing contract in most of the country, the *Exclusive Right to Sell* contract guarantees that you will pay the listing agent a commission on the sale of your home if the home is either sold during the term of the listing contract, or is sold after the expiration of the contract to someone who was introduced to the property during the term of the contract. What this means is that if you find your own buyer for the property, you still owe the agent a commission. Even if you cannot reach your agent because they're sitting on a tropical island drinking a spicy papaya margarita you still have to pay your agent. On the bright side, if you carefully select a good Realtor® who has a track record of service, they will be more likely to put a strong effort into selling the home. If the buyer is represented by another agent or real estate firm, the listing agent still collects his or her fee and splits the fee, in some fashion, with the buyer's agent.

Exclusive Agency Listing. Like the Exclusive Right to Sell contract, in an *Exclusive Agency Listing contract* if any real estate agent brings a buyer to your home, the listing agent gets paid his or her commission and generally splits the commission with the buyer's agent. The difference is that if you find your own buyer, you do not owe the Realtor® a commission. The obvious reason that most Realtors® resist this form of agency is that they do not want to spend hundreds or thousands of dollars and hours of their time marketing your home for you to sell it out from under them. Under an Exclusive Agency listing, agents are less likely to spend the money necessary to properly promote your home.

Open Listing. Open Listing contracts are most commonly found in extremely hot markets or resort areas. An open listing contract states that a property seller will pay a commission to the real estate firm that brings a successful purchase agreement to the owner. There is no single listing agent or agency because the seller will pay only the firm that brings the buyer. If the seller finds his or her own buyer, he or she pays no commission.

Listing Contract Clauses You Should Request

There are clauses you should try to negotiate with your agent, and some clauses you should watch for in listing contracts.

Exclusion Clauses. If you already have identified a buyer who has expressed interest in purchasing your home, do not wait to put the home on the market until that buyer makes a decision. You could lose valuable marketing time. Instead, ask the agent for an exclusion for ten days to attempt to close the buyer. If the buyer purchases the home after that ten-day period, ask the agent if he or she would be willing to handle the transaction for half the normal fee.

Early Termination Clauses. Ask your agent to include a clause that allows you a release from the listing contract if you are unhappy with the agent's service. This will keep the agent on his or her toes and insure against an agent who does not fulfill his or her promises. The release clause or early termination clause should spell out that you may list the property with another Realtor® immediately after the release.

Listing Contract Clauses You Should Be Wary Of

Cancellation Fee. Some real estate firms charge a fee if the seller cancels the listing. It may be called a *liquidated damages fee, cancellation fee,* or an *exit fee*. You should not have to pay a fee if the Realtor® does not provide the service promised. If you simply change your mind about selling, you will have to decide whether or not you feel you owe the Realtor® a fee for the effort he or she put into selling your home.

Document Preparation or Transaction Fees. Part of a Realtor's job is to handle all the paperwork associated with the transaction. Some Realtors® pass off part of their work to assistants and pass the cost along to you in the form of *transaction fees, conveyance fees, document preparation fees,* or similar charges. Although there are some areas of the country where this practice is common, you should not be paying any fees above the commission unless you agree to do so in writing when you list the property.

Holding the Home Off The Market

Some Realtors® try to convince home sellers that it is in their best interest to hold the property off the MLS or the open market for a few days or a few weeks. The Realtor® will offer the rationalization that he or she will have more control over the transaction and this will benefit the sellers, or that the Realtor® will give the seller a discount on the commission by a percent if the agent sells it him- or herself in the first couple weeks while the home is not in the MLS.

Do not do this. *Pocket listings* do not benefit the owner. They benefit the agent, who is using your home to try to attract buyers. They may have a tiny chance of *double popping*, which is handling both the buyer and seller, and therefore keeping the entire commission.

The reality is that you want everyone to know your home is for sale in those first few weeks. Rather than having only one agent working to find a buyer, with your home listed on MLS, you are opening your home up to all the Realtors® in the area and all the buyers those Realtors® are working with. When marketed by one single agent, you are not a whole lot better off than trying to sell on your own.

Your goal is to create demand for your home, and hopefully generate a lot of showings and multiple offers that bid the price up. Hiding the home from the open market for a few weeks does nothing for you.

There is a similar concept called a "Coming Soon" listing, which still brings the home to the open market. We'll discuss this option in the next chapter, but this can be a successful tool in a strong seller's market *if* the home truly is available to the entire public and all real estate professionals.

chapter 5:

Marketing Systems

Where do Most Buyers Come From?

A common misconception by home sellers is that they hire an agent to sell their home, and the agent will bring most of the buyers to their home. Although an agent handles a plethora of tasks, an agent is hired first to market the home and generate interest in the property. A successful realtor may be working with somewhere between five and ten active potential buyers. It is difficult to service more than ten buyers because an agent needs to be available to show them properties. What is the real likelihood that your agent happens to be working with a buyer who will purchase your home?

If my agent advertises the home, he or she be the one who finds buyers for it. While that's a nice idea, it is more likely that a buyer will see an ad and call the agent he or she is working with or find the home for sale on the multiple listing system. If your marketplace has one or two thousand real estate agents servicing the area, each of them may have three or five or ten buyers they are working with as well. In order to generate a demand for your home, you need to get everyone involved.

According to the National Association of Realtors 2018 Profile of Home Buyers and Sellers Report, 28% of buyers find an agent first, and then purchase a home using the resources of the MLS. For Sale signs only accounted for 7% of all buyers viewing the home.

This does not mean that your agent shouldn't bother marketing. On the contrary, I'm going to go through some guerilla tactics for getting your property noticed by buyers. What it does mean is that your agent needs to market not simply to the buying public, but also to other agents in the marketplace and to their buyers.

Where Buyers Found the Homes They Purchased

50%	Internet
28%	Real Estate Agent
7%	Yard Sign / Open House
7%	Friend, Relative or Neighbor
5%	Home Builder
3%	Directly from Sellers
1%	Print Ad

Source: 2018 Profile of Home Buyers and Sellers from the National Association of Realtors

2 - Source National Association of Realtors 2018

Using the MLS

Everyone's heard of the MLS, but what is it really? A multiple listing system or multiple listing service is a computer database that aggregates all the listings of real estate brokers in any region and allows the agents to share data in order to find the perfect home for their buyers. Once an agent begins working with a buyer, he or she will run computer searches of the MLS database to find homes that meet the buyer's search criteria. A buyer may only want three- to four-bedroom ranch homes with two-car garages in a particular school district. A multiple listing system allows realtors to narrow the search to just what the buyer wants.

Since we know that as many as 28% of buyers may be finding your home first on the multiple listing system, we have to find a way to entice them to set up an appointment to view the home. Making certain that the home falls into the correct price range so the home is competitive with others that are for sale in the MLS is critical, because at a high price the home may be missed entirely by searches. Other important methods of attracting attention to your home are good photographs, a strong headline, a well written description, and

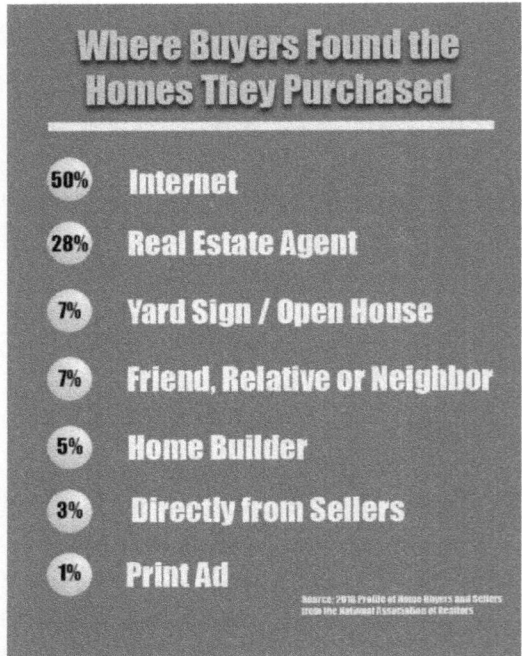

possibly a virtual tour. Your goal is to make sure your listing stands out among the thousands in the database.

In many areas, when a home initially hits an MLS system, an email alert is sent out to anyone using an *auto-prospecting program*. These programs alert buyers that a new home meeting their criteria has come on the market. You should ask your agent to make certain that an exterior photo is included in the listing prior to submitting the listing to the MLS. Buyers may overlook a home that comes to their inbox without a photo. You will not get a second chance to create that initial impact. Far too many agents enter a listing quickly and upload photos to the listing at a later time.

Homes that have more than one photograph are more likely to be clicked on than homes with only an exterior photo. Most multiple listing systems allow the agent to load multiple photos. Be certain that your agent makes use of this feature and includes photos highlighting the best aspects of your property.

Start with a photograph of the exterior of the home. Try to make sure the photo is taken without showing the street or sidewalk. If the photo *does* show the street and sidewalk, try to crop the photo with Photoshop or another program. Avoid showing power lines, street signs, and vehicles in the photo. Do your best to ensure the front of the home isn't shaded. You or your realtor may have to time the taking of photos in order to get the sun on the correct side of the home to shed light on the front of the home.

When taking photos of the exterior, when possible I suggest angled photos because they show the depth of the home rather than straight on photos of the exterior. Many agents have argued with me about this point, but I still believe angled photos are better than straight shots.

Make sure any interior rooms you photograph are well lit and show the width and depth of the room. As with any staging, photographs should showcase the home and entice the viewer into setting up an appointment to see the home. You want the photos to show bright and large rooms. If you are taking the photos yourself, try to use a wide-angle lens.

Unless your kitchen is hideous, make sure to include that particular room in the photos. When taking photos of the dining room, set the table like we described in the staging section of this text. You do not need to include every room. Some agents take photos of empty hallways, small bedrooms, and other areas that detract from the home rather than entice the buyer to set up an appointment. Incidentally, without a wide-angle camera, a bedroom shot is primarily a shot of the bed. That's not going to attract buyers.

3 - Sample screen shot of MLS posting

In addition to the photos, your agent has the opportunity to write a description or remarks about your home. Multiple listing systems generally restrict the number of words or characters used in the description, but a good realtor can use the space to entice the buyer. The description should always begin with a strong headline. You want buyers' attention to be drawn to your listing in the same fashion. The headline should provide the impact that leads the buyer to read the rest of the advertisement. Suggestions for strong headlines will be considered in a later part of this chapter.

For Sale Signs and Directional Signs

Many home sellers fear placing for sale signs on their homes because buyers may stop and knock on the door, or drive up their driveway without an appointment.

Example

Alex, a client who initially listed with one of our competitors, was absolutely against any sign being placed on the property. He pointed out that his home was not along a main road, and the only people who traveled through the area were the neighbors. Furthermore, his wife was home alone during the day, and he didn't want someone coming down their driveway and ringing the bell when she was by herself.

After a few unsuccessful months of selling, he canceled the contract with his initial agency and listed the property with our firm. We convinced Alex that he really needed to have a sign in the yard. Our compromise was that we would include on the sign that "Showings will be by Appointment Only." After only a week on the market, we received a call from Charlotte, a sister of one of Alex's neighbors. Charlotte said she had wanted to live in the neighborhood for years, but no homes had come up for sale. She hadn't been actively looking for a home, so she didn't know that Alex had his home on the market. When the for-sale sign went up, Charlotte's sister called her immediately. She paid full price for the home.

Signs are one of the best ways to attract buyers. Some of your neighbors probably already know someone who would like to live in the neighborhood. There are other buyers who are driving through your area right now looking around at what homes are for sale. Do not ignore the power of a professional-looking real estate sign.

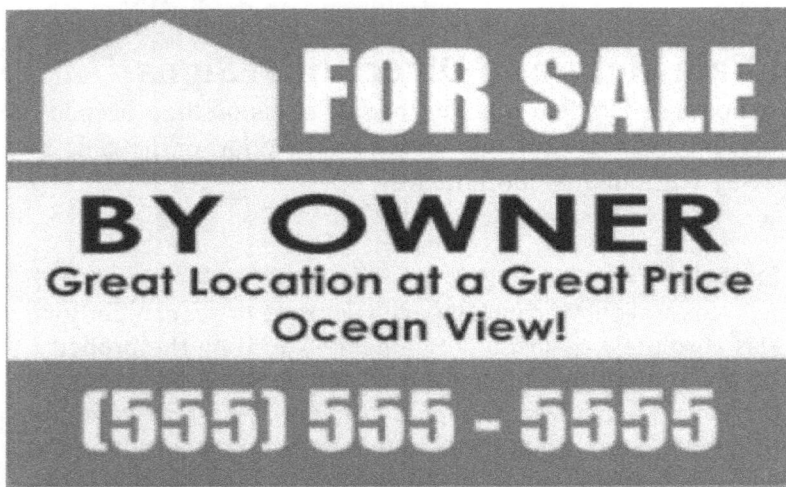

4- Having a Custom For Sale By Owner sign professionally designed makes you look more serious about selling your home

If you plan to sell your home on your own, make sure you have a professional looking sign installed in your yard. You want to convey to potential buyers that you are meticulous in everything you do. A generic sign from Home Depot with your phone number in magic marker lets buyers know that you did a quick job putting up the sign and may do the same with how you take care of the home. It also conveys that you may not be as serious about selling your property. Small sign companies are located nearly everywhere and can often have a professional-looking sign created for your home within a day or two. You can also order custom signs online at BuildASign.com or VistaPrint.

Directional signs can also help by leading buyers to your home. Buyers who are driving around an area looking for homes will home in on those little arrows and follow them to your house. A word of caution, though. If your agent places an arrow on a corner, the owner of that corner property may pick it out of their yard and throw it away. Some will even destroy the sign and leave it in place. Since you are the neighbor, and less likely to be seen as someone trespassing on their property, it would be better for you to contact the corner property owner yourself and explain how you are trying to sell your home and really would appreciate if they would allow you to have your agent place a directional arrow in their yard for a few weeks or months.

5 -Directional signs can be used to lure buyers from main roads to side roads to find you home for sale.

Marketing with Social Media

Social Media, like Facebook, Instagram and Twitter, have become more than a communication and sharing tool. Social media site developers have created the opportunity to directly target likely buyers for your home based on their likes, interests and their search habits. We never know exactly where a buyer might come from. According to the National Association of Realtors 2018 Home Buyer and Seller Report, 7% of home buyers purchase in an area where they know the neighbors.

I'm sure you've heard the concept of the "six degrees of separation." Originally the concept was that we are all connected by no more than six steps, or six social connections from each other. If

7% of home buyers purchase in a neighborhood where they know someone, imagine how many people you're connected with at work, or in the PTA or your place of worship who might know someone who knows someone looking for a home in your neighborhood? Social networking helps us to shorten the process of finding that potential connection.

Even if you simply add a photo album and ask your friends to share it, you may spark interest from the perfect buyer. There are many avenues to sharing your home listing and identifying likely buyers by using social media tools. Some of the many suggested campaigns and tools are identified in the next few sections.

The Photo Album Campaign

You can always start with simply creating a Photo Album on Facebook or Instagram of your home. Whether you're selling "by owner" or with an agent, select the best photos you can that showcase the highlights of the property and write a detailed description in the caption box for each photo. You can even include some hashtags for both the property location and each room. A hashtag for the location might be #PhiladelphiaHomeForSale or #ParklandSchoolDistrict. For a room description, you might include #GraniteCountertops or #ViewLot.

Set the album to "public" in your privacy setting so that anyone online can see them. This will not make your profile public. Finally, create a wall post referring back to your photo album, and ask your friends, co-workers and social network to share the album with their friends.

Share Online Listings to Social Media

Most online marketing platforms have a share button for top social media services. If your home is for sale on Realtor.com, ZapHomeSearch.com, Homes.com, Century21.com, Zillow or Trulia, simply click the Facebook icon near the listing and share it to your Facebook page.

| 4 bed   3 bath   1 pt. bath   5,566 sq ft $85 / sq ft   SFR |
| Lot Size 2.1 acre   Built 1994   On site 71 days |

Photos   Maps   Bird's Eye   Street View   Share:

1 of 33 photos

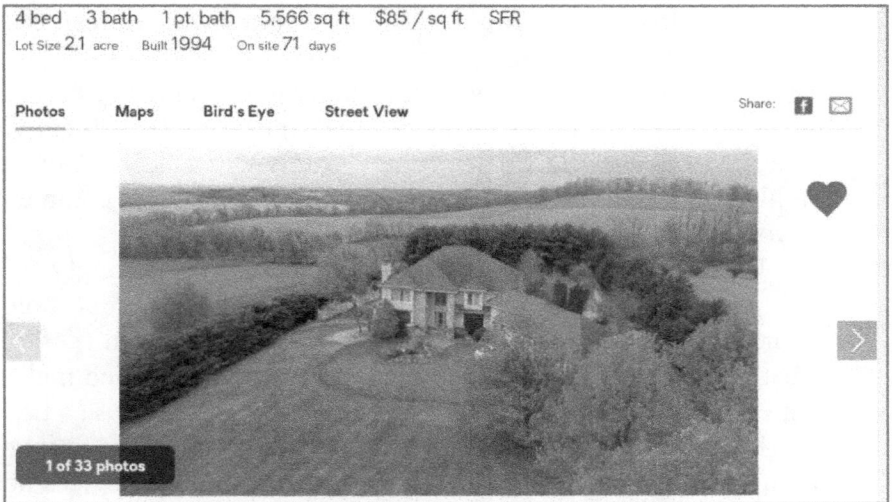

6 - Real Estate Websites generally have social media sharing tools

One negative aspect of sending potential buyers to check out the house on large aggregator sites, however, is that they will be looking at more than just your home. Chances are that they are searching on these sites as well, but you should be aware. A second negative is that sites like Zillow and Trulia sell the potential buyer information back to a Realtor®, so if you're selling on your own, that buyer will likely come with an agent charging a commission.

An alternate method is to create a website dedicated to your home with photos, video and details of the property. You can then link to that site through social media sites. Your network of friends, relatives and connections on Facebook can then share the link, increasing the reach of your marketing. There are also savvy real estate professionals who create unique property sites on all of their listings, in order to target likely buyers. We'll discuss that in a section on unique property sites.

Upload a Video

If you've hired a real estate agent who is going to pay for a stunning drone tour production with a stabilizer or a 360-degree home tour, then I would absolutely share that to every social media site possible. However, if you're selling on your own, you can create a short video without a professional camera.

Armed with a smartphone or iPad, you can either walk through the home or you can video each area separately and stitch the videos together with iMovie or nearly any free video editor. You might highlight the best features of each room by adding audio commentary, or you might simply play music in the background.

If you choose to video each area separately, I strongly suggest that you use a tripod. While most of us believe we can hold our smartphones still for video, the truth is that we can't. We are breathing and we have a pulse in our thumbs, both which makes the camera move. The end product is much cleaner if you use a tripod.

If you're walking through the home, you may want to invest in an inexpensive selfie stick stabilizer. These amazing devices help to keep the camera from bouncing while you move. Prices currently range from under $30 to several hundred. For the purpose of shooting a video to sell your home, the less expensive one is usually fine.

Again, share the video on Facebook, Instagram, YouTube and anywhere else you can, and ask your friends to share it with their friends.

Create an Event

You might consider holding an open house and creating a Facebook event for it. Invite everyone you can and ask them to invite their friends and social network. Remember to include the address and directions and make the setting public so others outside your network can see it.

Create a Fan Page for Your Home or a Marketplace Listing

Another option is to create a Facebook Page just for your house, then "Like" and share it. While Facebook only currently gives the options of Business, Brand, Community or Public Figure, many home sellers have constructed short pages around their home under the Community or Business sections.

Facebook also offers Facebook Marketplace. Select the "Item for Sale" section and under item category, you can select "Home Sale." You can add up to ten photos, a description, price and location.

Create a Targeted Ad through Social Media

Have you ever looked at a product online and found that same product or competing products or services popping up on other websites? That's because services like Facebook and Google track your online movements and record them to a profile. I was at a conference in Las Vegas a few years ago with a Facebook employee who claimed they know when someone is getting divorced before the couple knows they are getting divorced based on their ability to create profiles on every user of their service.

While this can be creepy, it does create an opportunity to tailor the targeting of your marketing to the most likely buyers at a very reasonable cost. There are buyers already online searching for homes that are searching in the price range of your home and in the same school district. While no Realtor® can specifically identify every likely buyer, Facebook and Google may have that ability.

Potential audiences for your home can be found using location-based targeting, demographic-based targeting, interest-based targeting, or behavior-based targeting. Any of these potential target audiences might allow you to narrow an advertisement to attract the most likely buyers. For example, if you believe the most likely buyers are going to come from within a ten-mile radius, you can use location-based targeting to narrow the group viewing your advertisement to a radius from your home, or the Designated Market Area. You can further narrow it to those living in the location, or those recently in the location or those traveling to the location. You can narrow your search by demographics by selecting those between 20 and 65.

Interest-based targeting can be used to find buyers for specific types of property. As an example, my firm listed a mountaintop estate for sale in excess of a million dollars. While the property was less than two hours from Manhattan by car, it was in a location that wasn't typically searched by buyers looking for retreats. The property had been listed by four firms prior to ours without selling. One of the unique features of the property was a helipad, which would make commuting to Manhattan, Philadelphia or any major area more convenient. Obtaining a permit for a private helipad can also be challenging.   We utilized a narrowly focused search to those individuals who owned or flew helicopters and had the income or assets to purchase and maintain a substantial property like the one we were marketing. The property was sold within days of our initial push to that target audience.

We have run targeted campaigns for as little as $5-per-day for seven to ten-day periods and had strong results.

Designing a comprehensive campaign to find a buyer for your home may be a bit beyond the scope of this book, but there are plenty of books, articles and YouTube videos available if you're interested in building a target audience.

Flyers and Brochures

The uses of flyers and brochures are many and varied. The type of flyer you or your agent creates to market you home depends on the target audience you are trying to attract, or where your flyer is placed. For example, if a flyer is placed in a brochure box in front of your home, it should have ad copy that will attract a buyer to view the home, but not give so much information that a buyer may eliminate the home without viewing it. A brochure placed in the home, for buyers to pick up during showings, on the other hand, should have complete information about the home including room sizes, taxes, and lot description so the buyer has something to refer to after the showing. Flyers and brochures can be used effectively to convey information about the home to potential buyers, realtors working with buyers, as well as friends, relatives, and coworkers of potential buyers who may tell them about the property.

Different kinds of flyers and brochures include the following.

Brochure Box Flyers

At times, a brochure box is helpful because buyers can take a flyer with them, without having to write down phone numbers, and call you or your realtor later to schedule a showing. The negative aspect of flyers in front of a home is that some buyers, after looking at the flyer, eliminate the home from consideration. For example, if the flyer in the brochure box has the taxes listed on it, the potential buyer may look at the flyer and determine the taxes are higher than they'd like to pay and cross the home off their list. Your home may have three bedrooms and a den, and the buyer may glance over the brochure, see three bedrooms and cross the home off their list without realizing that the home may work for their situation because they would be using the forth bedroom as an office. We have dozens of examples of buyers who initially refused to look at a home, because it didn't meet their desires, only to come back later and purchase the house they overlooked.

◆ FOR SALE

Price:	$474,990
Bedrooms:	4
Bathrooms:	3-5
Square Feet:	4028 (incl LL)

Beautiful views surround this pristine Magnolia Estates 4 BR, 3.5 Bath custom-built Colonial with in-ground pool. Just minutes from I-78, on a 1.36 acre country view lot, entertaining is a joy w/multiple decks & a patio from the walk-out lower level.

4875 Aziza Road, Lowhill Township

Loren & Theresa Keim
CENTURY 21 Keim Realtors

Phone: 610-969-7200
Cellular: 610-657-5095

Email: c21keim@gmail.com
Web Site: http://www.TheKeimGroup.com

Century 21
KEIM REALTORS

7 - Brochure Box Flyer

If you are planning to use a brochure box, select only the details that will positively impact most potential buyers. Use emotional words to describe the home and just enough detail to grab the buyer's attention. As with any other source of advertising, use a photo of the exterior of the home, a photo of the best feature of the interior, and a strong headline to convey a positive message about the home.

QUICK TIP:

By Owner Flyers

When selling on your own, you can create a flyer using Microsoft Word or one of the many word processing or publishing programs available. An alternative is to go to www.RealFlyer.com and select from its many real estate templates. The site provides an inexpensive method of uploading photos and text and having beautiful gloss flyers printed and shipped to you very quickly.

Brochure for Showings

You or your agent should prepare a several page brochure on your property to be given to potential buyers as they view your home. The brochure can have anywhere from six to twenty photos on it, highlighting the most positive features of the home. Descriptive text next to each photo helps paint a picture for the buyer.

"The dining room is large enough to accommodate a 120" table, which would easily seat ten comfortably and be perfect for holiday entertaining!"

"Spend a cold winter night snuggled up by the Moravian tile fireplace in the cozy reading nook off the family room."

"The kitchen is sure to please the gourmet in your family, featuring granite counters, stainless steel appliances, and beautiful, 42" solid oak cabinets. Sit with friends over a cup of coffee at the oversized center island."

"The luxurious master bedroom is a sanctuary away from daily strife, featuring a lavish bath and separate sitting area. Relax your sore muscles in the two-person whirlpool tub or unwind with a good book on your favorite chair in the master sitting area."

Elements that should be included in a full property brochure include:

- information on the area including information on local schools, distance to shopping, local parks, eating, and entertainment.

Remember that the buyer is purchasing a lifestyle as much as a home;

- information on the age and size of the home, number of bedrooms and baths, any amenities such as fireplaces or central air, and any upgrades to the home;

- lot size and information on the property;

- property tax information;

- a visual tour, including photos, of the highlights of the home; and,

- full contact information for your agent (or yourself if you are selling the home privately) so the buyer can easily set up a second appointment.

Flyer or eFlyers for Realtors®

Rather than simply relying on agents finding your home for sale in the MLS, or their buyers running across the home online or in a magazine, we want to improve the odds that the property is noticed. One way to do this is to create a flyer specifically designed for agents. An agent flyer can be as simple as a single sheet or double sided with details on the reverse.

The flyer should also be designed to catch the agent's attention. There are two ways to catch an agent's attention. The first is to use a great headline that may lead the agent to think about his or her clients and who that the home would be good for. The other way to catch an agent's attention is to offer the agent a benefit. You may offer a commission bonus or other incentive and use that as the headline to attract attention. Some agent incentives will be discussed in the next chapter.

There are several methods to get these flyers into the hands of agents. Many MLS systems allow a broadcast email to the membership either directly through the MLS or through a broadcast service such as MailChimp or Constant Contact. Your agent may be able to send out a broadcast email designed as a flyer, with built-in photos and video, or with an attached PDF flyer. Although emailing information to agents is the least expensive, I've found that it often produces the poorest results. Too many emails are caught by spam filters, and those that get through don't always get read.

Even in this high-tech society of Social Media, Twitter and text messaging, physical flyers still receive a solid response. That might partially be due to the fact that fewer and fewer people send anything by mail anymore.

Since most areas have at least hundreds, if not thousands, of active Realtors®, you or your agent may not wish to pay for a full mailing of a flyer or postcard on your home to all of them. Many agencies have a list of the top 10–15% of Realtors® in the marketplace and may be willing to send a flyer on your home to that specific list. Again, many MLSs will provide its members with a mailing list of the membership as well.

Another method is to simply stop by the major real estate companies in your market area and ask if they will allow you to post a flyer on their bulletin board, or better yet, put a copy of the flyer in each agent's mailbox. There may be half a dozen large real estate companies in your market area, depending on whether you are in a urban, suburban, or rural area. Hit the companies that have the most agents. You are proactively highlighting the property with this method rather than waiting for the MLS to work its magic.

Flyers to Neighbors

As stated earlier, your neighbors have friends, family members and coworkers who have expressed interest in living in your area. Take advantage of that by creating a flyer with the headline, "Pick your own neighbors!" and include language that reminds them that they may have a friend or relative who would like to live in the area. An inexpensive marketing idea is to print off one hundred or so of these flyers and walk the neighborhood, putting them in between the neighbors' front door and screen door.

Although it seldom produces significant results, you can also post these flyers on community bulletin boards at supermarkets, places of worship, laundromats, and anywhere else you find a bulletin board.

Flyers to Mortgage Brokers, Relocation Directors, Personnel Managers

There are many other sources you can hit with flyers or e-flyers. In addition to Realtors®, mortgage brokers also work with buyers. In some cases, a buyer will call a mortgage broker prior to a Realtor® in order to determine how much they can afford to spend on a house. If you can get permission to fax or email a flyer on your home to this group, you may also run across a buyer looking for a home like yours.

Relocation directors, personnel managers, and other human resource personnel are constantly moving people in and out of the area. We regularly target our personnel contacts at major corporations, hospitals, and colleges because they may pass the flyers on to people that they are relocating into the area.

Four Keys to Writing Successful Ads

Whether marketing online or in print, the four primary things most buyers want to know about properties for sale are:

1. the location

2. the asking price;

3. the type of home; and,

4. the size as expressed by number of bedrooms and baths.

Your goal as the seller is to keep them interested enough to read through the entire ad, and not provide so much information that the buyer eliminates the home from his or her list without setting up a showing.

Realtors will often avoid giving out the specific location in print advertising unless it is a very hot location. The reason for this is that the Realtor® wants the buyer to call, regardless of whether or not the home is located in an area the buyer wants. This allows the Realtor® to tell the buyer about other homes in his or her inventory that may fit the buyer's location needs. This is a very important and successful technique for Realtors® who are cross-marketing properties. Your property may help another one sell, and that property may help yours sell. If you're selling the home on your own, you have no need to do this, and would rather eliminate the call up front, so include the school district or township in the ad when selling by owner.

In advertising your home, you or your Realtor® should paint a broad picture of the home, describing it with words that evoke an emotional response. Each buyer has dreams of what the perfect home would be. Some buyers are looking for privacy or seclusion. Some buyers are looking for the perfect neighborhood for their children. Others are primarily concerned with a view lot, or an area to entertain, and still more are looking for something exotic or unique. Some buyers are thinking of one level living or being free of the heavy maintenance they have in their current residence.

First determine what brought you to the home. What was the draw that made you fall in love with this particular property? Was it the neighborhood and the proximity to parks and shopping? Was it privacy, having your own secluded paradise? Was the cul-de-sac important because you wouldn't have through traffic? Could it have been the exceptional view, or the way the sunlight streams through the kitchen windows?

Figure out what attracted you to the home, and then try to determine two or three possible target groups who would be interested in your home and why. Write several ads targeting different groups of people who may have different dreams and goals of the perfect lifestyle. Test the ads to see what appears to attract the most response.

Avoid flowery words that have no meaning because buyers will see right through them. Some of the most over-used words to avoid include "wonderful", "special", "fantastic", "lovely", "great", and "charming". Some strong opening lines are included on the list below.

- **Appealing to buyers interested in a prestigious address**
  - In an enviable location...
  - In a prized location...
  - When location truly matters...

- **Appealing to buyers interested in the property's setting**
  - Boasting a southern exposure and views of...
  - Enjoy the country life in this tranquil location...
  - A romantic hideaway...

- **Appealing to buyers interested in specific types of homes such as historic or contemporary**
  - This grand custom built...
  - Timeless appeal...
  - Thoughtfully designed...
  - Quaint and traditional...
  - The artistic craftsmanship...
  - This contemporary masterpiece...

- **Specific appeals**
  - A bright and airy home...
  - Designed to be low maintenance...
  - Natural sunlight streams through the large windows...
  - Nestled on a cul-de-sac in...
  - Featuring an open and flowing floor plan...

Emotionally Charged Words for Use in Property Descriptions		
Living Room	**Kitchen**	**Family Room**
Bold	Bright	Attractive
Captivating	Cheerful	Casual
Distinctive	Classic	Comfortable
Dramatic	Contemporary	Cozy
Elegant	Convenient	Inviting
Grand	Conventional	Relaxing
Impressive	Country	Spacious
Magnificent	Custom	Sunny
Posh	Designer	Tasteful

Living Room (cont.)	Kitchen (cont.)	Family Room (cont.)
Spacious	Eat-in	Technology-enabled
Stately	European	Warm
Striking	Galley	
Tasteful	Gourmet	**Master Bedroom**
Well-appointed	Impressive	
	Magnificent	Bold
Dining Room	Modern	Distinctive
	Open	Dramatic
Classic	Remarkable	Elegant
Distinctive	Southwestern	Grand
Elegant	State of the Art	Impressive
Formal	Step Saver	Posh
Grand	Sunny	Spacious
Impressive	Updated	Striking
Tasteful		Sunny
Traditional		Tasteful
Well-appointed		Well-appointed

Buyers also look for hot button features. Although hot features change over time, some of the most common hot features currently sought are a fireplace, whirlpool tub, granite counters, stainless steel appliances, hardwood floors, walk-in closets, and a location close to schools and shopping. These hot buttons may be included in advertising if space permits, and certainly should be included in any marketing brochures done on the property.

Internet Marketing

Most buyers do the majority of the early research for their house search on the Internet. The more locations your home can occupy on the Internet, the more easily the home can be found by potential buyers.

If you are planning to use a real estate agent to market your home, your agent should have a strong web presence. Hopefully the agent you select will have a website that is promoted, easy to find, easy to navigate, and contains lots of information about homes for sale.

Many agents use advertisements and social media campaigns to draw potential buyers to their sites in order to capture their imagination with colorful photos of homes for sale. Your agent should be updating his or her site often to include any price changes or changes you may request in the description of the property.

More important than your agent's individual site, though, is getting your home onto the largest national sites. Top sites for home searches include local MLS search sites, **Realtor.com**, **RealEstate.com**, **Homes.com**, **Century21.com**, **Zillow.com**, **ColdwellBanker.com**, **Remax.com**, Yahoo's Real Estate page, and **OpenHouse.com**. Other sites, like **MSN.com** have real estate search tools that pull listings from other sources, in this case **Realtor.com**.

If you are planning to sell your home on your own, several websites that allow owners to list their homes privately attract many buyers. Although sites like **Realtor.com** require the use of a realtor in order to be listed, top sites, like Zillow, allow an individual to place his or her own property for sale. You can set up a username on Zillow and enter information on your home.

Other sites that allow owners to privately list their homes include Craigslist and **Owners.com**. Craigslist is one of the most heavily trafficked sites on the Web.

Some sites allow a Realtor® to upload multiple photos of a home and attach virtual tours to the site as long as the Realtor® is a paid subscriber. Multiple photos on a listing tend to attract more potential buyers to click on the listing and review it. If your agent is not a paid subscriber, the most he or she can do is load the front photo and a very basic description of the home.

Virtual Tours and Video Tours

There are several different categories of marketing that fall under the term Home Tour or Virtual Tour. Each has a positive and a negative aspect and some can be quite expensive.

I have mixed feelings about virtual tours, because they must be done correctly in order to generate more showings for your home. I have found that clients are more likely to click on properties that have virtual tours, yet the showings on the properties with virtual tours in some cases have actually declined after the introduction of the tour. Virtual tours do allow home buyers to pre-screen homes, but it also leads to buyers eliminating homes from consideration that they may have truly considered had they toured the home in person.

There are some experts who argue that virtual tours increase the online traffic to a home's information and can eliminate the need for some showings because the buyer may not have real interest in the home if it doesn't look right on the screen.

The Virtual Tour or Slide-Show Tour

More than half of all virtual tours of homes online are truly only slideshows displaying the photos of the home. Several software packages pan photos as if they are video, while playing soft music in the background. While these tours are fine for the average consumer, they simply take buyers through the same photos that are likely on the agent's website.

The 3D Tour or Virtual Walk-Through

While some consider 3D tours to be a form of Virtual Reality, there are varying levels and quality of virtual walk-throughs from very poor to exceptional. A virtual walk-through is not a video. Instead, it allows prospective buyers to partially experience the home without actually scheduling a visit by navigating through the home on a PC, iPad, phone or with special glasses.

Early 3D tours were created with fish-eye lens cameras from the center of each room. The camera would be placed on a tripod in the center of the room and would pan the entire room. In many cases, the photographer was taking photos too close to plain walls and may actually have made the rooms appear smaller. While most of these tours have been replaced by higher quality software and equipment, beware agents using old technology.

The most common 360-degree tours are done using a special camera. Some of the cameras, like Ricoh Theta V's and Go Pro's

360-degree cameras, are available for less than $500 and produce solid quality images. One shot from a tripod in the middle of a room, controlled remotely, will produce a full photo in every direction.

Software allows the images to be sequenced so that a buyer can click on "hot spots" and move from room to room, using a mouse to turn and look through the entire home.

More expensive systems, like Matterport Tours, can run several thousand for the equipment or you can hire a local professional photographer who has the equipment. These tours are done by using multiple 360-degree photos of each room and area of the house to make moving through the home seamless. The software also creates interactive floor plans of the dwelling.

A buyer can even obtain a pair of 3D glasses and virtually walk through. Builders are more commonly providing 3D tours in order to allow buyers to see different model without having every model available in every neighborhood.

> ### QUICK TIP:
> ### Creating Your Own 3D Tour
>
> Computer savvy homeowners can create a 360-Degree tour using Google Tour Creator. While you need a 360-Degree camera, the software is free and relatively easy to use.

While these tours certainly have a *cool-factor*, I'm not convinced that most people purchase a home based on the tour. The benefit to having a 3D tour, however, is that they are a relatively new concept and your friends on social media will likely share the tour, leading to more people seeing your home for sale.

The Video Walk-Through or Drone Tour

Unlike a Virtual Walk-Through, where the user controls where he or she travels through the virtual home, a video simply introduces the property. Videos with a drone component, showing the home from above and the surrounding area, also has a *cool-factor* that leads to your social media friends and acquaintances sharing them.

A good video will show the highlights of the home and may wet the appetite of a potential buyer.

Beautiful 4 BR, 3.5 Bath Colonial in Northwestern Lehigh School District

Is a Tour Necessary to Sell Your Home?

Of course, the short answer is "No." A home that is priced right and staged well in a strong market-area is likely to sell regardless of the strength of the marketing plan.

Yet most buyers begin their search online and any tool that makes your home stand out to buyers or brings a buyer back more than once to view, is something to strongly consider. Technology will continue to evolve, but a strong virtual tour, 3D tour or video tour can help attract attention to your home.

In areas where buyers purchase second homes, a tour can be even more essential, as out-of-area buyers are more likely to extensively shop online prior to flying in to look at properties.

Open Houses and Coming Soon Listings

When I wrote my first book on selling homes, open houses were one of the least successful methods of generating a buyer. At that time, only 1% of buyers purchased a home at an open house. Today, the National Association of Realtors survey still has that number at close to 1%, but there is a way to use an open house to create an auction effect to get the highest price for your home.

As of the release of this edition, many parts of the country are experiencing seller's markets where there is an inventory shortage. Like all good things, this will eventually come to an end in the roller-coaster of the real estate market.

When there is high demand and low inventory, there are buyers statically in the market seeking the right property. When a home is initially placed on the market for sale, those buyers who have been looking at homes for several weeks will likely schedule appointments immediately to see the new listing. After that initial wave, the number of showings will typically drop, and the majority of showings will be to buyers just entering the market.

You may have seen a sign or an online ad for a home with the label "Coming Soon." A successful tactic in strong markets is to place a home for sale but hold back on showings until an open house. During this marketing period prior to the open house, you should not allow any buyers into the home. It's unfair to the rest, and it defeats the purpose of the auction effect.

Rather than a series of showings over the first two weeks, this can bring many buyers and their agents to the home simultaneously, creating a scarcity mentality that can lead to a better price and better terms if you receive multiple offers.

Pocket Listing

Some agents use the "Coming Soon" concept to sell their home sellers on holding the property off the retail market and MLS to build momentum but allowing their own showings during that period. Some agents even offer a discounted commission if it's sold during the pre-marketing period. In the industry, this is called pocket listing a property because the home is not truly available on the general market.

Pocket listings or pre-market listings are nearly always a bad idea for a home seller. Remember that the more broadly you market a property, the more likely you are to receive the highest price and best terms. This technique is a benefit to the listing agent who would like to double-dip and receive both sides of the commission.

Open Houses in a Slow Market

While open houses can attract buyers in a hot market, they are less impactful in a slow market. That does not mean, however, that you shouldn't do any open houses. Any attempt to market a home may generate the buyer who eventually purchases the home. Open houses do lead to some sales, whether the ultimate purchaser walks through during the open house or is told about the home by a friend or relative who walked through.

There are home buyers who skip over listings in the MLS because the photos do not look right, or the description wasn't exactly what they were looking for, only to show up at an open house and decide it was perfect once they actually walked through the home.

Your Realtor® may tell you that they have more effective ways to spend their time marketing your home. If your agent is very busy, you might suggest that the agent advertise the open house, and you stay in the property, allowing potential buyers to walk through.

Another effective tool is a *neighborhood open house*. If there are several similarly-priced homes for sale in your area, the different realtors or real estate companies that are representing the homes may elect to hold open houses on the same day. A neighborhood open house will often bring more buyers to view your property than an individual open house on just your property. This is true because different companies advertise different ways and are more likely to attract more traffic to the area. It is also true because buyers like to maximize the number of homes they view in a day and if they notice several open houses in the same area, they are more likely to visit.

Marketing Your Open House

There are several ways to maximize the impact of holding an open house. Buyers will find open houses online through social media, online classifieds like Craigslist, major real estate sites like Realtor.com, Century21.com and Zillow, newspaper sites, and on MLS systems.

Directional signs may lead buyers into the open house who did not see the ad. In a slower market, where for sale signs seem to be on every corner, you will catch more attention for your open house directional signs by attaching helium balloons to them. The motion of the swaying balloons will draw more drivers to read the signs.

If you are listed with a Realtor®, the Realtor® will hopefully have a sign-in sheet for visitors to the open house. This way he or she can follow up with the people who came through the open house and collect feedback or determine if any of them had serious interest in the home. If you are selling your home on your own, you should definitely use this same technique. Have the buyer fill out their name, address, phone number, email address, and how they heard about the open house.

For safety reasons, if you're holding an open house on your own, you should have another person at the house with you. The person could be your spouse, your neighbor, a relative, or a coworker. Having a second person in the house will discourage any possible theft or violence, or any accusations of misbehavior on your part. A second person is also helpful if multiple couples arrive at the home simultaneously. One person can chat with a visitor in the living room, while the other shows visitors through the home.

Make sure you or your agent has all the paperwork necessary to write an offer, should a buyer be interested enough to make one. If a buyer has a feeling for your home, your agent shouldn't aggressively pressure them, but should take advantage of that feeling while it lasts.

Finally, home sellers often complain that they do not appreciate the fact that the neighbors may come through the home during an open house. Something to keep in mind, though, is that the neighbors may know the eventual buyer. Since they will show up anyway, you may want to send them an invitation.

Specifically Targeting Likely Buyer Groups

Who are the buyers moving into your area? The most likely buyers may be relocation buyers for local large companies if you are in a transient or mobile neighborhood. Likely buyers may be move-up buyers from smaller homes in the same school district. If you are planning to sell a one-story home with a garage, the likely buyer may be an empty-nester or a senior planning to scale back to one level living.

When you determine who your likely buying audience is, you can affect a plan to prospect directly to that market. For example, if your home is a typical move-up residence, you may want to find the best way to communicate your property listing to buyers moving up. Earlier in this chapter we discussed using social media and targeted audiences. Another method is to compile a list of other homes for sale in the same school district or adjacent school districts where the home is a starter home or smaller than your home.

You may send a flyer or postcard to these potential purchasers. Postcards are a great tool for marketing because the reader doesn't have to open a letter, and too often letters that look like junk mail never get opened. Some people stand over the recycling bin reading their mail. If you are going to take the time to prepare something, you want to make sure it's read. Your agent may not be permitted to send out advertisements to homes listed with competing firms, so you may be on your own for this part of targeted marketing.

Examples of specific target marketing are as follows:

- **If you are selling a starter home, your target buyer is likely to be a current renter.** Try sending flyers or postcards to apartment complexes near your home. You may even try purchasing a mailing list from *infoUSA* or *SalesGenie* of renters within a certain radius of your home with a rental rate comparable to your mortgage payment.

  If you are selling a move-up home, your likely buyer is either a relocating buyer or someone moving up from a starter home to a home like yours. Try sending postcards or flyers to neighborhoods of likely buyers in your school district or adjacent school districts. Likely buyers include sellers of starter homes in the area, or renters of upscale apartments paying a comparable rent to your mortgage payment.

  If you are selling an upscale home, your likely buyer is either someone moving from a move-up home or someone

relocating into the area. You can target personnel departments at local companies, hospitals, and colleges. You can also send postcards to likely buyers in the same and adjacent school districts.

If you are selling a retirement home or single level home, your likely buyer is a single individual, young couple or family, or an empty nester who is looking for one level living. Options include targeting local renters if your home would appeal to first time buyers, as well as those selling larger homes because some will scale down to a smaller one story home.

- **If your home has some significant unique feature, target the group that is interested in that feature.** If your home has a small barn with horse stalls, send copies of a flyer to local boarding facilities with a note to please put on their bulletin board. If your home has a large garage, you may want to target automobile repair shops in hopes of finding a mechanic who wants a place to live and work on his own cars. Look for the potential buyer who would want the same unique feature that you did when you purchased or remodeled your home.

Broker's Open Houses

Broker's open houses are open houses for real estate agents. There are two reasons Realtors® conduct broker's open houses. The first is that the agent is trying to visually show you that they are proactively trying to sell your home. The second reason is that they hope if a lot of agents come through the home, they will be more likely to talk about the home with their buyers.

The sad truth, though, is that most Realtors® do not actually come to broker's open houses to see your home. They come because the listing agent is offering a free lunch and possibly a giveaway of some sort. The other issue is that Realtors® do not travel far from their offices to participate in a broker's open house. Since they are really coming for a free lunch, they don't want to drive twenty minutes out of their way. This type of open house works best if the home is located within a ten-minute drive of a concentration of real estate offices. If your home is further away, you may have to offer a greater incentive to attract agents to participate.

The bright side is that the agents do see your home, and agents introduced to your property during a broker's open house are more likely to talk to buyers about the home and show it. This can lead to a faster sale. Just like sending flyers about your home to top Realtors® in the area, the more who know about the home, the more likely they are to show it to their clients.

chapter six:

Guerilla Marketing Techniques

Guerilla marketing techniques are imaginative and unconventional methods of marketing the property to generate buyers. In a hot market in a hot area, homes will sell in days or hours. Some homes only need a for sale sign or minimal advertising. In a normal market, in a location where properties do sell, the standard methods for marketing, including MLS, signs, and Internet marketing on major sites will sell most properties, as long as they're staged properly. In a declining market or a slow market, you need to be the best home on the market in your price range in order to guarantee a sale.

When the market truly slows, you can do the same marketing as everyone else, and hope for different results, or you can attack the market with unconventional methods to find or create potential buyers. Guerilla tactics don't necessarily require a lot of money, just some innovative thinking and perhaps a little imagination.

Staying Ahead of a Sliding Market

If the market is sliding, you may need to position your price ahead of the slide in order to sell.

Example:
Keith had a townhome for sale in a nice suburban neighborhood, but in a depressed area. The home had expired

with another real estate firm. Because Keith had already finished the construction of his new home, he was paying on two mortgages. Keith's payment on his townhome was $1690 a month and his wife was expecting a baby in a few weeks. He needed to get the home sold fast.

Our initial evaluation of the market showed that there were thirty-two homes for sale in this large townhome subdivision. The prices ranged from $172,900 to $184,900, with the majority of the homes being priced between $172,900 and $177,900. There had only been eight homes sold in the prior four months, which meant approximately one out of every sixteen homes was selling in any given month. These were pretty poor odds of selling.

The most recent four sales all sold between $168,000 and $171,000, and sales prices had declined consistently over the past six months. The majority of home sellers In he neighborhood appeared to be listed around $175,000 hoping to get somewhere north of $170,000. Keith wanted to list along with everyone else at $172,900 to $174,900 because he needed to sell, but he wasn't going to give his house away.

We convinced Keith that he needed to price it at $169,900 because the home would appear to be the best value in the neighborhood. Keith also did a bit of home staging by putting up fresh towels, moving furniture, around and decluttering. We had two offers within two weeks and sold the home for full price. Keith and his wife were relieved that the pain of the two mortgages was over.

While $169,900 may have appeared to be lower than the rest of the neighborhood on the surface, it was actually higher than three out of the last four sale prices. Buyers perceived the value to be better because it was already priced lower than competing homes on the market. Keith's neighbors had just as nice a home listed at $174,900 and they may have been willing to let it go for $168,000, but Keith's home appeared to be a better value to the buyers. They bid the price to the full asking price.

When you're in a sliding market, you cannot simply maintain pace with the slide because you will end up taking longer to sell and ultimately receive a lower sales price. For example, if you only have a one in sixteen chance of selling next month, the odds are that you are likely to be holding onto the home for several more months. If the market continues to slide, the home may be worth less in three months than it is today. Moreover, you are making a mortgage payment every month during that period of time.

When pricing a home, be conscious of the market trends. If prices are rising, set a higher price and hope for buyers to pay it. If the market is stable, you should be priced competitively with other home sellers. If the market is falling, stay ahead of the fall, because you are likely to come out better than someone who hangs onto their home for an additional few months.

No Money Down Offers

Example:
Pam and Rick owned a typical 2-year-old. four bedroom, two and a half bath home for sale in a moderately upscale neighborhood in the Bethlehem area of Pennsylvania. As the market began to sink, the builder, who was still putting up new homes in the community, dropped his prices and started offering incentives, such as upgrades at little or no cost.

Most buyers would rather have new construction because they can have it built exactly to their specifications, and because everyone likes shiny new things. The resale homes on the market were suffering a lack of sales. With several homes on the market for sale in the neighborhood and even more in the area, Pam and Rick could not afford to drop their price to such a low level that it would guarantee a sale. Yet, Rick was starting a new job in Texas in a few weeks and couldn't rent the home and manage it from Texas.

Our solution was to try to find a mortgage program that would allow a buyer to purchase their home for little or no money down. A local mortgage banker found a mortgage product that would allow a buyer to purchase with no down payment as long as his or her credit score was above 690. The lender would loan the buyer 80% of the purchase price as a first mortgage and the other 20% as a second mortgage at a higher interest rate. Under this program, the seller could pay all the buyer's closing costs, effectively allowing a buyer to walk into the home with no money out of pocket.

Although the interest rate was a little higher than the average interest rate, the different approach appealed to buyers who had great incomes, good credit, but had not managed to save enough money for a traditional down payment. Instead of the typical advertisements that read "Gorgeous 4 Bedroom Colonial... $439,900," we were able to run a series of ads reading "No Money Down and only $3,480 per month!" When running ads that include a payment amount, be careful, because a law known as *Regulation Z* states any payment information must come with a full disclaimer of the annual percentage rate and term. Seek out advice before running any advertisement with a specific payment amount.

The advertising program attracted some attention and a few showings. Our next step was to put up a professional looking sign in front of the home that read "No Money Down—call for details." The sign generated some calls, but not as many as we expected. We replaced the sign with a bright sign that was handwritten in black magic marker. "No Money Down—call for details," and the phone began to ring. The fact that the sign looked like a handwritten yard sign attracted people to look over at the sign and read it. We put up handwritten directional arrows claiming, "No Money Down Home—This Way!"

The home sold to a couple within days of the signs going up. Sure, we had calls from neighbors who told us that we were making their neighborhood look cheap. We had calls from other Realtors® who said we were giving real estate agencies an unprofessional look by handwritten signs. Can't we afford real signs? The truth is that the handwritten version attracted the eye and worked to sell the home.

I have since repeated this feat a number of times. If the home is the right price range for a first-time home buyer, we have run ads on Craigslist and in the newspaper under 'Houses for Rent' explaining that they could purchase a specific home cheaper than rent. "3 Bedroom, 1.5 Bath townhome in west end near parks. Beautifully appointed. Only $795 per month to own with no money down using special financing program. Own this home cheaper than rent."

Even better, buyers of these properties often do not look at any homes other than the one advertised, because of the special financing program being advertised along with the home. The key to making this method work is to lower the barrier of resistance for the potential buyer.

As you have probably seen on the news, many of the 100% financing options have disappeared during the real estate market crash and the implosion of the subprime lending industry. However, options still exist by utilizing programs that allow a mortgage to be broken into first and second position loans, or for excellent credit risks, full 100% financing programs.

You or your agent should contact several home financing companies to find the best low or no money down product and apply the terms to your home. You need to be willing to pay the entire amount of the buyer's closing costs and you may need to go above and beyond the norm in your marketing efforts to contact those who may not currently be considering purchasing.

Paying the Buyer's Closing Costs and Buy-down Loans

Another alternative to a simple price reduction strategy is to target buyers who cannot purchase a home like yours because their available cash is insufficient to obtain a high enough mortgage. In this case, offering to pay part or all of the buyer's closing costs may make the purchase more palatable, or sway a buyer from another property to yours.

Although they sound similar, there are several differences between the strategy of offering your home 'No Money Down' and offering to pay some of the buyer's closing costs. First, the 'No Money Down' strategy can bring buyers into the marketplace that were not initially considering purchasing a home. Secondly, the cost to do a 'No Money Down' program is much higher for a seller than simply paying some of the buyer's closing costs, but it often brings in substantially more buyers. Paying buyer closing costs also allows a buyer a wider range of mortgage products than 100% financing.

In many cases, offering to pay $3,000 to $5,000 in buyer's closing costs works out better for a seller than dropping the price by $10,000 or $15,000 to bring the home into a different price range. It can be a win-win by netting you, as the seller, a higher price, and getting the buyer into a home by effectively financing his or her closing costs.

Another method of attracting buyers is to prepay the interest on a mortgage and offer a buy down mortgage. A *buy down mortgage* is a fixed rate mortgage, where the constant rate is bought down for the first couple years by prepaying the difference in interest. For example, if today's rate were 7% for a thirty-year fixed mortgage, using some mortgage products, the buyer can buy down the interest rate to 5% for the first year, 6% for the second year, and then 7% for the remaining twenty-eight years. The benefit to doing this is that on some buy down loans, a buyer may qualify on the first-year rate, which affords the buyer more house.

If a buyer is in a situation where he or she expects his or her income to rise over the next few years, he or she can still buy the home of his or her dreams with the expectation that he or she will be paying a higher payment next year and a higher payment the year after that. The difference between this type of loan and an adjustable rate loan is that the rate is fixed on a buy down. Contact a local mortgage banker or mortgage broker and find out what buy down programs are available, and the fees are to purchase a buy down. The common terminology

---

QUICK TIP:

Holding a Mortgage for the Buyer

Another financing alternative which is riskier to a home seller but may eventually net the seller more money, is to hold the mortgage for the buyer. For example, if you own a home valued at $250,000, a buyer who doesn't have to obtain a mortgage may be willing to pay a higher price for the home.

The risk is that the buyer defaults and you have to foreclose on the house and take it back. You should

(cont)

is a *2–1 buy down* if you are prepaying the interest to 2% below the prevailing interest rate for the first year and 1% below the prevailing rate for the second year. A *3–2–1 buy down* starts at 3% below the prevailing interest rate for the first year and follows the same pattern as the 2–1.

Allowances

If your carpeting has holes, the appliances are goldenrod, and your kitchen counter is chipped, very few buyers will consider making an offer. Most home buyers do not want to do any work on a home that they purchase and those that will work on the home will generally want to buy at a low price point.

Staging is listed as one of the top three critical factors that sell your home because, so few buyers want to do work on a home. If your house absolutely needs updating and you cannot afford to do the work yourself, you may consider offering an allowance for carpeting, appliances, or other repairs. An *allowance* is an amount of money you're agreeing to give back to the buyer at closing toward repairs or upgrades. Allowances, however, are not nearly as effective as actually making the repairs yourself in the first place.

require that the buyer pay a sufficient down payment that will cover the costs of foreclosure and any potential damage that could be done to the home. The other downside to holding a mortgage is that you don't receive your equity immediately, but instead receive it over a longer period of time.

The good news is that you may sell the home at a higher price, and you will get interest on your equity for the period that the buyer is making payments to you. When holding a mortgage for a buyer, you should always seek the counsel of an attorney for legal advice and a tax advisor to determine what tax implications holding the mortgage may entail.

Auctions

An auction on your home is an event where potential buyers come together to bid against each other for the privilege of buying your home. The number of real estate auctions in the United States have been increasing over the past five years. There are several benefits to auctioning a property. One major benefit of an auction is that it is a quick way to get a home sold. Another is that if the auction goes well, you as the homeowner get the luxury of selecting the time frame of the sale.

A strong value of auctions to the homeowner is that buyers must put down a significant deposit to hold the home, generally in the 5% to 10% range. This deposit is usually non-refundable. The seller also avoids having to go through the offer-counteroffer process of a normal home sale. If there are several bidders, the seller may even finish with a higher price than negotiating with a single party on the open market.

One of the negatives to auctions, however, is that auctions typically work better in a hot market than in a cooling market. In a hot market, buyers bid up the price of homes because a shortage exists. In a cooling market, buyers come to auctions primarily because they believe they can get a deal and purchase the property at a price that is significantly lower than the market value.

Additionally, an auction may generate a lower sales price than allowing the property to sit on the open market for a normal marketing period. Auctions can eliminate many potential buyers. Some buyers will not attend or purchase at auctions either because they are concerned about putting down a non-refundable deposit, or because they are planning on using financing to purchase that does not require as much down as they would need at an auction. One last detrimental feature of an auction is that it doesn't necessarily hit all the same marketing venues as the standard process of marketing through a Realtor®.

I have run simultaneous marketing with auctioneers where the auctioneer and my firm split the commission on the sale. This allows the Realtor® to use the normal marketing track and get the home in front of a significant number of buyers. The auctioneer puts up an auction sign with a date on it and advertises the auction. This auction date is a deadline, so buyers feel pressured to put up or shut up if they have a feeling for the home. In several cases, buyers have made offers prior to the auction in order to secure the home without having to bid on it at auction. If the offer is accepted, the auction is canceled. The auctioneer, however, must still be paid for his or her work and time.

There are two primary forms of house auctions—the absolute auction and the reserve price auction. At an *absolute auction*, the home seller accepts whatever the highest bid is, even if it is only one dollar. Some auctioneers waive any upfront advertising fees for absolute auctions because their pay is guaranteed. The reason that many auctioneers prefer this type of auction is that it generates more prospective buyers because the buyers believe they may have a chance of getting the property at a very low price. In reality, the higher turnout often guarantees a higher sales price. Despite many successes with this method, I find it to be too close to a roll of the dice and hoping for a good outcome.

Most home auctions are *reserve price auctions*. The home seller sets a minimum bid price that the seller will not go below. This minimum bid price is generally not disclosed to buyers. Instead, an opening bid price is advertised to tease buyers to attend the auction. For example, a homeowner may set a reserve price of $250,000, in hopes of selling the home for $260,000 or more. The auctioneer may advertise an opening bid of $215,000 in order to generate excitement about the sale.

Even if the reserve price is not met, an auctioneer may take the highest bid to the seller and give the seller the option of accepting something lower than the originally anticipated sales price. The high bidder may then negotiate with the seller through the auctioneer or the seller's agent.

Unlike typical home showings with a Realtor®, an auctioneer may set up several inspection dates where prospective buyers can all walk through the home in the same hour or two-hour period. Similar to an open house, this allows the seller to clean and stage the home a few times, rather than cleaning and staging the home each time an individual prospective buyer appointment is scheduled. If a potential buyer is interested in having the home inspected by a home inspector, or for termites, radon, or anything else, it must be done prior to the auction date.

If the auction is successful, sales contracts are exchanged and signed, the high bidder pays the required deposit by certified or cashier's check, and the bidder becomes legally bound to purchase the home or lose the deposit.

There may be additional expenses with auctions. Some auctioneers require prepayment of marketing expenses prior to the auction.

Lease Purchases

While I attempt to avoid lease purchases, they are sometimes a necessary tool to get a home sold in a spiraling market. A *lease option* is a contract to lease a home for a specified period of time, and then purchase the home at the end of the term. *Renting with the option to buy*, on the other hand, is a contract to lease a home giving the tenant the option to purchase at some point in the future. There is no real benefit to a seller in giving the tenant the option to purchase unless he or she is locked into a transaction. A true lease purchase has a definitive sales clause as part of the contract.

In a *lease purchase contract*, the purchaser, or tenant, pays a market rent plus an additional fee each month that goes toward the down payment he or she will eventually need to purchase the home. Even if you, as the seller, are willing to credit the buyer the entire rental payment toward the purchase of the home in order to get the buyer's down payment collected sooner, lenders guidelines typically will not allow anything other than an amount above market rent to be considered as part of the down payment or closing costs.

The primary reasons that buyers attempt lease purchasing a home rather than a straight purchase are that they do not have any money saved toward down payment and closing costs, or that they have credit issues that need to be straightened out prior to purchasing. Other possible reasons include that the buyers are going through a divorce or lawsuit that precludes their purchase of a property until the divorce is finalized or the lawsuit settled. The buyer may also have changed careers recently and needs more time in the field before a lender will write a mortgage.

There are several benefits to you as the seller for selling with a lease purchase. First, you probably won't have to negotiate much on your asking price. Lease purchases are in demand and few sellers are willing to do them. Consequently, you can command a higher price than the market. Secondly, lease purchase buyers view the property as their home, as opposed to tenants who see your property as a rental. They tend to maintain and take better care of the property than the average tenant. Finally, you may be able to get your property under agreement in a very slow market and have your mortgage payment covered rather than continuing to hemorrhage mortgage payments and utility bills for the property each month.

Just as there are benefits to lease purchases, there are many risks. The number one reason that buyers search for lease purchases is because they don't have money saved. While there are still specialized mortgage programs allowing buyers to purchase homes with very low or no down payments, they tend to come with tight restrictions, requiring most buyers to put more money down on the homes they purchase.

With so many low money down programs available currently, the may not qualify because of credit issues. My experience has been that lease purchase buyers will wish to get their credit cleaned up, but something will happen during that six month or year long lease term that will keep their credit from improving or make it worse. The buyer will either ask for an extension or bail out, and you are back at square one selling your home.

If credit is one of the buyer's issues, have the buyers provide copies of their credit reports prior to signing any agreement with them. Review the credit thoroughly with a professional to determine the likelihood that the credit can and will actually be corrected within the time frame of the contract.

If the buyer is waiting until a lawsuit is settled and expects it to happen any month, you may be surprised by extension after extension. Some lawsuits can last for years. An individual waiting for a divorce to be finalized may find that he or she has been hurt worse in the divorce than he or she anticipated and may be unable to complete the transaction. Even if everything goes well, some buyers will find issues with your home and decide not to go through with the transaction. They will attempt to back out and purchase another home.

There are several other risks as well. If the market turns and homes begin to appreciate, you may miss out on the increase in value because you are locked into a contract with this buyer. Another issue is that once you move out of the property for a few years and lease the property, it becomes an investment property in the eyes of the IRS, and you may be charged capital gains taxes when you sell. Speak to an accountant before signing any lease purchase agreement.

In writing a lease purchase agreement, your Realtor® or attorney should spell out every possible term or scenario. The agreement must include who is responsible for payment of utilities, taxes, insurance, maintenance, and repairs. You should also very carefully address what physical alterations the buyer may make to the property prior to settlement. Although a buyer may make improvements, a buyer may also change the property in a way that makes the home less appealing to other buyers, should the sale fall through. You, as the owner, should have the right to approve or disapprove any alterations to the property prior to settlement.

If you are having the buyer pay the taxes, insurance, or municipal utilities, you should include a clause that requires the buyer to provide proof of payment. If real estate taxes are not paid, the county can take your property. If insurance is not paid, and the home is damaged or destroyed, you will get nothing and still owe the mortgage. If municipal utilities are not paid, a judgment will be filed against you.

Include language in the contract that specifies what remedies you have if the buyer defaults on the transaction. Another important consideration is to require some sort of security deposit, as you would in a normal rental situation, in case damage occurs to the property and the buyer fails to settle.

Paying Realtor® Bonuses or Higher Commissions

A Realtor® working as a buyer's agent or buyer's representative is supposed to represent the buyer to the best of his or her ability. These agents have a *fiduciary responsibility* to the buyer, and therefore are required to attempt to locate the best home values for their buyers. The buyer's agent is not supposed to be swayed by bonuses or higher commissions. Unfortunately, there are real estate agents who will actually sort what listings they are showing buyers based on the commission.

Example

David and Adrienne had a classic cape for sale in Emmaus, Pennsylvania. The home had gorgeous wood trim, oak hardwood floors with a cherry inlay, and leaded glass French doors between the living room and dining room. The home had been on the market for six months with a competing firm without selling. David couldn't postpone his new job in Memphis any longer and had to relocate without his wife and two children. The home was in a quiet neighborhood in a popular school district and appeared to be priced competitively with other homes on the market, and appeared to be staged properly, but the market had gone soft and there were many competing properties.

The couple had been offering a 5% commission through their previous Realtor®, which was split 2.5% to the listing agency and 2.5% offered to the buyer's agency through the MLS. Looking through the most recent sales, I noticed that the majority of sales had 3% commissions offered to the buyer's agents. Worse, more than half of the competing listings were also paying a full 3% buyer's side commission and two were paying 3.5%.

No matter what the rules of agency relationships state, an agent knows that if he or she has a buyer who needs to buy, the Realtor® will make $1,250 more if he or she sells a $250,000 home with a 3% commission rather than a 2.5% commission. The Realtor® doesn't have to do anything wrong, necessarily. He or she just shows houses with higher commission splits first.

After looking at the raw statistics, David and Adrienne, who initially said they would not ever pay higher than 5%, listed their home at 8% with the agreement that we pay 5% of the commission out to the buyer's agency and only keep 3% on the listing side. We immediately sent out a flyer to the top agents servicing the Emmaus area with the headline "5% Co-Operating Commission on Gorgeous Emmaus Home." We followed up by calling all the agents who had competing properties and letting them know that should they have a buyer who did not like their listings, they would earn more selling ours than their own listings.

We received two offers within ten days. The home sold, in a soft market, for full price.

The problem wasn't that the home wasn't saleable because of condition or price. It just never made it onto many agents' lists of homes to show buyers. Once a number of buyers were introduced to the home, it was only a matter of time before someone fell in love with it.

In the interest of full disclosure, there is a huge class action lawsuit occurring during the publication of this book aimed at the major brokerages for this sort of activity, claiming that brokers are doing a disservice to their clients with this practice. I completely agree.

However, I also realize the reality of human nature. In slow markets, in order to increase sales, some builders offer high buyer-side commissions because it drives sales. By letting our sellers know that they have the option of paying a higher commission to buyer's agents in order to entice showings, we're attempting to give them the best advice to get their homes sold.

Another method of attracting Realtors® to show your home over others is to offer a flat fee bonus. Rather than paying an additional 1% or 2%, you can offer a $5,000 reward for the Realtor® who brings an acceptable offer to you by some specified date. Your listing agent can create a flyer to post at other real estate offices, to mail to top agents in the area, or to mass email it to agents throughout the area.

In some cases, the higher real estate commission works more effectively because Realtors® are trained to look at the little box on the MLS sheet that indicates the buyer's side commission. In other cases, a flyer announcing a flat bonus may attract more attention if it happens to hit an agent who is showing homes in your area and price range.

Right or wrong, a key to selling real estate is understanding what motivates people. Buyers are motivated by a home that fits their imagination for entertaining or family or childhood memories. Realtors®, who set up showings, are motivated by money or prestige.

Giving Away a Car or a Vacation

At the writing of this book, one of our sellers who has a property for sale in excess of a million dollars, is offering a brand-new convertible to the agent who brings in a successful offer on his property. Our mass emails and advertising flyers include a photo of the new car at the top of the page. Realtors® from other firms have called to ask whether the offer was real. The truth is that a $35,000 car is less than 3% of the asking price of his property. Rather than doubling the buyer's side commission, the seller is attempting to create a word-of-mouth campaign of agents talking about his property.

During the last downturn in the real estate marketplace, we tried to take the bonus idea a step further. Rather than simply offer a monetary reward to agents, we thought we would try to appeal to their imagination and give away trips. We found we could purchase blocks of timeshare weeks from companies at very good discounts. A block of ten timeshare weeks that could be used all over the world could be purchased for as little as $300 to $500 per week. We asked our sellers if they would be willing to purchase two timeshare weeks for the buyer and the buyer's agent if it meant a faster sale. Many were willing, so we ordered the transferable vouchers.

Our next step was to create a series of flyers for top agents that began with "Dear Agent—If you sell this home, we'll give you a paid week at a resort in Orlando, Las Vegas, San Antonio, Myrtle Beach, or San Francisco—your choice!" This may have been a long headline, but remember that the headline is what catches the reader's attention and draws them in. After the initial response, we included two photographs on the front of the flyer. The first was of a beach at sunset. The lower photo was an exterior photo of the home we were selling.

The flyers attracted the agent's attention. In order to attract the buyer's attention, we had sign riders made up that stated, *"Take a Vacation on the House!"* and placed them on each for sale sign of a home willing to pay for the timeshares. We added the wording to the MLS that the seller would provide the buyer with a paid week at a resort of their choice in more than one hundred locations worldwide.

I doubt that many buyers purchased a particular home simply because a vacation was included. However, it generated more showings on homes in a slow market that were not receiving showings. The more showings, the more opportunity we have to find the perfect buyer for the home. Also, if a buyer is comparing three very similar homes, a vacation or another package may just sway the buyer in your direction.

If you are considering this approach as an option to attract buyers, a vacation package may cost significantly more when only one is purchased, but you can still build that cost into the price of your home. Rather than a $5,000 price reduction, offer an $1,800 trip. You may be surprised by the response.

> ## QUICK TIP:
> ### Vacation Certificates
>
> Several companies offer vacation packages that you can prepay and use as an incentive for an agent to bring buyers to your home, or for a buyer as an additional incentive to purchase.
>
> One of the country's largest timeshare companies, Wyndham - RCI, offers a program with resort vacation certificates. The program is available to view online at:
> ResortVacationCertificates.com.

More Creative Uses for Flyers

Depending on the type of home you are attempting to sell, there are several creative ways to combine guerilla marketing techniques with flyers to create an impact that will attract potential buyers. Lease purchase offers, paying buyer's closing costs, or paying all the costs so the buyer can purchase your home with no money down are all effective marketing techniques to attract buyers who may not even be in the market to buy until they learn about your offer.

Flyers can be an effective resource when attempting to get the word out to potential buyers. Consider where your likely buyer might see a flyer, and then try to create a flyer that jumps out and grabs the reader's attention. Finally, give the reader a way to contact you without taking your flyer off a bulletin board, even if they don't have a pen and paper on them.

> ## QUICK TIP:
> ### Lender's View of Incentives
>
> When offering incentives such as cars or vacations, you should be aware that some lenders will view these gifts as a seller concession. The lender's view may be that by giving away something of value to the buyer, the seller may have an inflated price to cover that cost. These lenders may be less likely to approve the mortgage.

Where might the potential buyers see a flyer? If they are first time buyers, they may go to a laundromat where there is usually a bulletin board. If they are move-up buyers, they may be a mid-level manager at a company, and there may be a bulletin board at the water cooler. If the home is a larger home, perhaps a good place would be the bulletin board in the local country club's locker room or the local racquetball club's bulletin board.

Create a compelling headline. If you are planning to put a flyer together for a starter home and hang it at Laundromats all over town, a headline might read "*Washer and Dryer Included!*" Another approach would be to create buyers by showing them they could purchase your home with no down payment. "No

Money Down and $967 per month to Own!" might be an appropriate headline.

Finally, you want to make sure the flyer stays in place, but that the readers of the ad have an easy way to call you. Try making up a flyer with pull off tabs at the bottom. Take a sheet of copier paper, print your name and number several times across the bottom, take a scissors and cut strips to create pull off tabs. Potential buyers can rip off the small piece of paper and carry it with them until they call you. An example of this can be found here.

Stop Wasting Your Nights in a Laundrymat
The Washer and Dryer are Included!

No more hanging out at the laundry! This property comes with a washer, dryer and full ser of appliances.

Enjoy relaxing on the deck overlooking your new quarter acre lot in the Clearview area. The home features 3 bedrooms, 1.5 baths, a casual living room with hardwood floors, gracious formal dining room, and a sunny updated kitchen with oak cabinets and new countertops.

And best of al, this home qualifies for a special mortgage program. A qualified buyer can own this adorable ingle with a Low Down Payment and only $1296 per month!*

Call Mike Miller at CENTURY 21 Keim Realtors for more info on this great home and to see if ou qualify for this outstanding Low Down Payment offer! 555-555-5555

* Based on a 30 year fixed rate mortgage at 6.45% with an APR of 6.75%. This flyer is done for example purposes only

Washer & Dryer Included
Call Mike Miller of CENTURY 21 Keim
610-55-5555

chapter seven:
Other Property Challenges

Location-Challenged Properties

Location-challenged homes are properties with significant deterrents in the neighborhood or surrounding area. These challenges can include being located close to train tracks, busy intersections, blind corners, or airport runways. They can also include situations like being near or next to a mining operation, manufacturing plant, nuclear power plant, sewage treatment plant, or any other facility that gives off a lot of smell, makes a lot of noise, or makes buyers wonder if there is a safety issue. Appraisers call these types of homes *economically obsolescent* because they are devalued based on their surroundings.

The truth is that any home will sell at the right price. If you own a split level that is only fifteen feet from the railroad tracks and offer it for sale for one dollar, someone will live with the train. After all, you did when you bought the home, didn't you?

Whether you have a home in a difficult location or not, you still need to stage your home so that your home will appear the absolute best it can. Too many homeowners with location challenges say "Why should I put any money into it? There's only so much I can get out." If you think that way, you will treat your home that way, and no one will get a good feeling for the home when they walk through.

If—once you or your Realtor® are able to overcome the location challenge and attract a buyer to view your home—the buyer walks into a gorgeous, perfectly appointed home, you will be far more likely to receive an offer. If you can block out the view of the train tracks with folding shutters, then you will have more buyers seriously consider the home despite the location.

Visual Problems

If the problem is a visual problem, the situation may be reduced by carefully adjusting the viewer's perception of the property. For example, we had a client a few years ago whose home backed up to a major highway. He had tried selling the home with another Realtor® without success. I told him that the highway was a difficult situation to overcome.

"People keep telling me that, but I just don't see it. There has only been *one* occasion where a car flipped over the fence and ended up in the backyard. What are the odds of that happening again?"

I hadn't even considered the possibility that a car could actually come crashing through the yard. My concern was that while we were standing on the patio, we had trouble hearing each other speak, but worse, we could watch the cars whizzing by. I could just imagine what young mothers would think bringing their kids out in the yard to toddle around eighty feet from cars doing sixty-five miles an hour on the highway.

Always consider every situation from what the buyers will see. A buyer would open the back sliding doors and step out onto the patio. Just beyond the patio, between it and the highway, was a children's swing set. You may have to imagine looking at a swing set in the foreground with cars whizzing by behind. It was quite a sight.

I asked the owner to plant arborvitae across the back to at least visually change the landscape. I also thought that might limit the possibility of another car in the yard. The seller took the home off the market for a few weeks to find a landscaper. He was able to find someone to put in a row of eight-foot tall arborvitae. Additionally, he moved the swing set and play area to the side of the yard instead of directly out back. Couples looking at the home would turn left to look at a play area that had rows of other yards behind it, giving the property a totally different feel.

Although very little sound was deadened, the yard was transformed. The home was sold in a few weeks. He still received less for the home than a comparable home would in a different location, but he was able to sell the home at a fair price rather than sitting on it for several years.

Train tracks have been run next to some magnificent homes. Unfortunately, the home will not have the same value being this close to the noise and danger of the train.

By planting trees, putting up fencing, and moving outdoor furniture to attract the eye in a different direction, you are changing the focus of the potential buyer. Please understand that you are not hiding the problem, but you are lessening the impact in the buyer's mind.

Odor Problems

If the location issue you are facing is a problem with a strong, foul odor, such as the smell of a sewage treatment plant or a steel smelting plant, there is little you can do outdoors. A scented candle on the patio just won't do it. One method you can try to alter a buyer's perception of the outdoors is to plant arborvitae to block the physical view of the detrimental neighbor, and then plant a strong-smelling tree or plant on the near side of the arborvitae barrier. Orange trees or other fruit trees, in the correct climate, smell wonderful. Plants and flowers such as lilacs, rose bushes, honeysuckle, nicotiana, hyacinth, and even mint give off pleasant odors. In most cases, though, you cannot expect to truly negate the effects of the local treatment plant with some plants.

Even if the exterior is potentially a lost cause, you can at least attack the problem from the inside. If you don't have excellent thermal or multilayer windows, make sure the windows are caulked and strong storm windows are placed on the home. Place rubber strips on the bottoms of doors and look for any ways that odors might penetrate the home. Try to keep any odors out. Light candles when necessary to give the house a homey feeling.

In severe cases of odor that penetrates the home, you can add extra insulating drywall on interior walls. This will slightly lessen the space in your room but may help alleviate some of the noise. Remember that your ultimate goal is to sell the home.

Noise Problems

If the issue is a problem with loud noise, such as a train or neighboring manufacturing plant, outdoor changes are also probably not likely to help. The yard may still benefit from a row of arborvitae or other trees or fencing to help block some view of the offensive neighbor. Handling the noise issue inside requires sealing the windows and looking for ways to add soundproofing or insulation. A good set of storm windows on the exterior may help deaden the sound. If you don't have central air in the home, you may need to add central air and an air exchanger in order to keep the windows closed and show a quiet home during summer months.

During showings, you may want to turn on some soft jazz or piano music to set the stage for the buyers. Keep in mind that we are not trying to hide any defect in the property, but we are trying to help the home to appear in its best light.

As with odor, in severe cases of noise that penetrates the home, you can add extra insulating drywall on interior walls. Again, this will slightly lessen the space in your room, but may alleviate some of the noise.

Parking Problems

In older urban locations such as Philadelphia, Atlanta, and Boston, there are homes built along narrow streets without parking. Some homeowners and tenants still walk blocks to park their cars. As with any other challenged property, these homes tend to sell for less because they are more difficult to sell

In 1885 or even 1910 when these types of homes were built, there were few cars on the road and residents tended to walk to work. In the modern world, though, parking is a necessity for most people. To counter a lack of parking, you should compile a list of local parking lots that rent spaces and the cost to rent. You may even consider offering to pay the first year's parking fees in order to entice a buyer to purchase your home.

The offer to pay for parking will be likely to position your home higher on a buyers list than a similar property without such an offer, but your sales price is still likely to be lower than any comparable property that has either onsite parking or at least nearby street parking.

Electrical Towers

Another location challenge is selling a home that is adjacent to power lines or directly below power lines. Due to the height of the power towers, they can seldom be blocked by arborvitae, although I would certainly try to plant some tall trees in front in

> **QUICK TIP:**
> ## Airport Noise Reduction
> Some airports have been required by government regulations or lawsuits to provide financial assistance in reducing the noise in homes within a certain radius of the airport. Because these programs are not always advertised, contact the administrators at your local airport to determine if a program is offered in your area.

order to reduce the impact. There are two ways to attempt to minimize the impact of towers and lines on potential buyers.

First, contact your local power company. Every power company has literature showing there are no negative effects from having these lines close to your home. Have this information available during showings. Unfortunately, as many times as you might tell a buyer that there is no negative effect from power lines or power towers, standing under them in the rain or snow as they crackle sends chills up the spines of most buyers.

The second method to minimize the impact is to stage the yard so that the buyer's eye focuses elsewhere. Set up a picnic in the yard before showings, opposite the tower. Place the children's swing set or play set on the opposite side of the yard. Try to pull focus away from the tower so it doesn't appear as overwhelming.

Pricing Location-Challenged Properties

The second key is to price the home correctly. A client named Charlie once tried to convince me that it was great that his home was located very close to a large airport because it would be convenient for executives to fly in and out of town. Let me be honest. Unless the buyer is a deaf person who loves watching planes, being right off a runway is a negative. I have sold homes to and for several pilots, and every one of them was located in a rural area far from the airport. Again, that doesn't mean that I'm picking on those of you close to airports, and it certainly doesn't mean that your home can't be sold. It must be staged well and priced correctly.

There is a price at which the home will sell. Determining that price can be difficult. You need to figure out what percentage less than normal a location-challenged home will sell for. What I typically do is to try to find other properties that have sold recently along the same railroad tracks, busy street, or airport runway. If there aren't any recent sales, try switching your tactic. You can either find a similar situation in another area, or you can search historical records to get an idea of what a typical discount might be.

For example, instead of simply searching a small town to find homes along the railroad track that sold, pull out a map and find other local train tracks. Search similar situations in the entire county. If you still can't find them in the county, then search adjacent counties. Once you have found homes in similar situations, find out what other homes, similar to the challenged one but without the same issue, have sold for recently and compute the difference.

Let's say in your research you find two homes close to railroad tracks that were both ranch style homes of about twelve hundred square feet and they sold for $150,000 and $154,000 respectively. A search of other twelve hundred square foot ranch homes in the same township and schools, but without the challenge of being close to the tracks, sold in the range of $180,000 to $200,000. Divide the average challenged home price by the average unchallenged home. The average of the challenged homes was $152,000, and the average of the unchallenged homes was $190,000. $152,000 divided by $190,000 is 80%. This means a good ballpark for selling a home adjacent to train tracks in your area is that it will sell at approximately 80% of the mean selling price of other similar homes that don't have the same issues.

Keep in mind that this is *not* an appraisal method to calculate the fair market value as determined by appraisers and the banking industry, but it should give you a feel for the local marketplace based on recent sales.

If you cannot find similar current properties, try a historical approach. Research back a few years and check when the last time homes adjacent to the tracks sold. What were the sales prices at that point, and what was the difference between those sales prices and the sales prices in the same timeframe for the same type of property that didn't have the challenge of being adjacent to train tracks? Again, divide to get a percentage. Although this is not current market data, the percentages may hold true, and you can test the waters of marketing the home.

With a location-challenged property, you will not attract *every* buyer regardless of price. Some buyers will not live within the view of a nuclear power plant regardless of how little they may pay, although they may buy the home as an investment to rent out if it's cheap enough. Some buyers will never live at the end of an airport runway because they are afraid of planes.

If you are listed with a real estate agent, be patient with him or her when buyers don't show up for appointments. Too often, buyers will call from an online ad and set up an appointment, only to drive by and cancel it. This is common with properties that have glaring problems outside.

Marketing can also be a key to selling a challenging property. Use the techniques found in the previous chapter to find a buyer who isn't actively looking or is only casually looking. No money down programs or paying buyer closing costs may attract a buyer who feels they cannot afford a different home. Advertising like this will attract a different group of buyers than those looking at everything for sale.

There is one other thought on selling properties that are adjacent to factories, power plants, sewage treatment plants, airports, and other exterior factors that impede the sale of the home. Try approaching the owner of the factory or airport. We have had several occasions where the owner of the factory or power plant was willing to purchase the property in order to control the neighborhood or use it for their own offices or future expansion. Some factories may jump at the chance to buy adjacent property in case they ever need to expand.

In one case, our client had a home next to a commercial lot. A Burger King was eventually built on the commercial lot and our client began complaining that the smell wafting in her windows was driving her insane. She complained to the township and to the owner of the Burger King. Eventually, the owner of the Burger King purchased the property at a fair price. The purchase both eliminated the complaint and allowed the owner a place to lease to one of his managers.

Functionally Obsolete Properties

Functional obsolescence, when referring to a home, means that the home has a reduced usefulness compared with other homes because of a poor design, features that lacking from the home due to innovation in most other homes, or features that are part of the home that are obsolete and not useful to the average person. A poor design might be a home that has walk-through bedrooms, or the only bathroom is on the first floor of a two- or three-story home. In very rural locations, a home lacking features might include a home without a bathroom, having just an outhouse, or a home with no electric wiring to the second floor. A home with obsolete features might include a six-bedroom home, when family size has changed over time, making the additional bedrooms unnecessary.

Example:
A magnificent stone home west of Allentown had been in the same family for nearly fifty years, originally built circa 1860 by the marrying son and daughter of two very prominent local families. The home was named for the families and virtually everyone in the area knew the property. The home featured four fireplaces, gorgeous exposed beams, a second-floor covered porch, and hand-hewn wide plank flooring. The owner had regular parties in the large living room, and visitors to the home would often comment that if the owner ever wanted to sell, he should call them first.

When the owner passed away a few years ago, his heirs asked me to market the home, although they didn't think they really needed any marketing because *everyone* knew the home, and they were certain to have a bidding war within days. I surprised them by saying it would be a difficult sale. Despite how pristine the home was, or how unique it may be to have an authentic historic stone home in a beautiful setting, the home had significant functional obsolescence, which would not appeal to most buyers.

In the case of the historic home, there were several issues. First, there were four bedrooms, but they were all walk-through bedrooms. In order to get to the fourth bedroom, you would have to walk through the first three. Secondly, there was only one bathroom in the home, and there was no easy way to add an additional bathroom without taking away some of the character of the home or putting an addition on the home. Finally, there was no central air, which was common in the area for homes in this size and price range, and again it would be very difficult to add ductwork to the lathe and plaster walls.

True to my prediction, the farmhouse was difficult to sell. Within a few months, we had over three hundred showings on the property, which was a record for our company. Typically, a home receives an offer within twelve to fifteen showings. Depending on the market and the location, a home could receive an offer in only one showing, or may take thirty, but seldom more.

The sheer number of showings was created by the allure of the setting and the gorgeous stone front. Everyone who was looking for a home in or near this price range wanted to see the grand old home. Unfortunately, buyers would look at this home and end up purchasing new construction with a standard layout, a huge master bath, and central air for the same price. Eventually, two buyers appeared who bid against each other for the home. The owner still ended up with less than they originally wanted, but close to what I had initially suggested it would sell for.

When dealing with functional obsolescence, some homes are *curable*. In other words, modern conveniences can be retrofitted into the home. In other homes, it is a great challenge, or nearly impossible, to alter the home to compete with typical modern homes. When a home can be cured, the owner may want to cure the issues prior to listing the home for sale in order to obtain the highest price. If the owner doesn't have the funds necessary to make the improvements, he or she must understand that the home will have a limited market appeal. Most buyers do not want to do any work on a home they buy. They simply want to move in and live there. Those buyers who are willing to take on a challenge will pay far less for the home. A buyer will often overestimate the cost of the upgrades, and the buyer will want significant money off the price of the home for having to go through the trouble of making the upgrades.

Another option is to try to take on a partner to make the necessary changes to get top dollar. There are investors, handymen, or contractors who may be willing to make a deal to split the difference in what the property is currently worth and the amount you will receive after the repairs, renovations, or additions are done.

Believe it or not, we've had two cases of homes around 2010 that still had no indoor bathroom. Both of these Pennsylvania homes were owned by families from New York City, an hour and a half away, who used them as summer homes and never bothered to add indoor plumbing because the outhouses were fine. Oddly enough, the home next to one of these properties was likely to be in the million dollar plus range.

Even in cases where a four bedroom, two and a half bath colonial was built in the late 1980s or early 1990s versus those built recently, there is some functional obsolescence that causes buyers to be attracted to the new construction. Twenty-year-old construction may feature older master bathrooms with basic shower stalls. The current trend is huge master bathrooms with whirlpool tubs and separate showers. Additionally, newer homes tend to have higher first floor ceilings. These minor changes cause buyers to pay less for an older colonial, even though the interior layouts are virtually identical in most respects.

In many older cities, you will find townhomes, also called row homes or brownstones, that have five or more bedrooms. I am regularly faced with clients who tell me "Well, I understand that homes in this area are going for $100 per square foot, so I think my home is worth X dollars."

"That may be true," I respond, "but buyers have no real need for eight bedrooms, so you won't receive the same value out of additional rooms on the third and fourth floors."

Home sellers seldom want to hear this, because they've read articles and make assumptions that their homes are worth significantly more because of the size. Elements of a home or rooms in a home that are not useful to the majority of buyers are other forms of functional obsolescence.

A last example is a home we sold about fifteen years ago. A woman had passed away and the heirs wanted the home to be sold in a timely manner. The furniture had all been removed from the property and the heirs assured me that they broom cleaned it. While walking through the home, making notes, I entered the second-floor master bedroom. Directly in the center of the roughly sixteen foot by fourteen foot room was a toilet. I approached it and looked in. It was actually a working toilet. Apparently, the owner had used a first floor bath for the forty years she had lived in the home. When she became sick, she had plumbing run through a downstairs closet to the second floor. She located the toilet in the most convenient place for her—next to the bed.

If you have some renovation done to your home that is very specific to your needs, you probably won't get your money back when you eventually sell. Some owners build shelves into every wall of their family room to create a library. It's a nice idea, but it doesn't fit with most buyers' visions, so it makes the home more difficult to sell. Having a model train run along the ceiling from room to room through little holes you cut in the walls is really cool to watch. However, most buyers don't want to deal with closing all those holes up.

If the home is undersized for the area, the land value may be greater than the value of the house on the lot. You can either price the property appropriately, or another method is to search out a financial partner or a builder who would be willing to remove the smaller home and put up a larger home allowing you to profit from a different use of the property.

QUICK TIP:

Get Bids for Upgrades

Buyers often overestimate the cost to renovate, repair, or upgrade a home. One method to avoid this is to have two contractor's estimates prepared for the upgrades or renovations that most buyers will require. Have the estimates available for inspection by buyers. This may lead a buyer who likes the location to consider the home despite the deficiencies.

Properties in Difficult Regions

Just like economic obsolescence, where a home is affected by something in the neighborhood or an adjacent property, there are entire regions where homes are difficult to sell. In most cases, these issues are work related. In rural areas across America, there are towns where one major company employed a majority of the local workers. If the company closes or relocates, a large number of people become unemployed. This begins a trend, because all the local businesses that serviced that company or the employees of that company also take a hit in their income. Many of those smaller businesses close as well.

Younger people move out of the area in search of work. Some older people remain behind if they are able to retire. This has happened in textile areas, where clothing manufacturing has moved overseas. It has happened in coal mining regions where the dependency on coal has been largely replaced by oil and gas, and many other industries that were started in small town America.

Even in these areas, some homes do sell. There are still people working at local businesses who move from smaller homes to larger homes. There are still nurses, doctors, and lawyers who service the community. There are still investors who purchase homes based on their belief that properties will increase in value or their ability to rent the properties.

The problem is that in some of these areas, only a small percentage of homes put on the market are selling. For example, if only one out of every seven homes in a market is selling during its listing period, you need to increase the odds that your home is the one sold.

As with any other type of property, in order to do better than average, you need to stage your home well. With homes in modest price ranges, you have to be very conscious of how much you spend on renovations, repairs, and staging. You can certainly still deep clean the home, repaint the entire house, and stage the furniture. You may simply not be able to replace windows or siding, because the cost won't be returned in the sales price.

The real key I've found in more modest locations is an aggressive marketing campaign. The difficulty in finding someone to handle an aggressive marketing campaign is that local Realtors® have a tendency to market locally, and outside Realtors® don't want to work hard for the commission they will receive on homes in a more modest range. You may have to offer to pay for part of the marketing efforts in order to get significant marketing.

Aggressive marketing means several things for these properties. First, you want to market to any metropolitan areas within a forty-five minute to an hour drive of the property. You may find that a buyer would be willing to telecommute once they discover the great prices of properties in your area. Secondly, you may want to attempt to market a no money down program to attract buyers that may not yet be seriously looking. Combine these methods with advertising outside the area. "Own a 3-Bedroom Single home only thirty minutes away with No Money Down and a payment of just $560 per month including taxes!" This type of ad is sure to attract response.

If all else fails, you might try at least getting money out of the home on a monthly basis. Renting the home with the option to buy is unlikely to sell the home, but there's always a chance it will work out. Slightly better is a lease-option with a definite settlement date in the future. Other possibilities could be a seller-held second mortgage or possibly scheduling an auction for the home.

What to do with One Bad Neighbor

There are times when the issue isn't the neighborhood, the local economy, or a neighboring power plant. The problem is there is just one neighbor who is a slob. This neighbor has beer cans lined up along his front porch railing, a motorcycle on the front porch, a car under a piece of plastic or on blocks in front of the home, and a strand of Christmas lights half hanging off the porch in July.

Unfortunately, you cannot move your home. The first thing you should always try is to talk to your neighbor honestly. "Hey, Paul. I really like you, but I'm trying to sell my house and people are worried about who lives next to me. Don't get me wrong, I think you're a great guy, but I'm getting negative feedback from people looking at my home. Is there any way you'd consider cleaning up the front yard? I'd be happy to help."

Every once in a while, this approach works. It's the easiest, the most direct, and the best to get a neighbor to make changes that benefit your sale. If the problem is junk in the backyard, it may be easier to handle by planting trees or large bushes or even spending a little bit extra and putting up a fence between the yards.

Example:
One of our recent situations involved a neighbor whose home was attached to our clients. The neighbor had a severe roach infestation that was bleeding over into our client's home. Our client, Sue, was fastidious and her wits end. We approached the neighbor and asked if they would consider allowing us to pay for an extermination in their home in order to curb the bug problem. The neighbor slammed the door in our faces.

We had to move to stage two. We called the local health department, and she was temporarily removed from the home. During the removal, the property was completely sprayed, and bags of old garbage were removed.

While this was an extreme move, it was necessary to correct the problem and sell our client's house.

Example:
Another situation involved an owner who simply had car parts lying all over his front lawn in a beautiful area surrounded by very expensive homes. Buyers wouldn't offer on the property for sale because they were afraid of the neighbor they would get. In reality, the neighbor was a very nice gentleman, but was a slob. Nothing would change that.

Our client and his friends, moving quietly in the middle of the night, boxed up everything on the neighbor's front lawn and moved it to the back of his home. Please keep in mind this is illegal and is at the very least trespassing. However, it was an effective method of improving the view of the home when buyers first approached.

Each of these situations needs to be considered at on a case-by-case basis. If you have a neighboring property that is bringing down your property value, you may have to consider all the options before moving forward. Determine the impact of the neighbor. Try driving around the block and approaching your home as if you were a buyer looking at the property for the first time. Look at the home through a buyer's eyes.

In extreme case, where the neighbor refuses to either clean up his or her yard or allow you to clean up the area, you may be forced to speak with the local municipality or take legal action. You will have to determine which will cost more—the legal fees to force your neighbor to clean up or the loss in sales price by having a messy neighbor.

chapter eight:

Showings

You've spruced up your home, staged it for buyers, priced it for the market, and signed the listing contract. You're ready to show the home. Discuss with your agent when you will allow showings, how the buyer will obtain access to your house, and whether or not you should be home for those showings.

When Should You Allow Showings?

Always. While it's more convenient to have a lot of notice for a showing, and it may be more convenient to you to have showings two nights a week and on weekends, this kind of thinking limits your potential buyers. It is your goal to get twelve to fifteen serious, qualified buyers though your home in a reasonable period of time. Some buyers look at homes in the evening or on weekends. Some only have one free night a week. Other buyers can only look at homes during the day. If you turn down a showing, the buyer probably still has his or her choice of other homes on the market and is unlikely to come back to yours.

It is not uncommon for a home seller to initially tell us that they will only show their home Tuesday and Friday evenings between six and seven-thirty, and Saturdays between nine and noon. "If buyers want to see our home, then they'll have to follow our schedule. The kids have soccer. We have to work. Fifi needs constant grooming, and buyers will just have to understand our situation." Remember, buyers are not doing you a favor by looking at your home. They are trying to find a home that they want to buy. If your home is not available for a showing, the buyer will go on to the next property.

Your Realtor® may suggest putting a note on the listing stating that he or she would like twenty-four hours' notice for showings. While this helps you to clean up your house before any clients come through, it may also cost you possible buyers. Relocation buyers are notorious for coming into town for two days, picking fifteen homes, and wanting to see them at the last minute. These buyers are the ones who are pressed for time to find a home and are looking to buy quickly. While there are times when you simply must refuse a showing, you should try to keep it to a minimum.

QUICK TIP:

Showings by Owner

When selling a home on your own, you still need to make every effort possible to accommodate showings. If you are a couple and neither spouse is a stay-at-home parent, try to make sure one spouse is at least home each evening and on the weekends. If possible, find a way to make yourself available for lunchtime showings for relocation buyers. Some owners selling privately will speak with a retired neighbor and ask him or her to assist in letting potential buyers into the home.

To Lockbox or Not to Lockbox

A *lockbox* is a strong metal box that hangs on your railing or doorknob and has the key to your home securely locked in the box. An agent who wants to show your property will open the box, get out the key, and use it to open your home.

There are two primary types of lockboxes. The first is the standard dial or push button lockbox. Each box has a numeric or letter code, and agents who want to show the property must call for the combination in order to get in. The second type is an electronic lockbox. In many areas across the country, Realtors® carry electronic keys that open these boxes or have an app on their mobile device that opens it. The agent uses a code that he or she types into his or her key and points the key at the box. The key electronically communicates with the box and opens.

There are benefits and detriments to both systems. An electronic lockbox is more secure for several reasons. First, the person opening the box must have a Realtor's key and the code. Secondly, the electronic keys must be updated over the phone regularly. They become useless without being updated. Additionally, the electronic lockbox keeps a record of the Realtors® who showed the property, and the date and time of the showings. One last benefit is that an electronic lockbox can be set to only open certain hours. You may only want showings from nine in the morning to eight at night. These boxes can be programmed for that.

On the left is a typical Electronic Lockbox with an alphanumeric box on the right.

The dial or push button lockbox may not be as secure, because a client may see the code that is dialed or entered and may try to come back to the home later. However, electronic lockboxes are not universal. If your agent is part of one Board of Realtors or Multiple Listing System, and the showing agent is part of the MLS in the next county or town over, their keycards may not overlap, so the agent cannot get into the house. This can limit showings and is of particular importance if you are located in a suburban or rural area between two cities, counties, or metropolitan areas. You may end up limiting the showings to those agents who are part of the same MLS as your agent. An alternative is to have your agent meet the showing agent to let them in, but whether or not that happens depends on how available the listing agent can be.

When we discuss lockboxes with our home sellers, about half say something like "Please put a lockbox on my door. I do not want to be home for showings. I do not want to hear what people say about my house. Do you have one in the car?" The other half say "Lockboxes? My home will be broken into and robbed. I don't want that kind of liability. Someone will come into my home in the middle of the night and take Fifi."

Anything you can do to make your home more accessible, or at least to *appear* more accessible, will help you to get showings. There are agents in the industry who run property searches, and rank showings first by those homes that pay the highest commission, and second by those homes that have lockboxes. They believe that a home with a lockbox is easier to show, so they are certain they will be confirmed to show the home and will not have to add other listings later to replace those that refuse showings.

Even if you seldom leave the home and plan to be there for all showings, it's still a good idea to have a lockbox on the home to show Realtors® that your home is accessible.

There are still a few areas in the country where lockbox use is uncommon. Realtors® keep keys in their offices because they believe it is safer than placing a lockbox on the home. If you're located in an area that commonly uses a key, question your agent to make sure all keys are locked up at night.

Should You Be Home for Showings?

Many agents, brokers, and trainers believe a home seller should never be home for showings. They tell the seller that the buyer has difficulty emotionally moving into a home if the seller is present for showings. This might be partly true, but I believe the deciding factor is that sellers tend to hurt their own transactions by talking to the buyers directly.

When selling with a Realtor®, allow the Realtor® to show the home. Do not follow him or her around like a lost puppy. Sellers tell us that they know the house better than any agent and they can point out all the positive features. That may be true, but you are more likely to make the buyer feel uncomfortable than reassured. Uncomfortable buyers don't make offers. Buyers want to be able to mentally and emotionally move in. They are afraid to open closets and look closely at a home when the owner is with them.

Some buyers will walk through the home and try to pick it apart. Some will be outright rude. Smile and ignore their comments. These may be the purchasers of your home. They may be complaining on the outside about the workmanship, but inside they're thinking "Wow, this is really pretty nice. I wonder if my Tiger-skin sectional sofa will fit there?" There are buyers who believe that if they pick apart a home, the sellers will be more likely to reduce their price. Don't be offended.

If you are using the services of a Realtor® and you are in the home for showings, find a nice quiet corner somewhere and sit down with a good book or watch something on your iPad. Hold it right side up so that you can at least pretend that you are reading or watching something. When the prospective buyers have finished looking through the home, you can ask if they have any questions about utility bills or the neighborhood.

If you are selling your home on your own, walk the prospective buyer through the home, and point out the most positive features. You don't have to say things like "This is the fireplace." They can see that. You can point out benefits that aren't overly visible to someone viewing the home for the first time. You can also help set the stage by short statements, such as "This dining room has been great. We've had over a dozen people around the table at holidays." Make sure the statements are short. You want to give them a tour of the home without too much commentary. Let the potential buyers see the home their own way.

They will picture their own furniture in the home, or how they would alter it to fit their needs.

Open doors to rooms, turn the light on, and step back out of the way so the potential buyer can step in and view it as his or her own. If you are standing in front of them, they get a different feeling.

Try not to point out all the little flaws that you know about. In an initial showing, the buyer is feeling the house out to see if it's a fit for his or her lifestyle. Once he or she falls in love with the home, you can discuss full disclosure of potential defects with the buyer. Don't ever hide anything, but you can talk yourself right out of a sale by your commentary.

If you are asked questions, be careful how you answer them. Home sellers often give away too much information when speaking directly with buyers, potentially hurting their bargaining position. One of the primary reasons that Realtors® are often able to command a higher price for a home is that they negotiate as a third party without giving away your bottom line.

Example

As an example, one of our clients, Doris, had her home listed for $750,000, making it a luxury property in her area. She was home for a showing when the buyer told her that he wouldn't pay more than $700,000 for the home. He asked her directly if she would accept that offer. He said he didn't want to waste time writing it up if she wasn't going to accept. After thinking for a few minutes and doing some calculations in front of the buyer, she agreed to his price. The next day, his agent brought me an offer at $675,000. The buyer felt that if Doris would accept $700,000, she would probably accept $675,000.

Whether you are represented by an agent or not, you should avoid directly answering some questions that give away your position. Buyers seem to all attend a secret training school somewhere, because they all have the same questions for sellers. How you answer them can help or hurt your negotiating position. These three deadly questions asked by buyers are:

1. *"Are you negotiable on price?"*
    Variation: "Would you accept less?"
    Variation: "Would you consider an offer of ...?"

    Wrong Answer: "I'd be open to negotiation. I could probably go lower. What were you considering offering?"

    Correct Answer: "If you make a written offer, we will certainly consider whatever you offer." This vague response doesn't offend the buyer but doesn't give away any bargaining position you may take. Once buyers have made a written offer, they often emotionally purchase it, so you will have a better chance negotiating a higher offer.

2. "Why are you selling?"
    Variation:" Are you being relocated?"

    Wrong Answer: "Yes. We are being relocated and we need to move by November 1," or "I'm in the middle of a messy divorce and we need to get the home sold in order to settle," or "I'm going into foreclosure and if I don't sell it by Friday, I'm doomed. I'm lucky the electricity hasn't been shut off yet."

    Correct Answer: "We're moving to another area." This is an answer to many similar questions including a job transfer. It is an honest answer but doesn't let them know you have a timeframe in mind. Also correct is "We're planning to purchase a bigger home" or "We're planning to move to something smaller." These are intentionally vague answers. If you are retiring, the home may be too large, and you are planning to buy something smaller. If you're getting divorced, it's likely you are moving to something smaller. Don't let them think that you need to sell in order to settle a divorce.

3. *"When are you planning to move?"*
    Variation: "Is there a time frame you have to move by?"

    Wrong Answer: "My job starts in Oklahoma in six weeks." or "We bought another home across town and we need to settle on it in forty-five days." Again, with these answers, you are telling the prospective buyer that you are in a hurry to sell. You have a deadline, and he or she can make a lower offer because you may be pressed to accept it.

Correct Answer: "When the house sells," or "We don't have a definite time yet." Even if you need to be in Tulsa within sixty days, you don't have a specific date yet. By giving the buyer the exact time you want or need to move, the buyer feels they have leverage to offer you a lower price.

Stop talking

Home sellers can actually talk themselves out of sales by giving out too much information. There is a fine line between honest disclosure and scaring a buyer away. If you are home for the showing, let the buyer walk through your home and ask if he or she has any questions. Don't follow the Realtor® around and don't offer commentary unless asked. If the buyer asks you a question, stick to answering the question openly and honestly, but do not offer additional narrative. You could scare away a buyer.

Example:
    A few years ago, I was showing a property to a couple for the third time. They were just making one last walk through the home before going back to the office to write an offer. They were initially concerned about purchasing the home because it was on a very busy thoroughfare, only one door off the corner of an intersection. Ultimately, they decided that the home sat far back from the road and had lots of trees in the front. The backyard was a nice size, and they loved the layout and character of the home.
    As I was pulling the door shut to leave the home, the owner pulled in the driveway and hopped out of his car. He hurried up to us and asked us to go back in the house.
    "We're kind of in a hurry." I said.
    "This will just take a minute."
    We re-entered the home, he closed the door behind us and said, "Do you hear that?"
    "Hear what?" I asked.

"Nothing. You don't hear anything. You don't hear the noise from the road out front because this house was built right. It's brick with solid doors, and you do not hear the traffic noise in the home." he said.

Obviously, this had been an objection he had probably heard from his listing Realtor® over and over again, and he was trying to convince us that it was not the big problem others had made it out to be.

"That's great." I said, unenthusiastically.

"No, you don't understand. Everybody talks about the noise here. We don't hear it. As a matter of fact, there's an accident on the corner about once a week. We never know about them because the house is so well insulated, we never hear them."

At this point, the buyer started fidgeting and I knew the buyer was reconsidering. I think the seller saw it too and took it to mean that the buyer didn't believe him, so he stepped it up a notch.

"Actually, we've had accidents right in front of the home and never heard them. Ambulances, police, you can't hear them through these walls." He tapped on the plaster wall for effect. "As a matter of fact, my son's best friend was killed pulling out of our driveway last year. T-boned right out there and his car rolled onto our front lawn. There was an ambulance and the fire department. We didn't even know it. *That's* how well built this home is!"

In case you're curious, no, the buyer didn't buy the home.

Safety

In every walk of life, you need to be careful. There are child predators on the Internet, computer hackers stealing your credit card information, and the nice old man down the street might not be that nice. When you're selling your home, you are inviting a bunch of strangers into your private sanctuary. You need to be careful of theft, attack, and accusations.

Realtors® help insulate the homeowner from many of the risks of allowing people in your home. They will typically have contact information for the people they show homes to, so it's less likely they will have criminal intent in mind.

When you are selling your house on your own, you should verify that the person on the phone is not giving you an incorrect or phony phone number or other bad information. When someone calls to view the home, tell him or her you will have to get back to him or her about the time, and get the interested party's name and number. The act of calling back the number verifies that at least you know something about the person entering your castle. If someone stops by and tries to see the home, let him or her know you work by appointment only. This can happen even if you are listed with an agency. Buyers stop by and attempt to negotiate with you directly. Let them know that they will have to go through the agent.

> ## QUICK TIP:
> ### Pets During Showings
>
> Pets can become nervous as strangers regularly enter your home. For example, there are many cases where the friendliest of dogs reacts badly to a potential buyer and bites him or her, leading to a potential lawsuit. Even if your pet has never before bitten someone, you may be opening yourself up for a liability.
>
> Additionally, pets distract buyers from actually seeing your home. Some buyers are afraid of dogs and some buyers are completely turned off by cats. Dogs that are put in cages may bark, providing an additional distraction for buyers. When possible, remove your animals from the home before showings.

At the time of the showing, try to make sure there is more than one person in the home. A predator is discouraged from acting if the odds are against him or her. Additionally, a second person is a witness should someone visit your home and try to accuse you of accosting them. Unfortunately, these types of things can happen. When possible, take down the license plate number of the car the buyer is driving.

Before any showings, hide or remove any personal items of value. Put away any jewelry, handheld electronic devices, or loose cash. Any valuable items should be tucked away from sticky fingers. Your eyes or your realtor's eyes Realtor® cannot be on everyone all the time. Small mementoes that have sentimental value should be out of site as well, and you should take the time to go through medicine cabinets and make sure nothing is visible that someone might covet. It's better not to tempt fate.

The Most Common Misconception About Showings

Homeowners often believe that the home will be shown primarily by the listing agent or the listing office. As we discussed earlier, this is seldom true. A good agent may work with five to ten active home buyers at any given point in time. The likelihood that any of the agent's buyers want a home of your style, your size, and your decorating style in your neighborhood and school district is not very high.

Some of your agent's marketing efforts will bring potential buyers to your agent that may like or love your home. More likely, however, is that buyers will see the ads on your home and call the agent they are already working with. Advertising and marketing by your agent does not necessarily mean he or she will show your home more often, and just because your agent isn't showing your home doesn't mean he or she is not working to find you a buyer. The fact that you are getting showings is evidence that the marketing plan is working.

Feedback

If you have selected a good real estate agent, he or she will call or email you with feedback on showings. If your agent doesn't call, call him or her and request feedback. Find out what buyers liked about the home, what they didn't like, what they would change in order to sell it, and what they think the eventual sales price will be. What buyers liked about the home is a good way to determine what buyers feel are the most positive attributes of your property. You can then use that information in your marketing. What a buyer didn't like may allow you the opportunity to correct the deficiency prior to the next showing. If you ask what a buyer would change about the home, you can possibly get into his or her head and see how someone else views your property. What buyers expect the selling price to be will give you an idea of how the buyers compared your home with others in the neighborhood.

Beware of the feedback "We thought your home was well priced." They didn't buy the home. They may be trying to be polite to you. Research shows that between one- and two-thirds of buyers who view a home will buy one within thirty days. If they are not buying yours, they are buying a competing property. Your home will not appeal to every single buyer, but if you find that you have twenty-five showings and no offers, you are probably being compared unfavorably to other homes in the market

Example

For example, a few years ago we had a couple, Janice and Jeffrey, who were waiting for a particular style 1900s brick home to go on the market within a few blocks of Muhlenberg College in West Allentown. I happened to list a home that I thought met their needs. They were very excited and set up an appointment to view the home the same day.

As we walked through the home, they pointed out the French doors, the leaded glass, and the refinished hardwood floors and trim. They loved it. We went upstairs through the bedrooms, and finished in the kitchen, where the owners were sitting. They politely spoke for a minute with the owners and we left the home. Outside, Janice turned to me and said she wanted to keep looking. The home wasn't for them.

I was surprised by her reaction, so I called her the next day and asked what had changed her mind. She appeared to love the living room and dining room as well as the location and the features of the home. "I'm not being pushy, Janice. I'm really just curious what turned you off."

She asked "Did you notice the water stain in the kitchen ceiling? I didn't mention it because the owners were sitting

> ## QUICK TIP:
> ### The Four Questions to Ask Home Buyers
>
> 1. What did you like about our home?
> 2. What didn't you like, or what did you like lease about our home.
> 3. If you could change one thing about our home, what would it be?
> 4. I'm just curious, what do you believe will be the most likely selling price of our home.

there. My brother bought a home where the roof had leaked for months, without them knowing it. By the time they found out, they had thousands and thousands in damage. The roof on this house has to be replaced. That's probably $15,000, and we don't know how much water has leaked between the walls. That can cause mold or rot out the beams and then we're looking at ripping apart the whole back part of the house. No thank you."

"I understand your concern. Roofs are running about $5,000 to $6,000 for this style home at the moment but let me find out what the actual story is. Maybe the owners already replaced the roof."

It turned out that the roof was about five years old, but the leak hadn't been from the roof. Their grandchildren had been staying with them and splashed water out of the tub on the second floor. The owners had caulked around the tub and fixed the problem, but it only leaked once. The owners just didn't feel the need to repaint the ceiling.

Janice and Jeffrey bought the home.

If I had not persistently called the buyers to find out w*hy* they had decided against the home, the owners may have had a dozen or more showings with one buyer after another deciding against it.

When we know about an issue that's concerning buyers, we may be able to address it before it turns off more buyers. Feedback is critically important in the sales process.

Lookers or Buyers?

Not all people who set up an appointment and view your home will be serious buyers. Unfortunately, you will have to accept this premise in the beginning if you are planning to sell your home. Hopefully, your Realtor® will help to reduce the number of lookers wasting your time, but there are usually one or two that slip through.

There are several distinctive types of buyers in the marketplace. The first is the serious buyer who is qualified and wants to find a home. Luckily, these are the majority of buyers in most marketplaces. These buyers look at your home and compare it with other homes for sale and decide which one they want to purchase. Because your home is now well staged and priced correctly, they will hopefully decide on your home very quickly.

The second type of buyer is someone who really wants to buy but hasn't yet been able to get his or her financing in place. This buyer may have good credit, but little money saved toward the purchase, or he or she may have credit issues that still need to be worked out before purchasing. Unfortunately, the buyer's lack of current ability to purchase doesn't seem to discourage him or her from looking. On a positive note, Realtors® usually figure these buyers out very quickly and stop showing them homes.

The third type of buyer is someone who really wants to purchase but won't do it unless he or she finds the perfect home. This buyer's home is not sold yet and may not even be on the market. The offer this buyer makes may be contingent upon the sale of his or her home. That is not a good position to be in, but the buyer rationalizes that he or she does not want to give up his or her home and be stuck having to buy something else quickly without taking the time to find the new, perfect abode.

The fourth type of buyer is the discount shopper. This buyer is looking to find a steal in the marketplace and will keep hunting until he or she finds it. Discount shoppers may be investors looking for home sellers in trouble, or they may be buyers looking for a personal residence but wanting to pay below market. Discount shoppers often make many offers on properties until they find someone who is willing to take their offer.

The final buyer type is really not a buyer at all. This type of buyer spends his or her weekends house hunting at the expense of many Realtors' gasoline and car wear. They are called *lookers* or *window shoppers*. They dream of buying another home, and it becomes entertainment for them, just as if they were going to dinner or a movie. Realtors® try to minimize the number of lookers to whom they show homes. Some of these individuals show up regularly at open houses.

chapter nine:

Offers and Negotiations

The first offer just came in on your home and it's not even close to what you expected. You sit back in your chair and wonder why you went through all the trouble and hassles of cleaning, painting, and de-cluttering. Wasn't it just a year or so ago when buyers were bidding housing prices up to numbers much higher than the asking price?

Somewhere in the back of your mind, though, is the rational thought that buyers are conditioned to make low offers because they think that a low offer will get you to reveal your bottom line. A buyer may love your home but does not want to spend any more than he or she absolutely has to.

You may be tempted to cut the offer into *really* little pieces and send it back to the buyer in an envelope. Before you make this move, remember that every offer is an opportunity to sell your home for a reasonable price. Somewhere in between the offensive number on the offer and your asking price, you may be able to negotiate an offer that favors you in the transaction.

When you receive an offer, you have three choices.

1. You can accept the offer the way it is written.

2. You can reject the offer.

3. You can make a counteroffer or counter proposal to the buyer.

A counteroffer can be made on the price or on any terms that are part of the agreement of sale. Counteroffers should be carefully thought out and considered. You want to negotiate the best deal possible for you and your family without losing the potential buyer.

Your First Offer

Your first offer may be great, or it may be very low. Don't get too upset if you receive a low offer. Too often, home sellers become emotional and take offense at a low bid placed by a buyer. "How dare they come in with such a ridiculous offer. Don't they realize everything I've put into this house?"

I suggest that you always make an attempt at negotiations, even if you feel they are doomed to failure from the start. Many buyers believe that if they make a low offer, you will settle somewhere in the middle. Certainly, you will have to counter an offer where you feel comfortable, but our negotiating tactic is typically to counter within 30% of the difference.

For example, if your home is listed at $200,000 and the offer is $170,000, the buyer is probably expecting you to counter around $185,000 or at about 50% of the difference. My suggestion is to counter above $190,000, because you will be more likely to pull the buyer up to a higher number than $185,000.

In negotiations, you would probably be surprised by how many home sellers tell me not to bother countering the offer, or they make a silly counter because they are offended. For example, a home is listed at $250,000 and the buyer makes a low offer of $215,000. The seller counters at $249,870. This may make the seller feel good for a few hours, but seldom gets us very far in negotiations. Typically, the buyer becomes angry and walks away from negotiations. Had the seller countered with something that showed he was serious about selling, we would have more likelihood of putting a transaction together.

Remember that some buyers will make a low offer based on the expectation that you will counter the offer somewhere in the middle. Other buyers, however, really cannot quite afford your list price and make an offer based on what they can afford. You may not be certain which kind of buyer this is until you make a counteroffer, or unless the preapproval letter is very specific about his or her qualifications.

Before making any counteroffers, however, you should go over all the contingencies of the offer to purchase. The price is only one component of a sales agreement, and you need to be aware of the buyer's seriousness and qualifications, and any stipulations of accepting the offer.

Sales Agreements can be many pages and complex to review

The best buyers are both serious and qualified. There are some buyers who are very serious. They want a home so badly, they can taste it, but they may not be qualified. They may be really stretching and hoping that a lender will work a miracle on their behalf. There are buyers who are qualified, but not serious. These are the buyers with great credit and excellent incomes but are on the fence when it comes to actually purchasing. They hem and haw about the agreement and eventually write you an offer but are candidates that are likely to back out.

The way to determine whether a buyer is qualified is to require a full mortgage preapproval from a reputable lender. This mortgage preapproval should be from a mortgage banker or someone who can actually loan his or her own money. There are mortgage brokers who write loans for other companies and do not really have the authority to guarantee a mortgage. For example, ABCQ Mortgage Company doesn't really fund any loans. It writes its loans through Wells Fargo or other lenders. ABCQ issues a mortgage preapproval on your buyer, but really has not run the documentation past Wells Fargo yet. Three weeks from now, you can be on the receiving end of a very unpleasant call denying the loan. Always look for a lender who lends its own money or true underwriter approval. Your agent can assist with this task.

> ## QUICK TIP:
> ### Deposit vs. Down Payments
>
> A deposit is different from a down payment. *Down Payments* are the amount of cash the buyer will invest in the home he or she purchases. *Deposits* are the amount of money the buyer puts down on the home to secure it. The deposit is primarily made in order to guarantee the seller that the buyer will not walk away from the purchase. If the buyer backs out of the ale without cause, the deposit may be claimed by the seller. In some states, the disposition of the money may have to be determined by the courts.

The way to determine if your buyer is serious is to require a significant down payment on the home. Unfortunately, in most parts of the country, the days of a 10% deposit are just about gone. Buyers are less willing to tie up their funds to secure a home, and sellers are more willing to accept low deposits. However, a buyer of a $200,000 home can easily walk away from a $1,000 deposit. Discuss what you think is a rational number that the buyer will not walk away from if he or she happens to get cold feet or buyer's remorse. If the home is $500,000, the buyer should certainly be putting down $20,000 or more to secure the home. After all, you are taking the home off the market for this buyer for possibly sixty or ninety days.

When you receive an offer, you should respond quickly. A buyer can withdraw an offer at any time up until the offer is accepted, signed, and delivered back to the buyer's agent.

Example:
> Last year, we had a home seller who sat on an offer for four days, debating on the merits of the offer. Despite the pressure we applied, he said he was not going to be rushed into making a rash decision. Ultimately, he accepted the offer as written, but the buyer withdrew it prior to the seller signing the offer. Weeks later, the seller sold the property for less than that initial offer.

Buyers can get something called *buyer's remorse*. After writing the offer, they go home and consider whether they did the right thing. Was it the right house? Was it the right neighborhood? Did they jump too fast? Should they have kept looking? Is this going to stretch their budget to the limit? As time wears on, that anxiety can build, causing the buyer to try to back out of a purchase.

Purchase Agreement Analyzer

When I call a home seller with an offer, their immediate question is "What is the offer price?" While that's an important component of any offer, there are many other components that are also critical to discuss, like the deposit, the qualifications of the buyer and any contingencies. Is the sale contingent on selling another property? Is the sale conditioned on any inspections? What would your liability be under these inspection clauses? What is the time frame for you to move? What are they asking to remain with the house?

Sales agreements in many parts of the country are ten to twenty-five pages of legalese that is unintelligible to most people. In order to fully analyze any sales contract, I suggest putting the most important parts of the offer into a *Purchase Agreement Analyzer*. A *Purchase Agreement Analyzer* (PAA) is a one page fill-in-the-blanks tool that allows a property seller to review the highlights of the offer and determine what counterproposal the seller wants to make. If a seller gets into a situation of multiple bids on their property, they can use a PAA to help compare the offers and select the best one.

Purchase Agreement Analyzer

Offer Price:_____

Is buyer asking for closing cost assistance? _____ If so, how
much?_____

Actual net offer after closing costs: _____

Settlement Date:_____No. of days to settlement:_____
Possession date (if different): _____

Deposit with offer: _____
Full deposit on home:_____ In _____ days

Buyer has preapproval letter? ☐ Yes ☐ No

Inspections required:

☐ Home/Building inspection (buyer will accept up to _____)

☐ Well inspection

☐ Radon inspection

☐ Septic inspection

☐ Mold inspection

☐ Other inspection

Mortgage amount required by buyer:_____
Date of mortgage commitment: _____

Appliances, personal items, and fixtures to remain with home:

_____

Sale contingencies:
☐ Contingent on settlement of other property _____
_____
Copy of agreement on buyer's home included?_____

☐ Contingent on sale and settlement of other property _____
   _____

Details: _____
   _____

☐ Contingent on any repairs to property _____
   _____

Details: _____
   _____

☐ Unusual contingencies: _____
   _____

Conditions and Contingencies

A home sale can have any of hundreds of different contingencies. A contingency is a condition of purchase, such as, "The buyer will not buy the property unless the buyer is approved for a mortgage." The most common are that the sale is contingent upon mortgage approval of the buyer, contingent upon inspection results, and contingent upon the sale of another home. Any condition of sale or contingency can be negotiated, but you should have a solid understanding of what the options are in the most common contingencies. Remember, clauses vary from state to state, so make sure to review them carefully with your attorney or real estate agent.

Contingent on Financing

The vast majority of home sales are purchased subject to a mortgage approval. On most purchase agreements, if the buyer is turned down for financing, the seller or seller's agent must return the buyer's deposit.

Mortgage loans can be turned down for several reasons. Lenders approve or deny a mortgage based on four primary things, known in the lending industry as the *four Cs*. They are credit, collateral, capacity, and character. *Credit* is a credit score, as determined by one of the three national credit scoring agencies.

Collateral is defined as the value of the home that is being pledged for the mortgage. The lender generally requires an appraisal of the home by a licensed appraiser in order to determine whether there is sufficient value in the home so that should the borrower not pay the mortgage, the lender can foreclose on the home and resell it to pay off the debt.

Capacity is defined as the borrower's income and his or her ability to make the mortgage payments and repay the loan. Capacity is determined by comparing the buyer's income and other debt to the mortgage payments and determining whether or not the buyer's income and other debt fits into the loan program's debt to income ratio.

Character is whether or not the lender believes the borrower is likely to repay the loan based on his or her past history.

One of the most common reasons a loan is turned down is that the buyer's credit score is not high enough for the loan program to which the buyer applied. Another common reason for denial is insufficient income by the buyer to meet the lender's debt-to-income ratio. A failure of the home to appraise high enough for the mortgage is another reason the buyer may be denied a loan.

During slowdowns in the real estate market, appraisers tend to become more conservative in their estimations of value. One of their jobs is to protect the lender from over-mortgaging a home.

You can partially insulate yourself from the first two situations by requiring a written preapproval from the buyer prior to signing the sales contract. The third situation, under appraisal of the property, will be discussed in the next chapter.

Even with preapproval, problems can arise. A buyer's credit may change prior to settlement, or a buyer may lose his or her job prior to settlement. If buyers are denied a mortgage because they furnished false information to you or to the lender, you may be able to retain their deposit. Under these circumstances, I suggest seeking legal advice.

Part of the mortgage contingencies should also be a mortgage commitment date at which time the buyer must have a full written commitment from the lender. This commitment should be sent to your agent and forwarded to you. Mark the date on your calendar to follow up with your agent and be sure he or she gets that commitment. Missing a commitment date could be an indication of another serious problem with the loan. Additionally, missing a commitment date could allow you an escape from the contract.

Check the mortgage contingency clause for the maximum mortgage rate. This rate should be a half percent to a full percent higher than the current prevailing rate. Otherwise, your buyer may have a way out of the contract if rates rise prior to settlement or close of escrow. When negotiating or countering an offer, if this maximum mortgage rate is simply at, or worse, below, the current prevailing rate, counter with a higher number.

In any case, if an offer is made on your home requiring a mortgage, make preapproval from a lender a condition of accepting the offer. Should the offer on your property be cash, ask for proof of funds so that you are certain the property will close.

Contingent on the Settlement of the Buyer's Home

For move-up buyers, a clause making the sale contingent on the sale of the buyer's home is common. Your home sale becomes part of a chain of home sales. If the sale of the buyer's home falls through, so does yours. Although most home sellers would prefer to avoid this clause, most move-up home buyers and luxury home buyers are selling another residence in order to purchase yours. Even if the clause is not part of the sales agreement, chances are the buyer might not qualify to carry two mortgages if the sale on his or her current home collapses.

When an offer is made with a contingency on the settlement of another home, always obtain a copy of the sales contract on the buyer's home and information on the buyer of the buyer's home. Add a clause to your sales contract that you want a certain number of days to review the qualifications of the buyer of the buyer's home, and to review their sales contract. If the buyer's sale is shaky, your sale will also become shaky, so you want to make sure you have a solid agreement.

Contingent on the Sale and Settlement of the Buyer's Home

A *sale and settlement clause* means the buyer's home is not yet sold, and must be sold in order for the buyer to perform and buy your property. There are several versions of sale and settlement contingencies. Some of these clauses require the seller to take his or her home off the market for a period of time or indefinitely until the buyer's home sells. Other versions allow the seller to continue to market the property until another offer is made on the property, and the original buyer is given a period of time to secure financing without selling his or her home or release the agreement to the new buyer.

The first version asks you, the seller, to take your home off the market until the buyer's home sells. There is usually a time constraint on how long the buyer has to sell his or her home. This clause is almost never in the best interest of the seller. Because it is hard enough to sell your own home in a slowing market, there is no reason to take your home off the market and hope your buyer makes the right decisions to get his or her house sold.

The more common version is called a kick-out clause and allows the seller to continue marketing the property to other buyers. Should another buyer make an offer on the property, the seller is required by the original agreement to give a certain amount of time to the buyer to remove his or her contingency on selling his or her home. The first buyer may remove the clause by accepting a bridge or swing loan, which is borrowing equity out of a current residence to purchase a new home. Or, the first buyer may also remove the clause if his or her home happens to sell immediately.

Example

For example, a client, Eric, received an offer from Pam to purchase his home. Pam's home was on the market but had not sold. Eric and Pam agreed to an acceptable price and terms on a sales agreement but allowed it to be contingent on the sale of Pam's home. Eric was allowed to keep his home on the market with a forty-eight-hour kick-out clause.

A few weeks later, a second offer came in on the home from a different buyer. The offer was actually higher than Pam's sales contract. Eric told the new buyer that he would accept the offer, but he had to give Pam forty-eight hours to either remove the contingency on the sale of her home or to release her sales contract with Eric and let Eric sell to the new buyer. As luck would have it, Pam was able to secure financing to cover both homes within the forty-eight-hour period and purchased Eric's home. Because she had a signed contract, she purchased the home at the original price she agreed to with Eric, which was less than Eric's second offer.

There are several schools of thought as to whether or not to accept a sale and settlement contingency on your home. Many Realtors® and sellers believe it is unwise to accept this kind of contingency for several reasons. First, if the initial buyer is able to remove the contingency, you are bound to accept this price, even if someone else offers you a better price later. Second, buyers are reluctant to view homes that are under this kind of contingency sale because they are unsure whether or not they will be able to purchase the home, so they are more likely to pass it by without looking. Also, sellers argue that if the buyer loves the property, he or she can always purchase it when his or her home sells, if it sells first.

There are some benefits, however, to signing a sale and settlement contingency. First, buyers are often willing to pay more for the home in order to secure the contract. They realize they do not have as solid a contract as someone who doesn't have to sell a home, and they don't want to lose the home, so they offer a higher price. Second, you tie the buyer to the home. If the buyers sell their home without having a contingency sale on your property, they may find another home they like better in the meantime. Third, buyers who come back at a later time know that your property has been on the market longer and will often offer less for the same property.

Whether or not you accept a sale and settlement contingency depends on your situation. Talk to your agent and get his or her opinion of how accepting this type of offer would affect the sale of the home.

Contingent on a Home Inspection

A *home inspection* or *building inspection* is a complete inspection of the structure and systems of a property. The cost of a home inspection can be negotiated between the buyer and seller.

A sales contract on your home should spell out the time frame an inspection must be completed in, and who is responsible for repairs that are found to be necessary by the inspector.

Typical inspection clauses fall into two categories.

Take It or Leave It. This form of inspection clause allows the buyer the opportunity to perform a home inspection. Based on the results of the inspection, the buyer may cancel the sales contract and have all deposit money returned to the buyer. As a seller, this version is not feasible because the buyer could tie up the home for a few weeks and simply walk away from the purchase if he or she gets cold feet. The home inspection can be used as an excuse to cancel.

Seller's Right to Correct. In other versions of this clause, the buyer agrees to accept the property *as is* up to a pre-specified amount toward repairs. If the home inspection reveals more than that pre-specified amount, you as the seller, have the right to repair the difference, or credit the cost of the difference. If you refuse to contribute to or correct the difference, the buyer has the right to cancel the sales contract.

For example, a buyer and seller agree to a sales contract with a seller's right to correct inspection clause, where the buyer would accept the property as is up to $1,000 in repairs. The home inspection revealed several electrical issues and a furnace repair that were estimated at $2,400. If the seller was unwilling to pay the $1,400 difference or have $1,400 in repairs completed, the buyer is allowed to back out of the purchase.

Common Parts of a Home Inspection

Home inspections are generally broken into sections based on the part of the structure or type of system being evaluated. For example, the electrical wiring and the plumbing are both systems in the home, but they function completely independently and are placed in separate sections of any home inspection or building inspection report.

Structure and Foundation. The inspector checks for water penetration in the basement or other parts of the structure; structural integrity issues, such as cracking, sinking, or crumbling; and, other structure-related issues. Walls, floors, and ceilings are all examined for condition or possible issues.

Roof and Related Issues. The inspector checks the roof to determine the estimated remaining life span and any issues with the roof system. This examination also includes the gutters, down spouts, flashing, chimney, and the attic to check for water penetration or rotting wood.

Electrical. The inspector checks the electrical panel to verify it is properly grounded and properly installed. He or she checks outlets, junctions, and wiring for shorts, deficiencies, and issues.

Plumbing. A complete check of all tubs, sinks, pipes, and the entire plumbing system for leaks, clogs, and other issues.

Heating and Air Conditioning. An inspection of the furnace, air conditioning units, ductwork, air flow, and efficiency.

Appliances. Verification that appliances are in good working order.

Exterior Issues. Decks, patios, porches, retaining walls, site issues, and run off from down spouts are all part of this examination.

Contingent on a Water Inspection

A water test is generally performed on homes that are serviced by well water or spring water. Tests can be as simple as a check for coliform bacteria, or as complicated as a test for dozens of potential issues. Water issues include high metal counts, lead, petroleum, acidity, or dozens of other issues.

If your water tests high for acidity, you may need a neutralizer. If the water tests high for bacteria, it may be possible to correct it by *shocking* the well with chlorine. Over time, wells can develop a one-time contamination from bacteria. *Shocking* is a process of dumping chlorine into a well, which kills bacteria in a well, and then running water through the pipes in order to kill any bacteria in the pipes. If you retest the water a few days after shocking the well and find that there is still contamination, the problem may be ongoing contamination from an outside source. To ensure clean drinking water, you may need to install an ultraviolet light. Ultraviolet lights attach to the plumbing and kill bacteria in drinking water.

If, on the other hand, the water test reveals higher than normal levels of calcium, magnesium, or other metals, you may need to install a water softener. A high level of calcium, magnesium, or other metals is known as *hard water*. These minerals tend to clog pipes and slow down or halt soaps and detergents from dissolving properly. *Water softeners* remove minerals from the water.

Contingent on a Septic Inspection

Septic systems are diverse and include in-ground systems, sand mounds, cesspools, and spray irrigation systems, among others. Homeowners seldom know if a septic system is failing, and the replacement cost of a drain field can run into the tens of thousands of dollars.

Most septic systems are broken into two primary components—the holding tank, or tanks, and the drain field. The *holding tank* holds the solid waste, while the liquid is pumped through the holding tank out into the yard into a *drain field*. An older system known as a *cesspool* may have a holding tank and a leach field, which works in a similar fashion, but the liquid waste leaches out into a field instead of being pumped. In some rare cases where there is little land around the home or a high water table, septic systems are simply self-contained holding tanks that must be pumped out continually in order to remain functional. Since the majority of systems contain a tank and a drain field, a proper inspection checks both.

Tests vary from region to region and may be as simple as a *dye pack test*, in which the inspector flushes a dye pack down a toilet and checks the yard to determine if and where the dye comes up, or as complicated as a hydraulic load test, where the inspector flushes a few hundred gallons of water into the system to determine if the absorption area is able to handle the expected daily volume.

The most common test is a visual inspection to determine that the system is functioning properly. The inspector must check that solids are being properly deposited in the tank, that liquid is flowing properly into the drain field, and that the drain field is not oversaturated. In this test, the inspector typically requires the homeowner to have the tank lid open so he or she can visually watch the liquid flow into the tank. The inspector then flushes some water through the system and watches through the tank opening to ensure no solids are flowing through the pipe into the drain field. In many cases, inspectors require the owner to have the tank pumped out or cleaned out while the inspector is present. This allows the inspector to see the tank functioning, and then to view the tank while it's empty in order to check for cracking or other issues with the inside off the tank. Finally, the inspector uses a probe in the drain field where liquid is sent from the tank to make sure it too is functioning properly.

Contingent on a Radon Inspection

Radon is an odorless gas that can cause cancer. If your sale is contingent upon a radon inspection, the inspector leaves one or more test kits, consisting of a charcoal canister or an electronic device, for a few days in your home. The kits are picked up and analyzed to determine if your home has radon.

Should your home test positive for radon, remediation measures include sealing cracks in the basement and piping air from under the foundation to the outside using PVC pipe and a fan system. This repair can run from several hundred dollars to a couple thousand depending on the size of the home and severity of the problem.

Contingent on a Wood Destroying Insect Inspection

Termites, powder post beetles, carpenter ants, carpenter bees, old house borers, and other insects can damage or destroy homes. A common condition of an offer is that the home be inspected for wood-destroying insects.

Contingent on a Mold Inspection

Tests for indoor air quality and mold are becoming more common than just a few years ago. Mold can grow in ductwork and between walls. It can potentially be a health hazard.

Counteroffers and Successful Negotiation

You've filled in a Purchase Agreement Analyzer to visually see the various aspects of the offer. Next, you will have to decide what your best negotiating strategy will be, and what to propose as a counteroffer. Go over the conditions of the agreement and see what you like, what you can live with, and what you absolutely need to change. You may find that the only aspect of the offer you need to counter is the price. You may find that the time frame won't work, or that the buyer wants your antique chandelier and you absolutely will not leave it in the house because it's a family heirloom.

Consider what might make the offer more palatable. This will depend on your situation. Some offers are time dependent. If you have already moved out of your home and are paying a mortgage on the home, a lengthier closing period will cost you some of your hard-fought purchase price. For example, if you have moved from the home and your mortgage is $2,000 a month, a typical forty-five-day closing will cost you approximately $3,000 depending on your mortgage and what is owed on your principal. A sixty-day closing will cost $4,000 and a ninety-day closing will cost $6,000.

Rather than counter on the price they offered you, ask for a shorter settlement period or escrow period. "I'll accept your offer, but only if we can get this closed in thirty days." Countering a ninety-day closing with a thirty-day closing would save you $4,000. This makes up for some of the difference between your asking price and the price offered.

Some methods to negotiate a higher price or better terms include:

- writing a note to the buyers explaining your situation to create empathy for your move;

- throwing in the appliances—give the buyer value in a different way than price;

- giving an allowance for repairs—find out why buyers are making their offer and what their concerns are. If they're offering less because of necessary updates, it may be less expensive to do the updates yourself;

- agreeing to provide a home warranty—if their concern is the age of the heating system or other home systems, a home warranty may give them the peace of mind to raise their offer; and,

- trying to shorten the contingency periods—these contingencies can become exit or escape clauses for the buyer. The faster the contingency periods expire, the firmer ground your agreement is on.

Writing a Note to the Buyers

One method of negotiating a higher price is to stay firm on the price. The problem with this as a negotiating method is that the buyers tend to respond with a firm stand, and you won't get anywhere. Buyers make a specific offer in hopes of getting your home at a discount. When you make a counterproposal, their feelings often change. The buyer has thought about the home for the last twenty-four hours and believes they may have offered too much. When you come back with your counteroffer, they are at the point in their thinking that they believe you are just being greedy in asking that much for your home.

There is another approach that cushions this attitude of buyers. The approach is to respond apologetically, hopefully creating sympathy for your position. Since it is very hard to attract sympathy from a seller to a listing agent to a buyer's agent all the way to the buyers without losing something in transition, my suggestion is to write them a heartfelt note. Tug a little bit at their heart strings and point out what the buyer probably loved about the home that drove them to write an offer.

Dear Mr. and Mrs. Babbas,

We wanted to sincerely thank you for making an offer on our home. My husband had the chance to meet you when you came through the other day, and he thought you were a lovely couple. Your son is adorable.

Although we really do appreciate your offer, we unfortunately can't accept it the way it's written. We are moving to the West End to a new development, and in order to complete our move, we just can't accept less than $228,000. When we priced this home, we carefully spoke with several Realtors and reviewed every competing home. We believe this to be a fair price and our Realtor assures us, based on the number of showings and positive feedback from buyers, that we can realize this price in today's market.

We've owned this home for almost ten years, and we've really tried to keep it in top condition. I hope you'll agree. It has been a wonderful experience raising our family in this neighborhood and in this home. We've enjoyed it, and I hope that should you decide to purchase the home, you enjoy it as well.

Again, I'm sorry we can't accept the offer as written, but we'd love to see you purchase the home. We simply can't accept less than $228,000.

Sincerely,

June Cleaver

Include the Appliances in Negotiations

One method of negotiating the price higher is to stay firm on the price, but include something else of value, like the washer, dryer, refrigerator, and freezer. Again, you may want to approach the buyers almost apologetically, because you will be likely to get a more positive response. Work together with the buyer to figure out a solution to the dilemma. "I really need this much for the home. What can we do to make this work?" You want the buyers to be able to save face with their friends and relatives. "Yes, we paid a little more than we wanted, but we made them leave all the appliances and do a few other things for us, so I think we got a good deal."

All buyers want to be able to say they got a good deal or feel like they won something. Negotiations are give and take. The approach would be: "I really need to sell at a price of $X in order to move. What I could do, if you'd be willing to accept it, is include the appliances with the sale at that price. They're worth a few thousand dollars."

When I suggest this tactic to a home seller, they sometimes look at me with confusion. "That means we'll have to go out and buy new appliances! How exactly does that help us?" It's possible you might have to buy appliances when you purchase your new home, or perhaps you can negotiate the appliances in the next purchase. Additionally, there are expenses associated with moving appliances. Because of the time and effort it takes to move appliances, movers charge more for it.

Pay for home repairs or updates

Buyers make their offers based partly on what they really want to spend on your home, partly on what they believe the actual value to be in the current market, and partly on what they anticipate their costs will be to move into the home and update it to their needs. Some offers come with a laundry list of what's wrong with the house to justify their offers. This note is often very offensive to a home seller. If a buyer provides such a list, however, they are telling us what they would like to do to improve the home.

If the buyer does not include a letter, ask the buyer, or have your Realtor® ask the buyer, what he or she based this decision on. Is the buyer planning to do any work to the home? What you're trying to determine is what the offer is based on. Buyers have a tendency to estimate high on what the cost of repairs or upgrades might be. Additionally, buyers discount even further for having to go through the trouble of doing the work.

An alternative is to explain to the buyer that while you cannot take $18,000 off the price, you would be willing to replace the master bedroom carpeting with the color of their choice, repaint the living room ceiling, and replace the main bath vanity. These changes may cost you $3,000, but the buyer is estimating the cost at $6,000 and wants $9,000 because he or she would have to take the time to find people to do the work. Making an offer to update, repair, or upgrade for the buyer often works to get the buyer significantly higher in price.

Pros and Cons of Home Warranties

A *home warranty* is generally an insurance policy that covers the systems and appliances in your home for one year after settlement. Prices range from $400 to $800 or more depending on the size of the home and the coverage included. Most home warranties do not cover roof leaks, basement leaks, or conditions outside the home, although some warranties allow this coverage to be purchased as an additional rider to the policy. The coverage includes the systems—like heating, air conditioning, electrical, and plumbing—the appliances, and some fixtures. Most home warranties have a deductible if something goes wrong.

The truth is that if you are paying $450 for a warranty and there is an additional $500 deductible if something goes wrong, $1,000 would have fixed nearly any single thing in the house that would go wrong anyway, with a few possible exceptions such as the furnace. What you're paying for isn't necessarily a policy to fix stuff as it is a policy to give the buyer peace of mind.

If the buyer loves the location of the home and the layout, but is concerned that the furnace is older, the central air unit is a little rusted, and the water heater is probably on its last few months, the buyer will offer less for the home or not make any offer at all. Offering a home warranty, whether it's part of your marketing campaign to sell the home, or part of negotiations, gives the buyer the peace of mind that they will not have any serious expenditures during the first year of living in the home.

An added bonus to you is that you will not have the buyers or the buyer's agent calling you in six months to complain that the furnace died and that you must have known it was about to die. The home warranty company takes care of the problem, and you probably never even hear about it.

If you find that the buyer is making an offer predicated on the fact that he or she is worried about the age of the systems and appliances, you can counter that argument with a $450 home warranty rather than agreeing to take $3,000 off the price of the home.

Shorten the Contingency Periods

In any negotiation on your property, try to shorten the contingency periods. These contingencies can become exit or escape clauses for the buyer. You don't want to wait three or four weeks to be certain that your sale is going to close. In some areas, a home inspector may take ten days to get there and do an inspection. In other areas, it may be closer to five days. Find out what the average time is, and negotiate a reasonable period of time, without any additional time. The more quickly the contingency periods expire, the firmer ground your agreement is on.

Other Clauses to Watch for in Sales Contracts

There are several clauses you should verify are part of the contract. First, make sure if the buyer walks away from the purchase, the deposit money is paid to you. This clause is usually called a *liquidated damages clause*. If you are selling with a Realtor®, the clause is generally part of the contract. If you are selling on your own, the buyer is more likely to have an attorney prepare the sales agreement. The attorney may prepare an agreement that only favors his or her client, the buyer.

Second, the contract should spell out a *drop dead date* for the mortgage. If the mortgage approval is not received by a certain date, you can cancel the agreement and look for another buyer. The reason this clause is important is that without it the buyer has until settlement to produce a mortgage. If the sale is based on a sixty-day escrow or sixty-day closing, you could be tied up for sixty days. If the buyer only has twenty days to have a formal mortgage commitment, you will be able to remarket the home in twenty days if something goes wrong.

If your town, borough, or city requires a *code inspection* in order to sell a property, you may be required to pay for the inspection and pay for any required repairs. Ask your Realtor® about the local requirements or call the municipality to find out. Your sales contract may spell out a time frame required to have the inspection completed. If the repairs are negotiable, you may have to negotiate these as you would any building inspection.

If the agreement is contingent upon the buyer receiving *gift money* from a relative, make sure the loan pre-approval notes that the gift is acceptable. Generally, they are acceptable if they are from a parent, child, or sibling. They may not be acceptable if they are from a second cousin twice removed on their Aunt Ethel's side. There should be a clause spelling out when the gift money is to be given. If it is given at settlement, something could change in the gift giver's life that would stop him or her from providing the funds. If the buyer has insufficient funds at the last minute, the loan will be turned down, and the buyer will get back any paid deposit. So, make sure the gift money is given to the buyer as soon as possible, and a copy of the transaction should be made available to you as the seller.

If the agreement is contingent upon a *zoning variance*, you may have the home under agreement for several weeks or months and have the sale collapse because zoning turns down the use of the property. Zoning contingencies can result from a buyer who wants to use part of the home for a in-home business, a buyer who wants to have animals on the property or kennels, a buyer who wants to park a large vehicle such as an RV or a truck cab on the property, or even a buyer who simply wants to fence in the yard and install a pool. Call the zoning officers for your borough or township and try to gauge the likelihood of the buyer's request being approved.

Chapter ten:

What Can Go Wrong Will Go Wrong

At this point, many sellers think the sale is almost over. An offer is signed and they are ready for settlement. Unfortunately, this is often where the real work begins. The first step of selling your home is finding a buyer for your home. The second step is actually getting that buyer to closing by jumping through all the various hurdles of the sales process.

The process that started with negotiating and accepting the buyer's offer and will end with settlement or close of escrow involves three elements:

1. First, unless the sale is cash, the buyer needs to formally apply for the mortgage and submit all necessary paperwork to the lender.

2. Second, the buyer needs to hire an inspection company and schedule inspections, if inspections are part of the agreement. Any other inspections, such as code inspections or certificate of occupancy inspections need to be ordered.

3. Third, closing has to be set up with a title insurance company, attorney, or escrow company, depending on where you are in the country.

With inspections, mortgage, title work, planning your move, and repairs going on, you will probably feel stressed out from everything you have going on. Hopefully, your real estate agent will be handling most of the details to make the transaction as painless as possible. However, I believe it's prudent for you, as the owner, to keep track of everything that's going on for two reasons. First, you want to know where you are in the process and what needs to be done still to get to settlement or close of escrow. Second, you want to make sure that everything is done correctly, and sometimes agents miss something.

It is helpful to create a checklist of everything that may have to be done during a transaction and put in the due dates for each part of the sale, including the inspections and mortgages. A sample checklist is included. If certain elements don't apply, simply write "N/A" next to them or cross them off. This becomes a visual reference of everything to be done to get your home closed.

Sales Process Checklist

- ☐ Received fully executed and initialed copy of contract.
- ☐ Received an estimate of Net Sales Proceeds

Buyer's Deposits:

- ☐ Initial Deposit Due _____ Received _____
- ☐ Second Deposit Due _____ Received _____
- ☐ Third Deposit Due _____ Received _____

Mortgage:

- ☐ Mortgage Application must be filed by _____
- ☐ Mortgage Approval due _____
- ☐ Appraisal is due by _____
- ☐ Appraisal is received _____
- ☐ Mortgage Approval received _____

Inspections:

- ☐ Wood Destroying Insect Inspection completed by
  _____
- ☐ Wood Destroying Insect Treatment done (if necessary)
- ☐ Home Inspection completed by _____
- ☐ Home Inspection Repairs negotiated
- ☐ Home Inspection Repairs completed
- ☐ Well Inspection completed by _____
- ☐ Well Treatment completed (if necessary)
- ☐ Septic Inspection completed by _____
- ☐ Septic Repairs negotiated
- ☐ Septic Repairs completed
- ☐ Radon Inspection completed by_____
- ☐ Radon Remediation negotiated
- ☐ Radon Remediation completed (if necessary)
- ☐ Code Inspection / Certificate of Occupancy Inspection completed by _____
- ☐ Code Inspection / Certificate of Occupancy Repairs negotiated
- ☐ Code Inspection / Certificate of Occupancy Repairs completed

Title Insurance:

- ☐ Title Insurance ordered by_____
- ☐ Title Search received by _____
- ☐ Settlement Scheduled

Creating a Calendar

In order to have an accurate understanding of what's going on during the settlement process, ask your agent to contact you weekly and update you on inspections, the mortgage, appraisal, or any other issues. You may want to pull out a calendar and map out the contractual due dates according to the contract. For example, the buyer may have fifteen days to complete all inspections and get you the reports, twenty days to be approved for a mortgage, and only two days to put down the additional deposit money required by the contract.

Sun	Mon	Tues	Wed	Thurs	Fri	Sat
		Contract is signed 2		2nd Deposit is Due 4	5	6
		1	3			
7	8	9	10	11	12	13
14	15	16	Inspections are due 17	18	19	20
21	Mortgage Commitment Due 22	23	24	25	26	27
28	29	30	Expected Settlement 31			

Just because you have a signed contract in your hand, with a mortgage pre-approval sitting on your kitchen counter, doesn't mean you're finished. There are things could possibly go wrong during the transaction, so you can be prepared for them.

Obstacles to Closing The Sales Contract

A good Realtor's job is only half done when they find a buyer and secure an agreement of sale. The other half is getting the sales contract closed. There are many obstacles in the way, from inspections and the appraisal to mortgage commitments and title insurance.

The most common problems fall into seven categories.

1. **Buyer's Remorse**. The buyer has a panic attack and backs out of the purchase or picks the home apart.

2. **Inspection Issues**. The inspection company determines there are significant necessary repairs. Other inspection issues include an inspector who is overly picky or is an

alarmist, an inspector who frightens the buyer with repairs, or an inspector who makes mistakes.

3. **Mortgage Problems**. The lender didn't properly pre-qualify the borrower, the mortgage rates change, the mortgage program for the buyer is discontinued, or the mortgage company requires repairs to the home. Another mortgage problem is where the mortgage company pulls a bait and switch on the mortgage type, which puts a hardship on the buyer. In other words, they entice the buyer to apply for a mortgage with their company by offering a mortgage product that has a low interest rate or low closing costs, only to later change the borrower to a program with higher fees or a high rate.

4. **Appraisal Problems.** The home under appraises because comparable sales appear to be at lower prices, or because the appraiser is unfamiliar with the area or overly conservative. The home cannot be appraised because of a lack of any comparable sales in the area. The home doesn't meet the appraisal guidelines due to zoning issues, lot size issues, or other issues.

5. **Buyer Problems.** The buyer's gift money from relatives falls through; the buyer fails to turn in the necessary documentation to settle; the buyer finds another home he or she feels is a better deal; the buyer lies to the mortgage company about income or debts; the buyer tries to renegotiate the deal after it's signed; the buyer hires an attorney who tries to change the deal; or a job transfer, illness, or divorce changes the buyer's circumstances.

6. **Title Problems.** Title defects—such as an improperly signed deed or incorrect engineering description—cause the sale to be postponed or halted. The title company misses important information or important figures that change the sale.

7. **Seller Problems.** The home the seller is moving into isn't ready at the time of settlement on the seller's current

residence. The seller doesn't realize he or she has a pre-payment penalty on the mortgage until settlement or within days of settlement, making the seller bring money to closing rather than receive money at closing.

Buyer's Remorse

Buyer's remorse can be deadly to a sale. *Buyer's remorse* is fear or anxiety about the purchase that leads to outright panic and can lead normally sane people to act outrageously. Panic can take the form of anger or rage, and it can lead to lies and misrepresentations by buyers. Buying a home can be one of the most stressful times in a person's life.

The excited buyers write an offer on a house and then go home and discuss what they did. Did they offer too much money? Is the home in the right neighborhood? Did you realize how much the taxes would be each month? As they wait for a response on their offer, their anxiety grows. At some point, it could become a panic attack, which could collapse the sale of your home. Your goal is to try to keep the transaction moving forward toward settlement, without having the buyer walk away from the purchase.

Example

A few months ago, Ted and Gretchen put an offer on a home they felt would be their dream property. They were very excited when they viewed the home and wrote the offer. After the seller agreed to their terms, Ted started wondering if they may have paid too much for the property. With that thought nagging in the back of his mind, he became very critical of every aspect of the home purchase process.

The couple came into town during the home inspection in order to make sure everything was in good working order. The home passed with a few minor repairs being necessary, like most homes. The septic test came back fine and there were no wood-destroying insects. The only test that failed was the well water test. The home had a small amount of bacteria in the well. Since Ted and Gretchen had lived most of their lives in the city, they were used to municipal water and sewer systems. This became the point of explosion. Ted called his agent and told her that he wanted the sale cancelled immediately and wanted his deposit back. "And by the way, how dare they try to sell us a house with water issues."

The agent correctly explained that according to the sales contract, the buyers had to go through with the purchase if the sellers were willing to correct the problem. Furthermore, bacteria in wells is not uncommon. Bacteria can be found in some bottled spring water as well. A simple shocking of the well to kill any bacteria generally cures the problem. If there really is a source of bacteria getting into the water supply from somewhere, then the sellers may put an ultraviolet light on the water supply. That would kill any bacteria that could possibly come into the home.

The buyers told their agent to get them out of the deal any way she could. They would not buy a contaminated home. In the meantime, the seller had also received a copy of the inspection report and the recommendation by the inspector to shock the well with a chlorine treatment. The treatment was done the same day. Two days later, the water was retested, and no bacteria were found. The water was clean.

This was insufficient for the buyers, who had now spoken to a friend who told them that bacteria could come from a leaking septic system. Now the buyers firmly believed that they were being railroaded and that the septic tank had a hidden leak and sewage was seeping into the water supply. The seller was incredulous. "You just had a certified septic inspector test the system and he said it was absolutely fine, and there's not even bacteria anymore!"

The buyers didn't care. They sent back a reply to the inspection requesting that the seller dig a brand new well at a cost in excess of $5,000, have an ultraviolet system put on the new well for another $1,000, and move the septic drain field to another part of the yard, which may have cost between $12,000 and $20,000. The seller refused but agreed that if it would make the buyers feel better, he would install the ultraviolet light system to kill any potential bacteria, but if the buyers backed out, the seller would not release the deposit on the home.

The buyers hired an attorney who accused the sellers of refusing to repair obvious problems with the property, and he requested that the seller release the buyers' deposit, or he would file legal action against him. The seller eventually gave in and released the deposit rather than spending thousands of dollars in court fighting over the money. The seller had to start from scratch and look for another buyer for the home, after wasting several weeks with it off the market. It all started because the buyers started thinking they had made a mistake, and that mistake got bigger and bigger in the buyers' mind.

Dealing with Buyer's Remorse

The two primary keys to dealing with buyer's remorse are to hire a good skilled agent, and to require a significant deposit so the buyer cannot afford to walk away from the purchase. If the worst does happen, you and your agent will have to work through the problem and try to keep the buyer's fears at bay. Unfortunately, your listing agent often isn't the person working directly with the buyer, so you will have to rely somewhat on the buyer's agent to do his or her job correctly.

We train our agents to pull out all the statistics showing that the property values really are there to justify the price the buyer is paying on the property. We show trends and why buying a home is a good investment. We go back over the mortgage payments and rates and the buyer's qualifications. We have even put together some cartoons to help lighten the situation.

Ultimately, there is no single answer for how to handle buyer's remorse when it appears. Just be aware of the potential for a buyer to panic. If it happens, the buyer may try to withdraw from the agreement, or he or she may begin nitpicking the home because he or she is frustrated. Do not become emotional. Simply respond the best you can and use the deposit as leverage to keep the buyer from withdrawing from the purchase.

Handling and Negotiating Inspections

Example:
My first experience with a home inspector was nearly twenty years ago at a Cape Cod-style home in a commercial zone. I had shown the home to a buyer who was concerned about some cracking in the ceiling of the property. After viewing the home, I was interested as well. The home was perfect for a small real estate office and was well located. My buyer paid for a home

inspection on the property to determine the extent of the problems with the cracking ceiling.

The inspector looked at the crack, went over the foundation, crawled through the attic, and came up with his evaluation. The home was going to collapse. The front and rear foundations were sinking into the ground pulling the roof apart, and the home probably wouldn't stand another eight months. The home could be repaired but would require a firm to lift the foundation and concrete beneath it, in addition to making other repairs. The cost would be more than $60,000 and could get even more expensive depending on what the contractors found once they started the work.

The buyer walked away from purchasing the property, and the inspector had frightened me enough that I wasn't interested either. The owner was extremely angry, pointing out that the home was ninety years old, and it had been in the same condition for the last twenty. The inspector assured the owner he had better do something or it would collapse.

That was twenty years ago. I stopped at the property a few days ago. It hasn't moved. The crack is still there and hasn't grown. The home did not collapse.

Please don't misunderstand me. Home inspections are great for several reasons. First, the inspection partially protects you because an independent professional has gone over the home and looked for issues. It is harder for a buyer to argue later that you hid some issue with the home if an inspector went over it and did not find any problems. Second, buyers should know exactly what kind of maintenance and repairs they will be responsible for after settlement.

Home inspectors are certified. In order to obtain a license or certification, they must perform many hours of inspections under the supervision of an experienced inspector. They are also required to take continuing education classes. For the most part, they are professionals. However, home inspectors are paid to look for problems. Some of them will work very hard to find anything they possibly can to justify their fee, and they can scare a buyer right out of a sale.

Example:

A home inspector was hired last year to do an inspection on one of our properties for sale. The home was a semi-detached, twin-style, two-story home. The layout was simple. The front door opened into a living room, which led right into the dining room, the kitchen, and out the back door. In the living room was a big picture window facing the front porch, and two smaller windows facing the side of the home.

The inspector wrote in his report that the home was dangerous in a fire because the large picture window was fixed in place. He said it should be replaced with a new window that would open in case of fire. The buyers, after hearing the inspector tell them a horror story, demanded the window be replaced at a cost of over $2,000.

Here's the logic of the situation. If a buyer were in a burning house, and they had a choice of running backward through the open dining room and kitchen and out the back door, or escaping through the large side windows, or perhaps running right out the front door, why in the world would they need to go through the picture window? If the door—which was right next to the window—is on fire, you'd run the other way.

This inspector nearly cost the seller a sale on their home. There are quite a few overly picky inspectors who scare buyers. There are also inspectors who are influenced by the buyers they work for.

Example:

We had a case this year where the buyer and seller both followed the inspector while he inspected the home and tested the septic system. The inspector told the seller everything was functioning normally, and he had no worries. The actual report a few days later stated that the septic system may be failing and needs a full hydraulic load test.

My seller was flabbergasted. He said that he had discussed the septic directly with the inspector and the inspector said it was fine. I called the inspector and was told that he had a conversation with the buyer, and the buyer was very concerned about the slowness of the drain. Despite the fact that the septic tank appeared to be functioning normally and the drain field did not appear to be saturated, yet the buyer had voiced concerns to the home inspector, so he changed his opinion and requested more testing.

Whether the inspector is influenced by the buyer, is overly picky or simply makes mistakes, the inspection report influences the buyer's view of the home. The inspection also opens the contract up to negotiation.

When this happens, you and your agent must be prepared to sit firm and handle the buyers with logic and anecdotes. You may have to have a second inspection done in order to determine if there is a real problem, because buyers can back out of many agreements if they are uncomfortable with the results of the inspection, or if the seller refuses to repair a significant issue.

When an Inspector Discovers Real Problems

If the inspector finds that your septic system has failed and is leaking into the water supply, you have a serious problem. When an inspector discovers issues with your property, your response needs to be based on the type of inspection clause included in your agreement of sale.

If the inspection clause is a take it or leave it clause, the buyer can simply cancel the agreement and walk away. In this case, you may want to make an offer to correct the problem in order to keep the sale. If the inspection clause is a seller's right to correct clause, then you have to decide whether keeping this sale together is worth correcting the issue that has been discovered.

Many home sellers take a very firm stand: "I came down $12,357 from my asking price. There is no way I'm putting $10,000 into a new septic drain field." That feeling is certainly understandable but may cost you money in the long run. Consider that the buyers were purchasing your home based on the assumption that you had a functioning septic system. If you put $10,000 into the system, that does not increase the value of the property to this buyer or any other buyer.

The other concern is that if you let this agreement fall apart by refusing to negotiate on the repair, you will now have to disclose the problem to any future potential buyer anyway. Any future agreement is going to also be predicated on having that work done. Some sellers tell us they will simply raise the price of the home to cover the repair. If you must install a new furnace or septic system or upgrade the electric, you are not increasing the actual value of the property. All you are doing is bringing the property back up to the market value that is assumed with a fully functioning property.

To put it more simply—if it is a serious issue, you will probably pay for the repair one way or another. You need to seriously consider negotiating with the current buyer because settling the property now is generally better than gambling that you will get the same or better offer later.

If the inspection report, on the other hand, does not find any serious issues, but finds many small issues, such as improper grounding of wires, missing ground fault outlets near water sources, or clogged chimneys and leaking flashing, you may want to negotiate the repairs. If the buyer asks you to repair $2,000 in minor items, you may counter with a $500 or $1,000 credit toward the minor repairs. You can explain that you were unaware of the issues but have lived with them without noticing the issues for many years, so they probably will not impact the buyer's quiet enjoyment of the property.

Mortgage Complications

Both buyers and sellers assume that a mortgage company is a bank loaning money to people who want to purchase a home. That is not always true. There are two primary types of lenders writing loans for buyers—mortgage bankers and mortgage brokers. *Mortgage bankers* can actually loan their own money to a buyer. They may sell the loan to a third party after the sale concludes, but they have their own money to loan. A mortgage pre-approval from a mortgage banker is usually very strong, because they can back up the guarantee with their own funds.

A *mortgage broker*, on the other hand, does not actually loan any of his or her own money. They work as an agent for other lenders, finding loan products and providing them to customers. Mortgage brokers often have a wider array of loan types available because they may be writing or processing loans for many different banks or lenders. However, a mortgage approval on the letterhead of a mortgage broker may not be a full approval, because it may still have to meet the approval requirements of wherever the loan is being placed.

Example:

Alex's mortgage company was a mortgage broker and they were using a special program that allowed him to purchase a home with no down payment. His credit score was 680 and his income was perfect to qualify him for the mortgage. A week before settlement, the lender called and said the real mortgage company had discontinued the program, and he could no longer get funding for his mortgage. The mortgage broker added that he couldn't get Alex into any other similar 100% financing program, because he would now need a credit score above 700 to qualify for the other programs the broker represented.

Alex panicked because he had already given notice to his apartment that he was going to be out by the end of the following week. The sellers had already moved out of their home, in anticipation of settlement. Alex was able to secure a gift of 10% from his parents, which allowed him to close on the property on time.

Far too often, this situation ends in disaster for the home seller, who thought they had a solid sale, only to realize that it was based on a special loan program. In a hot market, you, as the seller, may have the luxury of reviewing multiple offers and selecting the offer that appears to have the best chances of closing. In a slow market, when offers are few and far between, you want to make sure you don't take the home off the market for an unqualified buyer. Carefully review the buyer's pre-approval letter and determine if the pre-approval is from an actual mortgage banker, or if it's a mortgage broker selling the loan to a third party. If the loan is from a mortgage broker, call the broker and ensure that the buyer is using a standard mortgage program that will be easily replaced with another program should this one be discontinued.

The mortgage is a critical component of the transaction, and many issues can short circuit the process. Other mortgage situations that may cause a transaction to fall include the following:

- **The lender did not properly pre-qualify the borrower.** In most lending institutions, someone takes a mortgage application, passes the package to a processor who pulls together all the information necessary to get the loan approved, including pay stubs, appraisal, credit report, and verifications. The processor then hands the loan to an underwriter who approves or denies the loan. When taking the application, the originator could miscalculate numbers, transpose numbers, or mistake the qualifying ratios of one loan program for another. In any of these cases, the buyer may not qualify for the loan or the program. This may not be discovered until the processor or underwriter catches it.

- **The mortgage rates change.** The buyer may be pre-approved for a loan based on a 6%, thirty-year, fixed rate loan. Unfortunately, the buyer may be at the very top of his or her qualifying limit. Rates change daily. If the rate rises to 6.5% prior to settlement, the buyer may no longer qualify to purchase the home and the loan will be denied.

- **The mortgage program for the buyer is discontinued.** Any special loan program that is available from small lenders, investment pools, or investment groups through mortgage companies may be available today and gone tomorrow. Mortgage programs change regularly. Unless the mortgage company can lock in funds or a guarantee of funds for a unique program, it could end prior to settlement.

- **The property does not qualify for Fannie Mae financing.** Most lenders in the United States follow a series of guidelines for mortgages set by the Federal National Mortgage Association, commonly known as Fannie Mae. These guidelines are followed in order to ensure that lenders can sell their loans in bundles on the secondary mortgage market. The Federal National Mortgage Association sets the standard for mortgage Association sets the standard for mortgage loans. Although most homes qualify, certain properties, such as small farms, commercially zoned homes, and other unique properties may not. Fannie Mae restricts the appraised value that can be added for barns, outbuildings, additional land, and other features that may benefit a particular buyer and seller but are not common to most homes.

- **The mortgage company requires repairs to the home.** Mortgage companies are investing in the purchase of the home as much as they are investing in the buyers. If the buyer does not pay the mortgage, the lender winds up with the home, and it wants to be protected. If the appraiser points out any issues the mortgage company considers significant, the mortgage company may require them to be repaired in order to close. In this situation, the repair should be done at the buyer's expense, since the buyer was buying the property with the defect. In some cases, however, in order to close the home, the seller may have to contribute something toward the repair. Mortgage company repairs are generally only requested if the home has significant defects or issues.

- **The mortgage company pulls a bait and switch on the mortgage type putting a hardship on the buyer.** At settlement, the buyer looks over the mortgage documentation and discovers that there is now a *prepayment penalty*, meaning that if he or she sells the home in the next several years, the bank will charge a large fee for paying off the loan early. Worse, the loan fees are $2,000 higher than the expected fees. At times, lenders believe they are helping a buyer by switching to a different loan program when the first one falls through, but buyers are surprised by the changes in rate, terms, or closing costs. There are also mortgage companies known as predatory lenders. These lenders have been known to make last minute changes to the mortgage terms in order to increase their income. A panicking buyer may walk away from the table and refuse to settle on your home. There is no easy way to predict whether or not there will be a problem, but if you verify that your buyer is using a reputable lender and has a full loan commitment in plenty of time for settlement, the odds of a problem decrease greatly.

Appraisal Issues

An *appraisal* is an evaluation of the property being sold for the purpose of determining the property's *fair market value*. This value is supposed to reflect the most likely sale price of a property in a reasonable period of time. Since a bank is investing in the property as well as in the buyer, the bank wants some assurance that the property is worth what the buyer is paying for it. Additionally, the bank wants to be satisfied that it can resell the home, should the bank have to foreclose on the home.

Appraisals, however, work with historical data. An appraisal, as described in Chapter 3, uses three methods of evaluation and gives weight to the method that the appraiser believes to be most accurate. The problem with historical data is that it depends on sales in the past. If a market is hot and rising, with prices increasing at 1% a month, a sale five or six months ago is going to be off in value.

Although an appraiser can adjust a value based on the time of the sale, many appraisers are reluctant to do so in a rising market.

In a slowing market, many appraisers are conservative and tend to appraise on the low side, which creates a problem for the transaction. The common declaration by home sellers when a home under-appraises is "Well, it only under-appraised by $10,000, so that shouldn't be a problem. The buyers are putting $15,000 down." Unfortunately, lenders do not typically want to lend the entire amount of the appraisal.

For example, a buyer may apply for a loan program that required 10% down payment, called a *90 LTV loan*. This means that the lender will loan up to 90% of the appraised value or the sale price, whichever is lower. If the home sells for $250,000, the buyer is expecting to put down 10% of that amount, or $25,000. Additionally, the buyer may have 6% in borrowers closing costs, adding another $15,000 to what they need. The buyer has $42,000 in their savings account, so they are fairly certain they will be able to close.

The appraisal on the home comes in low at only $238,000. That means the lender will only loan 90% of that $238,000 or $214,200. Now the buyer would have to come up with the $12,000 difference between $238,000 and $250,000, plus the 10% of $238,000 which is $23,800, plus the 6% closing costs. That adds up to a whopping $50,080 and the buyer no longer qualifies because he or she does not have sufficient funds to close.

Sale at $250,000			
		Under-appraised at $238,000	
Buyer needs:		**Buyer needs:**	
10% down payment	$25,000	10% down payment	$23,800
6% closing costs	$15,000	6% closing costs	$14,280
Total funds needed:	**$40,000**	Plus difference in price	$12,000
		Total funds needed:	$50,080

Sales agreements may also be contingent upon a successful appraisal. Even if the sale is not contingent on an appraisal, you will get a lot of flak from buyers who now believe they are paying too much for the property. In either case, the transaction may have to be renegotiated in order to make the transaction work.

The second problem that can occur is that the home doesn't meet the appraisal guide lines and therefore under-appraises.

Example:

Carl was a buyer purchasing a property near Scranton, Pennsylvania. The property he was purchasing was a small horse farm that included twelve acres, a four-bedroom, ranch-style home, and a twelve-stall barn. The purchase price was $285,000. Carl's mortgage lender told him the loan would be no problem, and he would be able to settle the property in forty-five days.

The lender hired an appraiser who performed a Fannie Mae appraisal on the property. The appraiser could not find similar homes on significant acreage in the area, so they compared the home with other ranch style homes. The appraiser added negligible value for the twelve-stall barn because barns have little value in a Fannie Mae appraisal. The appraiser valued the property at $215,000; $70,000 less than the sales price.

The home was off the market for over four weeks before the lender informed the seller of the appraisal issue. The borrower quickly reapplied at another mortgage company that had a program specifically for homes with acreage. The new mortgage lender processed the loan for two weeks before discovering the loan program had been canceled.

Ultimately, we were able to get the loan in front of an agricultural credit agency that approved the loan based on a different type of appraisal by an appraiser who gave value to the additional land and outbuildings.

Another appraisal issue that comes up happens because the appraiser was not local and did not know the market well enough, pulling what he or she thinks are comparable sales from an area that might sell at a lower price range. This is common when the appraiser is hired by an Internet company that doesn't have local appraisers to work with. The company may hire someone from the nearest metropolitan area who is unfamiliar with the local market.

Settlements or close of escrow can also be held up because the appraiser selected is too busy to get the appraisal done in a timely fashion. Although it is impossible to completely avoid appraisal issues, some methods to guard against the most common problems include the following:

- If the lender is not a local lender, ask that your Realtor® be able to submit potential appraisers to the lender so a local one is chosen.

- If the property is unique or unusual in any way, talk to the buyer's mortgage company to let them know your concerns. Hopefully they will select the correct loan program and correct appraiser to meet the type of property.

- If you know of sales within the last ninety to one hundred and eighty days of homes similar to yours in the same area that justify your sales price, have copies of the listings available to the appraiser when they view your home.

Buyer Problems

Changes in the buyer's life can stall or short circuit a sale, as well. Job transfers, unexpected divorces, illness, deaths in a family, or other reasons can halt a sale in its tracks. Other issues include a buyer who is negligent in turning paperwork in to the mortgage company or loses his or her job before settlement.

A buyer's credit may change prior to settlement, preventing the buyer from obtaining the type of loan he or she applied for.

This could be an innocent situation as well.

Example:

Alan was buying a home last year and although he qualified for the low-down-payment mortgage program, he was at the very top of his qualifications. What no one realized was that Alan's student loans, which had been in deferment, were just coming due. The loan officer knew what the payments would be, but did not realize when they hit Alan's credit, they would appear to be eleven separate loans. As soon as they did, Alan's credit score dropped forty points and he no longer qualified for the mortgage program.

Example:
> Angela was 22 and just out of college. She was buying a home based on a gift of nearly $20,000 from her father. Just before settlement, her father had a stroke and was moved into a nursing home. She was no longer able to receive the gift because the nursing home explained that Medicaid could take the money back, and her father needed all of his assets to pay the bill.

These types of issues are difficult to predict or plan for. If the sale is contingent on a gift, the buyer should have the gift placed in his or her name immediately after the signing of the contract to avoid most problems.

Example:
> Eric was being transferred from California to Pennsylvania for a high-tech job. His wife, Karen, flew in and selected a new home, putting down a significant deposit. Before the move was to take place, the engineering company changes plans and asked Eric instead to move to Arizona. Although the seller could have tried to sue for *specific performance* and force the sale, the seller graciously allowed the buyer out of the sales contract. Unfortunately, the seller lost six weeks on the market and had to start over.

Title Problems

Lenders require an insurance policy to protect the lender and the buyer from any potential losses that arise from errors in the chain of title or fraud in the chain of title for the home. This insurance policy is called *title insurance*, and it also guarantees that any current mortgages or liens against the property are paid off at the time the property closes escrow or settles so that the lender can take a first lien position on the property. The lender needs that first lien position in order to foreclose if the buyer does not pay the mortgage. If a mortgage or other lien is discovered after the buyer takes ownership, the insurance pays off the mortgage or covers it to make sure it is satisfied and the lender keeps the first lien position.

In some states, like California, title insurance is the responsibility of, and paid by, the seller of the property. In other parts of the country, such as Pennsylvania, title insurance is paid for by the buyer. In either case, the seller has to be able to grant clear title to the property, and the lender requires insurance to cover any potential loss.

Different states also handle title insurance differently. In many states, title insurance may be purchased from either an attorney or a title insurance company. Some states require an attorney to provide the insurance, and don't allow title companies to directly operate with consumers.

Because title insurance is required by banks and lenders to protect their interest, the amount of title insurance required is usually equal to the loan amount. However, most buyers choose to spend the slight difference and insure the property for the full purchase price. The required lender's policy only insures any loss by the lender. An owner's policy, which is only a slight increase in fee, will cover the owner's interest as well. A third type of title insurance, called extended owner's coverage, protects the purchaser from prior violations of covenants or building permit violations.

Why is Title Insurance Necessary?

In a capitalistic society, we are allowed to own property. The deeds to property go back hundreds of years in some parts of the country. During those hundreds of years, ownership of the homes and the land they sit on have changed many times over. If, during any time in the history of the property, fraud was committed in the transfer of the deed, or a signature was missed, or a loan that was taken against the property was not properly recorded as satisfied at the local recorder's office, there may be someone out there who has a claim to your new home.

Property titles or deeds are recorded in a central government office. This location may be a courthouse or a Recorder of Deeds office but it is a place where the information is public so that anyone can look up information about property ownership and mortgages or liens. In order to guarantee the title, a *title search* is performed by the title company, abstract company, or attorney. A title search includes an examination of the deeds and the mortgages against the property. A *full title search* also includes examination of any county and municipal records to determine if there are any liens or judgments against the property.

If, for example, a tax lien is placed upon the property by the school district or municipality, and is missed at the time of settlement, the property owner owes that outstanding debt. Even though the debt was incurred under the prior owner, the debt stays part of the property. If the owner had work done by a carpenter and refused to pay the carpenter, the carpenter could have filed a mechanic's lien on the property. Likewise, if the city or borough ran new sewer lines to the property and they were not paid for, a municipal lien is filed.

Other restrictions affecting a property include easements. An *easement* is a legal document that grants someone else the use of part of your property, or access through part of your property. For example, at some point in the past, a utility company may have used the process of eminent domain to file an easement across your property for future sewer lines, or an electric or gas company may have purchased the rights to run a power line or gas line across your property. Easements generally keep owners from fencing in those parts of the yard, or from putting anything permanent in the easement, such as a pool, shed, or garage. If the buyer is unaware of these restrictions, and the local electric company shows up to start putting up power towers, you'll be likely to be sued.

The title searcher must check any municipal office or tax authority office to find any possible tax liens, judgments, mortgages, easements, and any other type of encumbrance on the property. When the title search is completed, the title company or attorney issues a policy insuring the buyer and the buyer's mortgage company against any future claims and legal fees as a result of some past issues.

Types of Title Insurance Coverage

- *Lender's Title Policy Coverage.* This type of policy protects the lender up to an amount equal to the loan against any previously recorded mortgages, mechanic's liens, unrecorded liens, unrecorded easements, and other defects in title. The lender's policy amount declines as the loan balance declines. Lender's policies are also assignable to a lender who may purchase the mortgage.

- *Owner's Title Policy Coverage.* The owner's policy protects the owner for the value of the property against unsatisfied mortgages or liens during a prior ownership. It also covers incorrect or forged signatures, lack of competency, defective recording, fraud, and lack of a right of access. The owner's policy guarantees clear title but is not assignable to other parties like the lender's policy.

- *Extended Owner's Coverage.* The extended policy covers the owner for errors stemming from errors in subdivision maps, incorrect surveys, claims for *adverse possession* (when a neighbor claims they have used the property for a significant period of time and now legally own it), buildings encroaching on a neighboring property, off-record liens (such as unrecorded mechanic's liens or estate tax liens), and preexisting violations of zoning ordinances.

Unlike most insurance, owner's title insurance protection lasts for the entire term of ownership. The term of ownership includes the owner and their heirs. However, the insurance protects solely against losses from events that occurred prior to the date the insurance was issued.

Title Problems That Can Stall Settlement

Example:
Last year, a home seller named Craig asked our firm to represent him in the sale of a rural home on a little over eight acres. It was a beautiful post and beam home setting far back from the

road. Craig had purchased the property just two years before and was relocating out of the area. At the time he purchased the rustic retreat, it already had a barn and a run-in shed for horses on the property.

The buyer's mortgage was approved, and settlement was scheduled with a local title insurance company. The title insurance company plotted the deed description and found that it had not closed properly. After a bit more research, they found that the deed description for the property was incorrect.

At considerable expense, Craig hired a surveyor to delineate the lot lines and write a new description. Based on the original subdivision done years before, Craig did not own the pasture where he was keeping his horse or the run-in shed. Worse, the surveyor determined that each of the adjoining properties had incorrect deed descriptions as well.

The township required that the properties go back through the subdivision process to approve the new lot lines that were suggested by the surveyor. This required some engineering work, filing fees, and review fees by the township. After thousands of dollars invested and four months of delays, the property finally settled.

Craig had purchased title insurance when he bought the home two years before. The title insurance company missed the discrepancies in the deed. The delay in settlement almost cost Craig the buyer of the property. The delay also cost Craig several months mortgage payments in addition to the fees to correct the problem.

Unfortunately, when purchasing the home, Craig relied on a title insurance company that failed to properly research the property. To avoid a similar fate, as a home buyer, you should be certain to hire a reputable title insurance, escrow company, or attorney with many years' experience. You should also require a copy of any title binder that shows the research the company or attorney performed on your behalf, and you should inquire as to whether or not they actually plotted the deed to ensure it properly closed.

As a home seller, you may want to order a title search from a title insurance company or attorney when you first put the home on the market. If a problem comes up on a title search, it may take several months to correct, so the sooner you know about the problem, the more likely you are to close on time on the sale of your home.

Example:
   Another recent situation involved a 220-year-old log home in the middle of ten acres of land near Allentown, Pennsylvania. The attorney handling the title search discovered that one of the prior deeds was not filed correctly. It was missing the signature of one of the owners. The property had transferred without it, but that individual or her heirs could come back after partial ownership of the property. The buyer's attorney contacted the attorney who had handled the original transfer. The missing signatory was still alive, and they were able to contact her and get her signature on a revised deed. Had the original seller passed away, settlement could have been significantly delayed until the title issues were resolved.

   Our suggestion on the seller's side of the transaction is to try to get a title search ordered as quickly as possible, so that if a problem is discovered, it can be corrected in a timely manner without delaying settlement.

Seller Problems
   There may be reasons why you change your mind about selling your home or your reason for selling disappears. This can happen because a job transfer falls through, or a couple reconciles rather than divorces. Some older couples decide that they cannot leave their home of forty or fifty years because too many memories are tied up in the home.

   In these cases, if the buyer has a firm written sales contract on your home, the buyer may be able to sue you for specific performance and force you to sell. You may have to agree to pay damages to the buyer in order to cancel the sales contract, or you may have to proceed with the sale even though you no longer have a reason or wish to move.

There are also reasons you may be unable to sell. A home inspector may find significant issues that you cannot afford to repair. This does not mean that you, as the seller, were aware of the problems. A bad septic drain field or a structural problem could lead to tens of thousands in necessary repairs. Alternately, there may not be any large repairs, but there may be dozens of minor issues that add up to a significant repair bill. A title search may find bad or unmarketable title, which may take months to correct. The buyer may not be willing or able to wait that period of time.

In the case of repairs that you are unable or unwilling to correct, the sale may be cancelled with no penalty under most agreements of sale. You will have to check with your Realtor® or attorney for verification. In the case of title issues, you may be responsible to reimburse the buyer for any expenses he or she incurred to purchase the home, including inspections, mortgage application, and appraisal expenses. Again, you should check with your Realtor® or attorney to verify.

chapter eleven:

Settlement

The Final Walk Through

It is customary in most areas for the buyers to be able to perform a final walk through of the property prior to settlement or close of escrow. This final walk through is done the day of settlement or the evening before. The buyer will use this opportunity to verify that all the systems are still in working order, anything remaining with the home is still in place, and no damage has occurred to the home since the buyer wrote the sales contract.

Let the buyer run the faucets, flush the toilets, and test the range. You want him or her to be completely comfortable with the home. Once this is done, use this opportunity to have the buyer sign a release stating that he or she has done a pre-settlement walk through and is accepting the property in the condition it's in at that time. This is a way to avoid the buyer making claims after settlement.

The Settlement or Escrow Process

Depending on where in the country your home is located, when a contract has been written on your home and you accept it, it is considered *pending, under agreement,* or *in escrow. In escrow* means that a third party, called the *escrow company*, holds the deed for the seller and the money for the buyer. The escrow company then exchanges the deed for the money after all the conditions of the contract are met. In escrow states, this is called *close of escrow.*

In most East Coast states, the deposit money is held in escrow by the seller's attorney or the listing real estate company. The settlement is held by a title insurance company or an attorney, and the money is given to the title insurance company or attorney to facilitate the transfer at closing.

In either case, it is the end of the sales process. The mortgage should be approved and the money wired or delivered to the closing entity. Any required repairs should be completed, and any required municipal inspections and approvals should be completed. In most cases, at settlement, the property seller receives their proceeds check, and the buyer receives the keys, the deed and possession of the property they are purchasing. In some areas, the move-out date, or the date the buyer receives keys, may be different than the date the seller receives their money and the paperwork is signed. During settlement, however, the buyer signs all the necessary loan documentation and the buyer and seller sign a plethora of paperwork.

Practices and customs vary from area to area for settlement, but all settlements involve a settlement statement that itemizes all fees paid by the buyer and all fees paid by the seller. In most jurisdictions, the settlement agent collects one check from the buyer and delivers checks to the seller, the current mortgage lender, the Realtors® and any other parties that must be paid out of the transaction. Most settlement agents require the buyer to provide certified funds at time of settlement.

Also, depending on where in the country you are located, you may be alone with the settlement agent or you may be in a room packed with the buyer, Realtors®, mortgage lender, and settlement agent in addition to yourself.

The HUD Settlement Statement

The *HUD Settlement Statement*, known as a *HUD-1*, is the final accounting of your home sale transaction. This settlement sheet breaks down and itemizes all the various credits and expenses that are part of the transaction. Any credits to the buyer, mortgage payoffs, tax prorations, taxes due, commissions, and settlement costs are listed on this form. This statement is prepared by the closing agent and should be reviewed carefully for mistakes. Any mistakes can cost you thousands of dollars.

If possible, try to get a copy of the settlement sheet prior to settlement, so you can thoroughly review it. This is sometimes impossible because many lenders have a tendency to fax or email their final figures to the title or escrow company the morning of settlement. However, it is always worth asking.

Explanation of the HUD Settlement Statement

The HUD Settlement Statement is two pages in length and is set up almost like a balance sheet. The first page is an overview of the transaction, and the second page breaks down the specifics of your costs in selling the property. Both the buyer's and seller's figures appear on the same two-page settlement sheet. You will see a blank HUD-1 form included in the next couple pages of this book.

On page one, the top part of the form outlines who the buyers, sellers, mortgage company, and settlement agency are for the transaction. The twin columns below separate the buyer's side of the transaction from the seller's side. The left-hand side, labeled "J—Summary of Borrower's Transaction" is the buyer's side and the right-hand side, labeled "K—Summary of Seller's Transaction" is your side as the seller. The section that is of most importance to you is obviously the right-hand column, labeled "K."

Your column has sections with 400s, 500s, and 600s, ending in line 603, which gives you the bottom-line number that you will walk away from settlement with. Again, the first page is an overview of the transaction starting with how much you receive, and then reducing it by your deductions and coming up with a final figure on line 603.

Previous editions are obsolete

form HUD-1 (3/86) ref Handbook 4305.2

A. Settlement Statement

U.S. Department of Housing and Urban Development

OMB Approval No. 2502-0265

B. Type of Loan

1. ☐FHA	2. ☐FmHA	3. ☐Conv. Unins.	6. File Number	7. Loan Number	8. Mortgage Insurance Case Number
4. ☐VA	5. ☐Conv. Ins.		8663106		

C. Note: This form is furnished to give you a statement of actual settlement costs. Amounts paid to and by the settlement agent are shown. Items marked "(p.o.c.)" were paid outside the closing; they are shown here for informational purposes and are not included in the totals. WARNING: It is a crime to knowingly make false statements to the United States on this or any other similar form. Penalties upon conviction can include a fine and imprisonment. For details see: Title 18 U. S. Code Section 1001 and Section 1010.

TitleExpress Settlement System
Printed 07/09/2019 at 11:04 KLS

D. NAME OF BORROWER:	Cash Buyer
ADDRESS:	
E. NAME OF SELLER:	John Seller
ADDRESS:	
F. NAME OF LENDER:	
ADDRESS:	
G. PROPERTY ADDRESS:	2702 Wayne's Manor Dr, Gotham, NY 10101
H. SETTLEMENT AGENT:	Settlement USA, Inc.
PLACE OF SETTLEMENT:	2299 Brodhead Road, Unit J, Bethlehem, PA 18020
I. SETTLEMENT DATE:	08/09/2019

J. SUMMARY OF BORROWER'S TRANSACTION:		K. SUMMARY OF SELLER'S TRANSACTION:	
100. GROSS AMOUNT DUE FROM BORROWER		**400. GROSS AMOUNT DUE TO SELLER**	
101. Contract sales price	515,000.00	401. Contract sales price	515,000.00
102. Personal Property		402. Personal Property	
103. Settlement charges to borrower (line 1400)	8,900.50	403.	
104.		404.	
105.		405.	
Adjustments for items paid by seller in advance		**Adjustments for items paid by seller in advance**	
106. City/town taxes 08/09/19 to 12/31/19	257.02	406. City/town taxes 08/09/19 to 12/31/19	257.02
107. County taxes 08/09/19 to 12/31/19	484.65	407. County taxes 08/09/19 to 12/31/19	484.65
108. School Taxes		408. School Taxes	
109.		409.	
110.		410.	
111.		411.	
112.		412.	
120. GROSS AMOUNT DUE FROM BORROWER	524,642.17	**420. GROSS AMOUNT DUE TO SELLER**	515,741.67
200. AMOUNTS PAID BY OR ON BEHALF OF BORROWER		**500. REDUCTIONS IN AMOUNT DUE TO SELLER**	
201. Deposit or earnest money	2,000.00	501. Excess Deposit (see instructions)	
202. Principal amount of new loans		502. Settlement charges to seller (line 1400)	36,410.00
203. Existing loan(s) taken subject to		503. Existing loan(s) taken subject to	
204.		504. Payoff of First Mortgage Loan	
205.		505.	
206.		506.	
207.		507.	
208.		508.	
209.		509.	
Adjustments for items unpaid by seller		**Adjustments for items unpaid by seller**	
210. City/town taxes		510. City/town taxes	
211. County taxes		511. County taxes	
212. School Taxes 07/01/19 to 08/09/19	557.93	512. School Taxes 07/01/19 to 08/09/19	557.93
213.		513.	
214.		514.	
215.		515.	
216.		516.	
217.		517.	
218.		518.	
219.		519.	
220. TOTAL PAID BY/FOR BORROWER	2,557.93	**520. TOTAL REDUCTION AMOUNT DUE SELLER**	36,967.93
300. CASH AT SETTLEMENT FROM OR TO BORROWER		**600. CASH AT SETTLEMENT TO OR FROM SELLER**	
301. Gross amount due from borrower (line 120)	524,642.17	601. Gross amount due to seller (line 420)	515,741.67
302. Less amounts paid by/for borrower (line 220)	2,557.93	602. Less reduction amount due seller (line 520)	36,967.93
303. CASH FROM BORROWER	522,084.24	**603. CASH TO SELLER**	478,773.74

SUBSTITUTE FORM 1099 SELLER STATEMENT: The information contained herein is important tax information and is being furnished to the Internal Revenue Service. If you are required to file a return, a negligence penalty or other sanction will be imposed on you if this item is required to be reported and the IRS determines that it has not been reported. The Contract Sales Price described on line 401 above constitutes the Gross Proceeds of this transaction.

You are required by law to provide the settlement agent (Fed. Tax 'D No: _____) with your correct taxpayer identification number. If you do not provide your correct taxpayer identification number, you may be subject to civil or criminal penalties imposed by law. Under penalties of perjury, I certify that the number shown on this statement is my correct taxpayer identification number.

TIN: ___ - ___ - ___ / ___ - ___ - ___   SELLER(S) SIGNATURE(S): _____ / _____

SELLER(S) NEW MAILING ADDRESS: _____

SELLER(S) PHONE NUMBERS: _____ (H) _____ (W)

settlement 219

Previous editions are obsolete

U.S. DEPARTMENT OF HOUSING AND URBAN DEVELOPMENT File Number: 8663106

form HUD-1 (3/86) ref Handbook 4305.2

SETTLEMENT STATEMENT

PAGE 2

TitleExpress Settlement System Printed 07/09/2019 at 11:04 KLS

L. SETTLEMENT CHARGES			PAID FROM BORROWER'S FUNDS AT SETTLEMENT	PAID FROM SELLER'S FUNDS AT SETTLEMENT
700. TOTAL SALES/BROKER'S COMMISSION based on price $515,000.00 @ 6.000 = 30,900.00				
Division of commission (line 700) as follows:				
701. $	15,450.00	to Century 21 Keim Realtors		
702. $	15,450.00	to Century 21 Keim Realtors		
703. Commission paid at Settlement				30,900.00
800. ITEMS PAYABLE IN CONNECTION WITH LOAN				
801. Loan Origination Fee	%			
802. Loan Discount	%			
803. Appraisal Fee				
804. Credit Report				
805. Lender's Inspection Fee				
806. Mortgage Application Fee				
807. Assumption Fee				
808.				
809.				
810.				
811.				
900. ITEMS REQUIRED BY LENDER TO BE PAID IN ADVANCE				
901. Interest From to @$ /day				
902. Mortgage Insurance Premium for to				
903. Hazard Insurance Premium for to				
904.				
905.				
1000. RESERVES DEPOSITED WITH LENDER FOR				
1001. Hazard Insurance	mo. @ $	/mo		
1002. Mortgage Insurance	mo. @ $	/mo		
1003. City Property Tax	mo. @ $	53.92 /mo		
1004. County Property Tax	mo. @ $	101.67 /mo		
1005. School Taxes	mo. @ $	436.33 /mo		
1009. Aggregate Analysis Adjustment			0.00	0.00
1100. TITLE CHARGES				
1101. Settlement or closing fee				
1102. Abstract or title search				
1103. Title examination				
1104. Title insurance binder				
1105. Document Preparation to Settlement USA, Inc.				100.00
1106. Notary Fees			5.00	10.00
1107. Attorney's fees				
(includes above items No:		)		
1108. Title Insurance			3,658.00	
(includes above items No:		)		
1109. Lender's Policy				
1110. Owner's Policy	515,000.00 - 3,658.00			
1111.				
1112.				
1113.				
1200. GOVERNMENT RECORDING AND TRANSFER CHARGES				
1201. Recording Fees Deed $ 87.50	; Mortgage $	; Release $	87.50	
1202. City/County tax/stamps	Deed $ 5,150.00	; Mortgage $	5,150.00	
1203. State Tax/stamps	Deed $ 5,150.00	; Mortgage $		5,150.00
1204.				
1205.				
1300. ADDITIONAL SETTLEMENT CHARGES				
1301. Final Water Sewer Escrow				250.00
1400. TOTAL SETTLEMENT CHARGES	(enter on lines 103, Section J and 502, Section K)		8,900.50	36,410.00

HUD CERTIFICATION OF BUYER AND SELLER

I have carefully reviewed the HUD-1 Settlement Statement and to the best of my knowledge and belief, it is a true and accurate statement of all receipts and disbursements made on my account or by me in this transaction. I further certify that I have received a copy of the HUD-1 Settlement Statement.

Cash Buyer

John Seller

WARNING: IT IS A CRIME TO KNOWINGLY MAKE FALSE STATEMENTS TO THE UNITED STATES ON THIS OR ANY SIMILAR FORM. PENALTIES UPON CONVICTION CAN INCLUDE A FINE AND IMPRISONMENT. FOR DETAILS SEE TITLE 18: U.S. CODE SECTION 1001 AND SECTION 1010.

The HUD-1 Settlement Statement which I have prepared is a true and accurate account of this transaction. I have caused or will cause the funds to be disbursed in accordance with this statement.

SETTLEMENT AGENT: _____ DATE: _____

The 400s are an itemized list of what is owed to you. Breaking it down a bit further:

- line 401 is the actual sales price;

- line 402 is for any personal items that you are including in the transaction, but are being paid for above and beyond the price of the home;

- lines 406 to 410 itemize what taxes the buyer has to reimburse you for (Many property taxes are paid ahead. If your taxes are prepaid, the buyer needs to reimburse you for the unused portion.); and,

- line 420 totals your credits, or what is the gross amount due to you.

The 500s are a list of your expenses. These expenses may be further broken down on the second page of the settlement statement:

- Line 502 is the total of all your settlement charges from page 2. These charges include any state or local transfer taxes, commissions to real estate agents, notary fees, deed preparation, filing fees, title charges and so on.

- Line 504 is the amount owed on your mortgage on the home. If you have an equity line of credit or additional mortgages on the home, they will go on lines 505–506.

- Lines 510 to 512 are reimbursements back to the buyer if your property taxes have *not* been paid and you owe a portion of an upcoming or past due bill.

- Line 520 totals your expenses.

The 600s are simply the total due you less the total expenses to give you a bottom line on line 603.

The second page of the settlement statement itemizes all the expenses from Line 502 on the first page. Again, as the seller, your column is on the right side of the page. The numbering system works like this:

- The 700s cover your expense in paying the Realtor's commissions.

- The 800s are generally for the buyer's side of the transaction, because they deal with fees charged to the buyer by the mortgage company. There should not be anything in your column in the 800s unless you are contributing toward the buyer's closing costs.

- The 900s are a buyer expense as well. These are costs associated with the buyer paying insurance, mortgage insurance and interest.

- The 1000s are again a buyer expense. These are the numbers used to set up an escrow account for the buyer's mortgage company to pay the buyer's taxes. Again, you should have no fees in this section unless you are paying costs on behalf of the buyer.

- The 1100s are title insurance charges, deed preparation charges, and notary fees. On most settlement statements, there are charges to both the buyer and seller. Depending on where you are in the country, you may have more or less of these charges on your side. Typically, however, you will be paying for some document preparation, such as a deed preparation on line 1105 and some notary fees on line 1106.

- The 1200s cover filing fees and transfer taxes. These fees depend on your location. In most areas the seller is responsible to pay some transfer taxes.

- The 1300s are where you should pay the most attention. If the mortgage company, Realtor®, escrow company, or title company is going to hit you with additional junk fees, they will be in this area. We'll discuss various junk fees in the next section.

- Line 1400 totals up the expenses on your side. Match this line to line 502 on the first page. The numbers should be the same.

Common Questions about Settlement Statements

Why is My Mortgage Payoff Higher than My Principal Balance on My Mortgage Statement?

Most owners pay their mortgage payment on the first of each month. That mortgage payment is for the previous month's principal and interest. What that means is that the day you pay your mortgage payment, your principal balance might be exactly what is on your statement. However, each day that passes after the first of the month, you accrue interest on the balance of the loan. If you sell the home on the fifth of the month, you will owe interest for those five days at settlement. If you settle in the middle of the month, it's safe to assume that your payoff will be approximately half a month's payment higher than your last statement's principal. This depends, of course, on how many years you've been paying on your mortgage. Additionally, some mortgage companies charge fees to satisfy the mortgage.

My Property Tax Payment is Made in March. Why is it Being Prorated as of January 1?

Prorating taxes appears more complicated than it really is. The county, school, and local taxing authorities set up a time frame that you are paying property taxes for. For example, the county may say that they charge taxes on a calendar year. That means the property taxes run from January 1 to December 31 each year. That doesn't mean you pay the taxes on January 1. In some areas, you may do just that. In others, you may pay the taxes in December for the following year, or you may pay them in March, but it back dates to January 1.

Doesn't the Buyer Pay Half the Commission? Why am I Being Charged the Entire Thing?

Your agent should have done a better job explaining the commission charge. Although half the commission, in most areas, does go to the firm of the buyer's agent and the other half goes to the listing agent's firm, the seller typically pays the entire commission.

What is a Tax Service Fee?

Some taxing authorities charge the title company or escrow company to verify that your taxes are current. This fee is often passed along to you.

Junk Fees

Some organizations try to pass on *junk fees* to home buyers and sellers as part of the closing package. Fees to watch out for include the following:

- **Conveyance Fees.** These are typically fees paid to the seller's real estate company for processing the transaction. They are very common in some areas. However, check if you agreed to pay such fees as part of your listing contract. If not, ask them to be waived.

- **Processing Fees.** There should not be any processing fees on your side unless you are paying part of the buyer's closing costs.

- **Document Preparation Fees.** Some title companies, attorneys, and escrow companies charge you, the seller, for the preparation and handling of documentation. Unless you have an unusual situation where you are holding a second mortgage for the buyer, or you need to prepare and file a power of attorney in order to sell a property, the document preparation that a settlement agent or an attorney will prepare for the seller's side of the transaction is generally limited to the preparation of a new deed conveying the property from you to the buyers. Fees for preparing a deed vary from region to region but are generally not more than two hundred dollars. If you find that you are being charged several hundred or several thousand dollars for document preparation, require the settlement agent to show you what was prepared and how he or she arrived at your charge.

- **Courier Fee / Express Mail Fee.** If you are paying off a mortgage or several mortgages, the escrow company or title company must have the payoff sent to your lender by express mail or courier to insure timely payoff. However, this is an area where many companies pad the bill. If you are paying $35 or $40 to express one check, you are paying too much. Ask it to be reduced.

- **Warehousing Fee.** This fee is for the title company to store documents on your transaction for many years in order to comply with regulations. However, most companies do not charge this, so you really shouldn't pay it.

Prepayment Penalties

When you purchased your home, you probably took out a mortgage. Over the last several years, more mortgage companies than ever have added *prepayment penalties* to their mortgage documents. What this means is that if you sell the property anytime in the first few years, you may owe the lender a penalty that can range from a few hundred to a few thousand dollars. This same penalty applies if you refinance the loan. In either case, you're paying off the original mortgage.

When you are attempting to determine how much you owe on the property, pull out your mortgage documentation and review it to determine if there is any prepayment penalty and what the charge might be. Typical penalties decline the longer you own the home. Although these vary widely, on a declining penalty, you may pay 3% of the mortgage balance if sold any time in the first two years, 2% the third year, and 1% the fourth or fifth year.

This is a critical issue to determine because you may be squeaking out of the home with just enough money to make a move. Sellers are put into a difficult position if they find out just before settlement that they owe an additional 2%. On a $200,000 home, that amounts to $4,000.

chapter twelve

When All Else Fails

Some home sellers don't have the luxury of waiting for a buyer to come along because they're in desperate need to sell quickly. They may be attempting to avoid impending foreclosure on their home and a ruined credit rating. Rising adjustable rate mortgage payments or a loss of income may have put their mortgage payment above their ability to pay.

Other home sellers don't have the ability to accept the current market value for their home. They may owe more on their home than they can sell for in the current market and are forced to sell by a divorce or to settle an estate. In cases like these, home sellers must consider their worst-case scenario and determine the best method to move forward.

"We'll buy your home cash!"—Investor Offers

In order to generate a quick sale on your property, you may try an auction, or you may try a company that advertises "We will buy your home cash." You've seen the signs. They're bright yellow and tacked to telephone poles all over the country. They often have huge ads in the yellow pages, or simply type "buy your house" into the Google search engine and see how many thousands of online ads come up.

There are always three types of buyers in a marketplace. There are those buyers searching for the perfect property. There are those buyers searching for a good deal and will buy a home if the price is right. Finally, there are those buyers who invest in real estate and are looking for a wholesale price.

I have heard many home sellers tell me that they are going to contact a *buy your home for cash now company* because the company says in its advertising that they pay top dollar. "Really, they just want to own a lot of real estate. That doesn't mean they want it at a discount." Of course, they want it at a discount. If they wanted homes at market price, they wouldn't be wasting thousands or tens of thousands of dollars to advertise on the radio and television or place signs all over town. Instead, they would be stopping at every real estate office and making offers. Again, sellers hear what they want to hear.

Investors are not always a bad alternative, though. If you are in a market where home sales are very slow and you need to get the home sold quickly, these investors or groups of investors will allow you to cash out of your home, eliminating the debt you are carrying in order to get on with your life. The right investors will buy your home and settle quickly. If you are in a position of desperation, you may want to find out what an investor would pay for the home.

Beware, though, that some investors have made a living by smooth talking sellers, using scare tactics and showing statistics and projections that panic a seller into signing a contract. Any contract you receive from an investor should be reviewed by your attorney.

When looking at an offer by an investor, talk to your Realtor® about whether you could beat the offer in a relatively short time. Remember that talking to one investor directly is not allowing the open market to compete for your home. If you simply kept your home on the market and slowly reduced the price, you are more likely to sell to someone looking for a good deal who will pay you above the wholesale price of an investor. You may also find another investor who would be willing to pay more.

Renting Out Your Home

Is it better to keep trying to sell your home, paying that mortgage and upkeep on the home month after month, or is it better to rent the home until the market turns around? This is not an easy question to answer because there are many variables to consider. On the negative side, tenants do not generally take care of homes as well as owners. They may make it difficult to show the home to other buyers, and if you rent the home too long, you may get nailed with capital gains taxes on selling the property. On the positive side, tenants may help pay your carrying costs on the home long enough that you are able to sell at a higher price in the future.

Renting your home might not even be a viable consideration, depending on your financial position. If you are moving to a larger home and need the equity in the current home to purchase the next one, you may find you are unable to rent your home. If you are moving across the country for a job transfer, you may need to rent your current home in order to even rent an apartment in your new location. The primary reason sellers rent homes is that they *have* to move and they owe more on the property than it is currently worth in the marketplace.

The Positives of Renting Your Home

The most glaring positive is that renting your home will likely cover the outstanding mortgage and upkeep of the home. If your mortgage payment is $1,800 a month, with taxes and insurance, and you're able to rent the home for $2,000 a month, you may even end up ahead. Keep in mind that you may have to do repairs or remodeling to the home once you get it back from the tenant, so budget for that as well.

If the home is rented through the end of a down cycle in the market, you may be able to sell the home for more when the tenant moves. This is a risk, however, because no one can truly accurately predict the real estate market.

There are also tax benefits to renting the home on a short-term basis. Landlords have tax write-offs. Repairs and maintenance, you put into the property are expenses to be taken off your taxes. Your accountant may also be able to depreciate the property, saving you money in yearly income taxes. If you elect to sell the home and take the capital gains tax deduction as a former live-in owner, you will be taxed on what you depreciated.

The Negatives of Renting Your Home

Tenants do not take care of homes like owners do. Unfortunately, the mind-set "It's a rental" is the way most tenants feel about your home. Many tenants will not treat your home with the same care and respect an owner would. Further, because tenants do not typically take the same excellent care of the home, you may need to do some remodeling, painting, cleaning, and repairs when the tenant moves.

If you still plan to market the home while it's rented, tenants can make the home very difficult to show. Tenants may not allow as many showings as you would, because they don't want to be inconvenienced, and they feel that they are paying to stay there, so they should have the quiet enjoyment of the home. Second, most tenants will not keep the home in clean and show condition for showings. In many cases, the home shows worse with tenants than vacant. If you wait until the lease is up to market your home again, you're back in the same boat of having a vacant home on the market that you're paying for.

The other consideration you will have to make is the implications of taxes. At the writing of this book, the federal government has an exemption on capital gains for owners selling their primary residences. If you live in the home, and have lived there for at least two years, there is no capital gains tax on the first $250,000 if you're single, or the first $500,000 if you're a married couple filing jointly. In other words, if you bought the house ten years ago for $150,000 and are selling it for $400,000, as a couple, you owe no capital gains taxes at all under the current rules.

However, if you rent the property out for the next three and a half years and then sell it for that same $400,000, the government will nail you with a Capital Gains tax on the profit you made on the home. You should talk to your accountant about the exact figures, but based on this example, the capital gains tax could amount to $37,500 at the current rate, as of the writing of this book. Worse, there are always politicians arguing that the capital gains rate should be raised higher. As political administrations change and new presidents are elected, the rate may change and hit you even harder in the pocketbook.

If you are only planning to rent your home for one or two years, you should still be free from Capital Gains taxes. The current rules state that you must have lived in your home as your primary residence at least two out of the prior five years. There are exemptions to all rules, and you should always seek advice from a knowledgeable professional such as an accountant.

Renting Your Home

Pros	Cons
Renting is likely to cover your mortgage and upkeep.	Tenants don't maintain the home like owners do.
Your home may appreciate while being rented.	Your home may need repairs when tenant moves out.
Your mortgage is being paid down by your tenant.	Your home may be difficult to show to buyers if tenant-occupied.
There are potential tax benefits of owning investment property.	Renting could cost you your capital gain exemption.

Other Considerations When Renting Out Your Home

If you are purchasing another home, can you afford to carry both mortgages if your present home becomes vacant?

Example:
     Several years ago, a client of ours rented her home rather than sell it. The tenant filed bankruptcy and listed the landlord

as a creditor. According to the homeowner, the tenant was able to avoid being evicted and paid no rent for eighteen months.

If this happened to you, would you be able to weather the cost?

Another question is, do you believe the home is likely to appreciate in value during the term of the rental? As discussed in Chapter 3, if the home is unlikely to appreciate, you may be better off investing the money into a mutual fund, money market, or other investment vehicle that will generate a better return than the property.

Before doing anything, find out if the rental market is any better than the sales market. If you are in a depressed area where industry has closed and jobs are scarce, the rental market could be just as bad. Even if you rent the property, you may end up with long periods without a tenant. You may be better off to use creative methods of marketing and selling the property.

Finally, are you cut out to be a landlord?

Example:

Just before Thanksgiving a few years ago, I needed to file eviction on one of my tenants. I had let it go far too long and they were now four months behind with no prospect of actually paying the rent. I had a mortgage to pay on the property and had to get them out. My assistant, Michelle, collected rents from my rental properties, and I asked her to please call them and let them know that they were now four months behind, and if I didn't see any money by Friday, I'd be starting the eviction process.

I came back from an appointment, and Michelle was nowhere to be found. I asked my other assistant Wendy where she went. "She talked to those tenants and they told her all about the fact that the husband couldn't find work, and their son was sick, and... well, anyway, she went out and bought them a Christmas tree." I explained to Michelle when she returned, that everybody always says they can't find work, and our unemployment rate was around 4%. The reality was that they were driving a brand-new car that was nicer than mine and I noticed a big screen TV last time I was at the house.

Example:
> One of our clients came in our office a few weeks ago to sell a seven unit. He said that only four of the units were paying because the others had really sad stories about family members who passed away and lack of work and so on. He had left one couple in an apartment for eleven months without paying.

Being a landlord is not for the faint of heart. You have to sort out the truth and the lies from tenants that appeared to be very good in the beginning but have lots of excuses today. You have to be able and willing to handle phone calls in the middle of the night that a pipe broke, or the furnace isn't working properly, or someone broke a window and they don't know who. The other option is to hire a property manager, but then you are paying out 8–10% of your rental income to a manager, netting you less on the property.

Unless you're planning to build a portfolio of rental properties, taking advantage of the tax deductions and building equity, I do not often recommend a seller rent his or her property if the seller can sell it without taking a loss. The reason is that the variables are too unknown.

Understanding Taxes and Capital Gains

As explained earlier in this chapter, capital gains, as related to real estate, is a tax paid on the profit you receive from selling a property. If you sell an investment property, for example, you will pay part of any profit to the government in the form of capital gains. There is a way to delay paying this tax by reinvesting the money through something called *1031 exchange*, which we'll deal with in the next section. When selling your primary residence, there is an exemption of up to $250,000 for an individual owner, or $500,000 for a couple. In order to qualify for this exemption, you must have lived in the home for 2 of the past 5 years, and you must not have sold another principal residence during the last 2 years.

If You're Selling Your Primary Residence

If you're selling your *principal* or primary residence, meaning the home that you live in most of the time, and you haven't sold another principal residence in the last two years, you can make a profit without paying capital gains.

In order to determine your actual gain, according to the IRS rules, you need to subtract your original purchase price from your new sales price. From that difference, you also need to subtract any costs you incurred to sell the home, such as commission, transfer taxes and similar expenses. You can also subtract any capital improvements you've made to the home. A *capital improvement* is an improvement that increased the value of the home, prolongs the life of the home, or expands the home. Capital improvements do not include maintenance of the home or minor repairs.

If you are audited, you'll have to provide evidence of the repairs you made to the home. Actual receipts for the materials and labor of the improvements are certainly what the IRS wants, but you may be able to provide evidence photographically. The problem is that you'll have difficulty proving the actual expenses based on pictures you took.

Example:
    You and your spouse paid $200,000 for your home in San Francisco eight years ago, and recently sold it for $720,000. You paid closing costs of $43,000 to sell the home. The IRS calls your $200,000 investment in the home your *basis*. Subtract your basis of $200,000 from the $720,000 you sold the home for and then also subtract your costs to sell.

Sales Price:	$720,000
Less Basis (Purchase Price):	- $200,000
Less Capital Improvements:	- $0
Less Costs to Sell:	- $43,000
Total Gain:	$477,000
Deduction:	$500,000
Capital Gains:	**$0**

There are several rules associated with this exemption. If you have any questions, you should seek out professional advice from an accountant. The current rules are as follows:

- The home was your principal residence 2 out of last 5 years. Even if you never rented the property, if you didn't live in it as your primary or principal residence in 2 out of the last 5 years, you will be hit with capital gains taxes. If you split your time between Boston and Orlando, you can only use the exemption on the one where you spend the most time living.

- You have not sold another principal residence in last 2 years. This exemption is only good once every two years.

- Your gain is not greater than $250,000 for an individual owner or $500,000 for a couple.

There are other ways to reduce your exposure to capital gains, if you need to move in under two years. You can exclude part of the gain if your move is based on a job relocation of more than 50 miles, an illness or an *unforeseen circumstance*, such as death, divorce or a natural disaster. In these cases, you will need significant documentation to prove your case, and, if allowed, you will be taxed on a percentage of the declared gain.

If you qualify under one of the partial reduction rules, you pay capital gains based on the difference between the period of time you lived in the home, and the minimum capital gains exemption period of two years or twenty-four months. Divide the number of months you used the home as your principal residence by 24 to get the percentage of time you can deduct. Then multiply this percentage by the $250,000 maximum deduction if you are an individual or $500,000 if you are a couple. That is the amount you may exclude.

Example:
     A couple used a home as their primary or principal residence for 16 months, and sold because of a job transfer. What is the maximum gain excluded?

16 months / 24 months = .667
.667 x $500,000 (because the owners are a married couple) = $333,333.33
The maximum gain excluded is $333,333.33

Partial Reductions in Capital Gains

A Change in Place of Employment
     If you are selling because of a job relocation and have lived in the home less than 2 years, you may exclude part of the gain. The job relocation can be to take a new job, or a transfer from your current employer. If you are audited, you should have transfer paperwork to provide the IRS.

Health
     If you are selling due to medical reasons and have lived in the home for less than two years, you may exclude part of the gain. For example, you may not be able to go up steps and you're living in a three-story townhome. If you are audited, you should have an explanation from your doctor explaining your condition.

Unforeseen Circumstances
     Unforeseen circumstances are a reason that the IRS will accept. On www.IRS.gov, you'll find Publication 523, which outlines the following examples of unforeseen circumstances:

- an involuntary conversion of your home;

- natural or manmade disasters including war, terrorism, which destroy your home;

- death, unemployment, divorce, or multiple births resulting from the same pregnancy;

If You're Selling a Vacation Home, a Second Home or an Investment Home

If the home you're selling is not your principal residence and you have not lived there for 2 out of the last 5 years, you will have to pay capital gains taxes on the gain. On an investment home, you may have depreciated the home during your ownership. You may also have written off your capital improvements on the home. These will have to be added back in before your tax is paid. This is called an *adjusted basis*. Rather than simply use your original purchase price, you need to deduct what you depreciated to determine your adjusted basis.

Example:

You paid $100,000 for your second home in Orlando more than 10 years ago, and recently sold it for $200,000. Your closing costs were $12,000. You depreciated $35,000 off the home on your income taxes. Subtract your depreciation from your original purchase price to obtain your adjusted basis.

To determine your adjusted basis:

Original Cost:	$100,000
Less Depreciation:	- $ 35,000
Adjusted Basis:	$ 65,000

To determine your realized gain:

Sales Price:	$200,000
Less Cost of Sale:	- $ 12,000
Less Adjusted Basis:	- $ 65,000
Realized Gain:	$123,000

Your capital gains taxes will be based on a realized gain of $123,000.

Common Questions asked about Capital Gains

Some common questions home sellers ask include the following:

I'm Over 65 Years Old, So I Don't Have to Pay Capital Gains on a House Sale, Right?

Wrong. There used to be a rule that a seller would have a one-time tax exclusion when they hit 65 years old. That tax exclusion was eliminated by the new capital gains rules. Regardless of age, if you have a gain in excess of $250,000 for an individual or $500,000 for a married couple, you must pay capital gains.

I Only Made $20,000 After Paying Off the First and Second Mortgages, So I Don't Have to Pay Capital Gains Taxes, Right?

Wrong. The mortgage amounts have nothing to do with whether or not the IRS determines you had a gain. If you paid $200,000 for a home and mortgaged $500,000, your basis or original cost is still $200,000.

I'm Losing Money on the Sale of My Home. Does that Mean I Can Deduct the Loss on My Taxes?

Unfortunately, it does not. The IRS only cares if you *make* money. There is no current deduction for any losses on a principal residence.

Deferring Capital Gains Taxes with 1031 Exchanges

If you *are* going to have to pay capital gains taxes in order to sell your home, second home or rental home, there is a powerful tax law that allows you to pass through your capital gain to another real estate investment without immediately paying taxes on the gain. The program allows an owner to sell one property and use the full proceeds as a down payment on another real estate investment by deferring the taxes.

Although the process is not very complicated, to properly complete an exchange and defer the taxes, I suggest you seek the advice of a good accountant and possibly an attorney who is well versed in exchanges to assist you in navigating the legal waters. Using an exchange, the capital gain is not eliminated, but the taxes that are due are postponed until you eventually sell the new property.

When you sell the new property, you may be able to exchange again, trading up again without paying the capital gains taxes on either property because you've postponed the gain. This capital gain is forgiven when you pass away, and all your heirs pay are inheritance taxes under the current regulations.

The gain can also be passed to almost any type of real estate investment. For example, if you sell a second home at the beach or in the mountains, you can use a 1031 exchange to reinvest the money into a commercial property, apartment building, or a second home somewhere else. You may even be able to sell the property and use an exchange to put your money into certain real estate annuities like TICs, which own shopping centers, medical buildings or office buildings and pay returns on your investment.

Another possibility is to sell your property and use a 1031 exchange to reinvest the money into more than one property. For example, if your beach front condo is now worth 5 times what you paid for it in the 1980's and you've depreciated it on your taxes to nearly nothing, you can sell the condo and use the money as a down payment for 2 or 3 investment properties, creating an income stream for yourself. Doing this, you're leveraging your equity.

There are three rules that must be carefully followed in order to avoid paying the capital gains tax when you sell

- For an exchange to work, the IRS states that the property must be sold for a *life-kind property.* Don't panic. Our experience has been that any real estate investment can be considered a like-kind property. That means virtually any real estate can be substituted for any other real estate property. Whether you are exchanging a second home for a farm, or a shore condo for a multi- unit, the new property is seen, in the eyes of the IRS codes, as a continuation of the original investment.

- You cannot ever touch the money. You cannot take possession of any funds received at closing. Your profit or gain will be given, at closing, to a certified Exchange Agent. The Exchange Agent then transfers the money to the settlement for the next property you are purchasing.

There are time limits on every aspect of a 1031 exchange. The rule is that you must identify, in writing, the property which you want to purchase for the exchange within forty-five days of the date you sold the original property. You can identify more than one property, just in case one doesn't work out because of an inspection or some other issue.

You only have one hundred and eighty days to complete the entire exchange, and the IRS has no provisions for extensions. If you're selling one shore home to buy 2 or 3 investment properties, all purchases must be closed within one hundred and eighty days of the sale date of the original property.

The other restriction is that you may not take any other thing of value during the transaction. You can't have the buyer put a roof on your home, give you a boat or car, or give you cash on the side. The IRS considers this to be 'boot' and disallows it. To be safe, have an exchange company or attorney carefully review all aspects of the exchange so you don't make a mistake and cost yourself a significant capital gains tax.

Upside Down in your Mortgage: Dealing with Short Sales

A few years ago, some lenders offered 100% financing, 103% financing, and even 125% financing. Borrowers took out first mortgages, second mortgages, and equity loans. With a falling real estate market, many homeowners are upside down in equity. They actually owe more than the home can be sold for in the current market.

If you are a homeowner in this situation, you have several choices. You may not have to sell the home. If you can stay in the home for a few years, try to make extra payments on the loan balances, known as the *principal*. Principal balances go down very slowly over the first few years of a loan because you are paying primarily interest. Over time, your property will hopefully appreciate in value.

An alternative is to rent the home and use the rent to pay your mortgage payments. Renting can be risky as well and put you in a poor situation, as we described in the previous section. If you're renting, try to pay ahead on the principal loan balances.

When you *need* to sell the home, whether it's due to a divorce, or because you cannot make the payments, you may need a more creative solution. Purchasing a home is an investment in real estate. The banks or mortgage companies that loaned you money are also invested in your home. This may work to your advantage when you need to sell.

Should you walk away from your home and give it to the bank, the bank generally loses money. Foreclosure and reselling a property is very expensive for a lender. Additionally, you may ruin your credit to the point that you may not be able to purchase another home for a decade.

If you have more than one loan on the property, the second-place lender or equity loan may receive nothing at all out of the sale of the house if the first lender takes possession of the property in a foreclosure.

For example, let's say you purchased your home for $100,000 using an 80/20 loan a few years ago. An *80/20 loan* means you borrowed 80% as a first mortgage and 20% as a second loan so you could step into the home with little or no money down. It also means that you are writing two mortgage payment checks each month. The first is on the $80,000 first mortgage, and the second is on the $20,000 loan. You then took out an equity line of credit from the local credit union for $6000 in new windows. That becomes a third-place loan. You owe a total of $106,000. If the home is foreclosed on, in all likelihood, the first mortgage holder of $80,000 will end up with the property and the second and third liens will not get anything out of the sale. This can work to your advantage in negotiating a short sale or short payoff.

A *short sale* is a transaction where the lender accepts less than you owe them as a payoff of the loan. Although some lenders will not accept short payoffs, many will consider them because they may lose less by discounting the principal balance on your mortgage than in going through a full foreclosure. The foreclosure process can cost a lender tens of thousands of dollars. In some cases, the bank will lose less by foreclosing and in other cases, such as the lender being in second or third lien position, the bank may lose everything if the property goes into foreclosure.

If you currently owe $200,000 on a property that is worth $180,000, you would ask the bank to allow you to sell the home for $180,000 at which point the bank would net the $180,000 less any seller closing costs. If the seller closing costs for Realtor® fees and transfer taxes adds up to $12,000, for example, the bank would actually net $168,000. The bank will take a loss, in this case, of $32,000 between what was owed and what they actually received.

In a perfect world, the bank considers this a loss and writes it off. You go on with your life, free of the debt. In some instances, the lender feels that you are perfectly capable of paying off the balance of the loss over time. They may write a personal loan to you for the difference, and you would make payments on that. Paying on $32,000 each month is still better than paying on $200,000. The alternative is that the bank or lender files some sort of deficiency judgment against you for the balance and tries to collect it using the court system.

It has been my experience that lenders do not typically come after the sellers for the difference. I have only encountered one lender, in my last ten years of doing short sales, who attempted to collect the difference. However, you should speak with an attorney to know your rights and obligations.

Attempting a short sale should be a last resort for desperate home sellers. There are many drawbacks to taking the short sale route. First, my experience has been that lenders are more willing to talk to you about a short sale if you are already behind in your mortgage payment. This is risky, however, because you are destroying your credit by missing payments on your mortgage or equity loans.

Second, you will not be allowed to take any money out of the transaction. The bank is losing money, so it will not allow you to receive a check at settlement or closing. Additionally, you should not have any significant liquid assets. The lender will certainly expect you to cover the loss before it will kick in any money. If you owe $200,000, the property is worth $180,000, and you have $10,000 in CDs, the lender will expect you to use that $10,000 toward the loss.

Finally, some lenders will not consider a short sale until you have a written sales contract on the home. In other words, you market the home below what you owe, with the hope that the lender will accept the short payoff of the mortgage. You then submit the offer to the lender and hope it is accepted. In this case, you must write a contingency into the sales contract that will allow you to cancel the sale if the lender is unwilling to accept the short sale. Some buyers will not proceed with a contract like this because they are not guaranteed that they will be able to purchase the home.

Steps to Requesting a Short Sale

Your first step in attempting a short sale is to contact your lender and ask who you should speak to in order to get a short sale approved. The part of the bank that handles short sales is often called a *work out department*.

If your real estate agent or attorney is working on the short sale for you, you will need to give the bank or lender authorization to speak with you. Write a letter to the bank stating that you want to give authorization to your agent or attorney. Include in the letter your name, social security number, loan account number, property address, the reason for requesting the authorization and the name of the person or persons you are authorizing to speak with them.

Whether you speak with the lender directly, or speak through your attorney or Realtor®, the lender will probably either send you a package of information it wants completed, or it will request certain information. In either case, you will most likely need the following things.

- **Hardship Letter.** We used to call these *cry letters* because the goal is to explain why you need to sell the home without paying the entire balance off, and why you cannot pay the difference. Explanations about job losses or illness may evoke the best response from the lender, but my experience has been that most of them are very objective. Your lender will want concrete reasons why your only other alternatives are bankruptcy or foreclosure, neither of which is high on the bank's list of goals.

- **Competitive Market Analysis.** This is a realtor's estimate of value, comparing the home to recent sales and those currently on the market, as described in Chapter 3. Your Realtor® should be happy to prepare a written statement, including comparable sales and listings, for your lender.

- **Preliminary HUD Settlement Sheet or Net Sheet.** The bank wants to know exactly how much it is likely to net on the sale of the property, so it can make a determination of whether or not to allow the short sale. A *net sheet* should account for any expenses you need to pay to sell, including real estate commissions, transfer taxes, notary fees, filing fees, tax prorations, and other expenses common to the area or specific to your home.

- **Income, Expense, and Asset Form.** The lender wants to know exactly how much you are earning, how much your expenses are, and what assets you might have besides your home. If you try to hide something, it's likely the lender will find it on your credit report or original application for the mortgage anyway, so it's better to be completely truthful. The lender is trying to determine if you can handle paying part of the difference, or if you really need a short sale.

- **Copies of Pay Stubs**. Just like when you applied for a mortgage, the lender wants to verify what you tell them. Pay stubs will tell them if you are being accurate on your income.

- **Copies of Bank Statements.** Again, verification of your assets. They may ask for two or three months of statements to determine if you quickly withdrew money from the account last month.

- **Sales Contract.** Some lenders will discuss short sales with you without having an offer on the table, and some will not discuss it without a fully executed offer. This will depend on the lender.

- **Broker Price Opinion or Appraisal.** Some lenders will require an unbiased opinion of the value of the property. To do this, they may request a broker price opinion or an appraisal of the property. This appraisal may be at your expense.

Although banks and lenders differ on what documentation they require, the list covers most lenders. Be prepared to answer some hard questions about how you got into this situation, and why the lender should agree to forgive part of the debt.

If you have more than one loan against the home, it is unlikely that the first-place mortgage holder will accept less than full payment. In a foreclosure situation, the secondary liens may lose everything, so they may be more willing to negotiate a short payoff. However, the percentage loss on the second or third loans would be greater, making them look harder at your circumstances.

For example, if the property is currently only worth $180,000 and you owe $160,000 on the first mortgage and $40,000 on the second mortgage, the second mortgage company would have to take a minimum of a 50% hit on the payoff. With closing costs, the second mortgage company may only be receiving 25% of their mortgage back. That may be a tough sell, unless you are far enough behind in your mortgage that the second mortgage company feels foreclosure by the first mortgage company is imminent.

Short sales can also be negotiated, sometimes, that the lender reports to the credit bureau that the debt was paid off in full. Although there is no guarantee a lender will do this, it will help your credit rating.

Ultimately, short sales are a tool of last resort when attempting to sell a home. There are home sellers who get into a position where they need to sell and cannot make up the difference or loss between current market value and the debt that is owed on the property. In this case, short sales may be viable options.

What if You're in Foreclosure?

Just as we've described in the previous section, lenders do not want to foreclose on your home. They are in the business of investing money, in expectation of a return. The foreclosure process costs a lender thousands or tens of thousands of dollars.

You may have purchased this book in hopes of finding the quickest method of selling your home and avoiding a foreclosure on your credit. First, you need to determine if you really want to or need to sell.

If you choose to attempt to keep your home, there are several methods to prolong or stop the foreclosure process. If you find you may not have the ability to keep the home, you should contact a Realtor® immediately and attempt to sell as quickly as possible. Missed payments, late fees, attorney's fees, and court costs add up very quickly, and make the home more difficult to sell without coming up with providing additional funds.

Keeping Your Home

Don't ignore the calls from your lender. You'll need to negotiate a plan to move forward and keep your home. Some lenders will allow you to create a payment plan or a mortgage modification. In some cases, you may need to contact an attorney to negotiate on your behalf or to file a bankruptcy to stall the foreclosure or prevent it.

Methods of stalling foreclosure include the following:

- **Forbearance.** Some lenders may allow you to delay payments for a short period of time. Credit Unions and small banks have allowed forbearance in cases where the owner experienced an illness that prevented their working. To secure a forbearance, you should call the lender as early as possible. Explain that you will be out of work for X months. To be approved for a forbearance, you must have a solid repayment plan including a higher payment for a period of time to catch up to missed and delinquent payments.

- **Repayment Plan.** If you're several months behind on your mortgage, the lender has likely filed for a foreclosure. Unlike forbearance, in which a lender may allow a period of time to elapse with minimal or no payments, a *repayment plan* requires the borrower to immediately begin paying on the outstanding balance. You, as the borrower, have to prove to the lender that despite the fact that you haven't made the last three payments, you will make every payment from now on, and you'll pay a portion of the missed payments until you are caught up on your mortgage payments.

- **Reinstatement.** Up until the time of the sheriff's sale, you have the right to pay the outstanding balance of missed payments, late fees, and attorney's costs to bring your mortgage current. If you have a large sum of money coming from a tax refund, estate settlement, disability settlement, or bonus, a lender may stall the foreclosure sale if you can provide solid proof that the outstanding debt will be paid. If you are receiving a sum from a lawsuit, the lender may be more reluctant because lawsuit settlements can be prolonged almost indefinitely.

- **Mortgage Modification.** If you fell behind on your mortgage payment due to an illness or death in the family, but can show you can make the payments now, the lender may allow a mortgage modification. The difference between a modification and a repayment plan is that in a repayment plan, you make additional payments to catch up your mortgage. If you are unable to pay additional money, a *mortgage modification* might mean adding those payments on the end of the loan or refinancing the loan to include the new balance owed.

In any of these cases, the lender does not have to work with you. It can simply continue the foreclosure process. Your only ace in the hole is that the lender knows you can file bankruptcy. Bankruptcy will stall the foreclosure process and possibly force the bank or lender to negotiate with you.

Not Keeping the Home

If you find that keeping the home is not your choice, or is no longer an option, you need to determine your course of action to minimize the damage to your credit.

The common question I'm asked is "Why shouldn't I just ride it out and not pay? I'll get several free months of rent. My credit is already shot from my late payments." The truth is that late payments will affect your credit for a period of time. A foreclosure hurts your credit for a very long time. If you're 30 years old now, you think you have your whole life ahead of you to turn it around. Imagine that at 40 years old, you're trying to convince a lender to give you a mortgage and they want documentation and answers to why you walked away from a property ten years before.

You have three choices if you choose not to keep the home or you are unable to keep it:

1. *Foreclosure.* Stay in the home as long as possible until the Sheriff removes you.

2. *Deed in Lieu of Foreclosure.* You voluntarily give your home back to the lender. In return, they forgive the balance of the debt. This will still damage your credit, but not as significantly as foreclosure.

3. *Sell Your Home*. Certainly, your best choice, because it will show on your credit that the loan was paid off. Your lender may allow you an extension on the foreclosure to sell the home, or they may allow a short sale. In either case, you must communicate with the lender.

One of the primary keys in selling your home before the foreclosure is to act quickly. Don't stall because of embarrassment.

Example:
A few years ago, Doris's husband passed away. Her husband left her debt free because a life insurance policy paid off her home. A few months after his death, she felt she had to redecorate in order to change the look of the home and move on with her life. She borrowed $20,000 against her $150,000 townhome, using an equity line of credit. At Christmas time, she took an additional few thousand to buy presents.
Doris didn't pay the mortgage and went into foreclosure. She was too embarrassed to tell her kids what she did and too ashamed to call a Realtor®. I was asked by the lender to secure the property after the Sheriff sale. She lost more than $120,000 in equity because of pride.

In foreclosure, you're racing against the clock. Don't be embarrassed. Ask for help, talk to the lender about options and call a Realtor®.

Don't Wait Too Long

Example:
Lynn was in foreclosure when she first spoke with me. She said that she owed $180,000 on a property worth $300,000. The average market time was over 60 days. I explained that she should list between $250,000 and $265,000 to attract investors or wholesale buyers for a quick sale. "I'm not going to give my house away," she said.
"You don't have enough time to hold out for top dollar," I explained.

"The sheriff's sale is 65 days away! That's over 2 months!"

"But it's common to take 45 days to settle. We need to market this home and sell it in the next 20 days. That's a third of the time it takes to sell most homes in the area."

Timing is critical when attempting to avoid foreclosure. You may need to underprice the home by 10–20% for a quick sale so you don't lose all your equity.

chapter thirteen:

When to Panic

In order to sell your home for top dollar, you have to avoid panicking. If you're in a declining market, you'll need to carefully consider your options and make absolutely certain you are one of the best values on the market. However, that doesn't mean you have to give your home away either.

If your property in on the market for 3 weeks without selling. That's okay. Don't get excited. If 5 or 6 potential buyers have looked at your home and none has made an offer, that's okay too. Far too many home sellers have unrealistic expectations about the market. That has been even more true lately in markets that have gone from hot to cold in only a year or so. Sellers remember their neighbors selling their home in just a few days or a few hours.

In a normal real estate market, you're likely to have a dozen or more showings before anyone makes an offer on the home. There are several variables to keep track of when marketing a home. First, you need to get honest feedback on showings and gauge the reactions of buyers who walk through. Remember that, although your home was the perfect home for your family, it is not the perfect home for every buyer. Listen objectively to their feedback.

Secondly, you need to determine what is the average market time is for a home like yours in your area. Home sellers get very impatient very quickly. Although the average home seller has expectations of the home selling in ten to twenty days, a realistic time on the market may be closer to sixty days.

Last, you need to determine what percentage of homes like yours in your area are selling monthly. This is called an *absorption rate*. For example, if you own a townhome in a school district or township where there are fifty relatively similar townhomes are for sale and ten are selling each month, you have a ten in fifty chance of selling in any given month. This is only a one in five chance of being the one sold. In a case like that, you need to improve your odds of selling through staging and price. Remember marketing, gets buyers to look at your property, but staging and price actually sell the home. When you are *very* similar to competing properties, such as when you own a townhome or a condo, price becomes a more important factor.

If you're in a foreclosure situation, or you're behind in your mortgage payments, you may need to reduce your price to the point where it is lower than the competition in order to insure a sale. Something is always better than nothing.

One of the questions I'm asked most often is "There's something wrong. People are going through my home and they seem to like it. It can't be the price. They would just make an offer if it were the price, but I'm not even receiving any offers!"

Buyers look at ten to fifteen homes before they make a decision to purchase one. Some buyers look at dozens or more before making a decision, much to the chagrin of Realtors®. The buyer will make an offer first on the home he or she gets the best feeling for. That is often generated by staging. If several homes are similar, the buyer will make an offer on the home he or she feel is the best value for the price. If they like your home just a little more than your neighbors', but your neighbor's is priced $10,000 below yours, he or she will probably make an offer on your neighbors' home.

If your home is on the market more than the average marketing time in your area, and you haven't received an offer, you could have a price problem, or you could have a problem with marketing. Buyers either feel you're priced above the competition, or enough buyers aren't finding out about the home. If you are using a Realtor® to market your home, sit down and discuss both situations with him or her.

If your home has had two dozen showings and it hasn't sold, marketing is not the issue. If you are getting activity, but no offers, don't call your agent and yell that they are not pushing people to make offers on your house. That's not the problem. The problem is either staging or price. There may be some issue in the house that is causing buyers to walk away, or buyers are finding enough homes in the marketplace that they feel are better values that they're making offers on those houses instead. Again, it's time to re-evaluate your position in the marketplace with your agent.

Being Logical in a Home Sale Rather than Emotional

Every step of the way, you need to take a step back from the transaction and emotionally detach yourself. I realize that this is *your* house. You raised your family there. You hung that old tire off the tree in the back yard. You and your brother Buddy were the ones who finished that basement, hanging the drywall and dropping the ceiling.

You can't look at this as your home. You need to consider it a valuable asset. When you're selling a stock or a car, you look up the value in a book of values. In the case of a car, you add or subtract based on the mileage and the car's condition. While no two homes are exactly alike, the value can be determined within a few thousand dollars and the home *is* an asset.

If you have the home on the market and it's not selling, you should step back and look for another approach. As much as you might not want to, you may have to bite the bullet and reduce the price. Try to look at the home logically. Maybe there is a problem with staging. Perhaps those bright orange walls are turning off buyers. When attempting to sell a home for top dollar, there is not room to think of the color as '*the color that matched my daughter's hair when she was 3.*'

If you have the home under agreement, you may come to a point where the sale needs to be renegotiated because the home inspector has found a significant issue, or because the home under appraises. You may become angry and shout *"how dare they try to do this to me,"* but the truth is that you have to keep your ultimate goal in sight. That ultimate goal is probably to sell the home at a reasonable price. If an inspector finds that you have significant termite damage, it is not the buyer's fault. They will not pay more for the house to cover your loss.

In order to negotiate the best transaction possible, you have to take a deep breath, step back and lay out all the positives and negatives of any difficult situation you encounter. If a buyer will back out of the sale if you refuse to repair or replace the septic, write down what the possible outcomes are. You can fix the septic. You can put the home back on the market and disclose the septic issue to every future buyer. Is there a likelihood you can sell the home for more if the septic is corrected?

Emotional detachment is very hard to accomplish in something as close to you as your home.

Conclusion

It may seem like a simple matter to sell your home. Put up a For Sale sign, get your home on Zillow, run a few ads, and wait for the buyers to bid on your home. Unfortunately, the home selling process is seldom that simple. In fact, selling a home can be one of the most stressful times in a person's life. Before making the decision to jump into the real estate market, you should carefully consider your motivation to sell. Do you need to sell in order to settle a divorce, an estate, or because you're behind in your mortgage payments? Are you selling due to a job relocation, or are you simply selling because you'd like to move into a larger home?

Is now the right time to sell the property? Is your home located in a seller's market or a buyer's market? If you are trading up to a larger home and the market is not as hot as you'd like, weigh the pros and cons of moving now or in several years when the market changes.

Remember that you cannot control the location of your home. The three primary components of a successful sale that you *can* control are staging the home for buyers, pricing the home for the current market, and detailing a strong marketing plan to attract the most likely buyers, In order to stage your home, take some time and go through your home as if you were a buyer. Use the reference material in this book to determine what needs to be decluttered, repaired, enlarged, neutralized, deep cleaned, and staged so the home shows its best.

You will want to maximize the net amount of money you realize from the sale. Take some time to calculate how much you will need to make your move and consider the costs associated with selling and moving. Carefully select your price by comparing your home with other similar homes that have sold recently in the area and watch the pricing of other homes for sale because they are your competition.

Decide whether it's better under the current market conditions to try selling your home on your own or to hire a real estate agent. Then, if you choose to hire an agent, select him or her on the strength of his or her marketing and servicing program to get your home in front of likely buyers. If you choose to market your home yourself, determine the most likely buying groups and use the techniques outlined in this book to attract attention from those buyers by utilizing the best marketing resources available.

If you find that your home is not selling, consider all your options in the guerilla tactics section of this book. Should you reduce the price? Can you afford to reduce the price, or should you consider renting your home? Should you offer an incentive in order to sell?

Once you find the buyer, carefully analyze the offer on a purchase agreement analyzer and negotiate the best deal possible. Whether or not you are using a real estate agent, keep track of all the details to ensure the buyer handles inspections, deposits, and the mortgage application in a timely fashion. Plan for settlement, and if there are a few bumps in the road, refer back to the sections of this book that deal with sales issues.

Again, good market or bad, homes are selling. There are buyers in the marketplace who desperately want or *need* to buy. These buyers may be buying because of job transfers, divorces, or the need to purchase a larger or smaller home. As you move through the process of selling your home, keep your eyes on the light at the end of the tunnel. The prize may be a beautiful new home of your dreams in the neighborhood where you have always wanted to live, or the relief of getting to your new location. Follow the steps in this book and get your home sold in *any* market.

Glossary

A

agency. The relationship that exists between property sellers or property buyers and their real estate agents. The agency is formed through a written contract that describes the duties the duties and obligations of the agent to the principal (seller or buyer).

agreement of sale. The sales contract or purchase contract for the sale of real estate.

appraisal. A written evaluation of the value of property as determined by a licensed appraiser based primarily on recently sold comparable properties in the same area.

appraised value. An opinion of the value of a property as determined by an appraiser. Lenders generally require appraisals in order to ensure sufficient value in a property prior to loaning money to a borrower or home buyer.

appraiser. A licensed professional whose job it is to determine the value of a property.

B

bait and switch. A process by which someone advertises something that sounds good and then attempts to talk the respondents into something else. In lending, a mortgage broker may advertise a very low interest rate, but it may only apply to a very select group of clients or properties. When a potential borrower calls a mortgage broker, the company then attempts to switch him or her to another lending program that is less beneficial to the buyer. In real estate, a Realtor® may advertise a property that has a very low price, but in a very rural or distant location, and then attempt to switch the caller to other properties in order to pick up a buyer.

below grade. Any room or area below or partially below ground level. Homes that have finished basements have rooms that are below grade. Bi-level style homes are often partially buried, offering rooms that are below grade as well.

broker. A person employed to represent another person. In the real estate industry, a broker has a license to list, market, and sell real property.

building inspection. A home inspection or building inspection is a complete inspection of the structure and systems of a property.

buyer's agent/buyer's broker. A real estate agent or broker in a property purchase who exclusively represents the buyer.

C

closing. Generally refers to the end of the sales process where the property ownership transfers. In some states, the closing is the meeting of all parties to sign documents and exchange money. In some states, the sale is not considered closed until the deed and mortgage are recorded.

closing costs. Fees that are paid by the buyer or seller at settlement in order to settle and transfer the property are considered closing costs. Costs paid by the seller may include Realtor® fees, recording fees, notary fees, transfer taxes, and even title searches in some parts of the country. Costs paid by the buyer may include lender points, appraisal fees, credit reporting fees, title searches, title insurance, proration of real estate taxes, and prepaid fees such as a portion of real estate taxes and insurance.

closing statement. Also known as a *settlement statement* or a *HUD-1*, this is the document outlining the final accounting of all fees paid by the buyer and seller and the net amount due from the buyer and the net amount paid to the seller (if applicable).

commission. Fee paid to the Realtor® for his or her services in marketing and locating a buyer for a property.

comparable sales. Generally used to evaluate the most likely sales price of a particular property, comparable sales are properties that have sold recently in the same area that have similar features or are of a similar size and age. In the case of very unique properties, appraisers or brokers may have to base comparables on characteristics of other properties. Comparable sales are often referred to as *comps*.

condominium. A type of property ownership where an owner takes ownership of the interior of the home or apartment, but the land and exterior are owned commonly with other owners.

contingency. A condition of the purchase or sale of the home that must be met prior to settlement. If the condition is not met, the sale may not occur. Examples of a buyer's contingency are making the home sale conditioned on the approval of a mortgage, an appraisal of the home, or home inspection results that are satisfactory to the buyer. An example of a seller's contingency is making the home sale contingent upon the seller finding a suitable home to move into.

contract. Although a contract may be any written or oral agreement, in real estate, a contract is generally referred to as either the written agreement between a buyer and seller to purchase a home, or a written agreement between a client and a real estate broker for representation by the broker.

credit report. A report generated by one of the major credit reporting agencies (Experian, Equifax, or TransUnion) that displays a record of a borrower's credit activities. Credit reports show loan balances, including credit card balances, payment history, and judgements or actions taken against the borrower as a result of late payments or unpaid bills. Credit reporting agencies often analyze the person's history and assign a credit score.

credit score. A number assigned by credit reporting agencies by analyzing a person's credit-worthiness based on his or her history of borrowing activities and payment activities.

D

deed. The legal document conveying ownership in a property.

default. (1) When a buyer or seller fails to follow the terms of the sale agreement, that party is in default of the contract. An example of a default is when a buyer fails to settle on a home even though all contingencies have been met and he or she has been approved for a mortgage. (2) When a borrower fails to pay his or her mortgage and the home goes into foreclosure, the borrower is then in default.

deposit. Generally refers to money paid by the buyer that is placed into escrow as good faith that the buyer will proceed with the transaction. If the buyer defaults on the purchase agreement, this money may be given to the property seller as liquidated damages, depending on state laws and practices.

down payment. The portion of the home price that the buyer pays in cash, or the portion of the purchase that the buyer does not mortgage.

E

earnest money deposit. Also known as a *deposit*, the term refers to money paid by the buyer that is placed into escrow as good faith that the buyer will proceed with the transaction. If the buyer defaults on the purchase agreement, this money may be given to the property seller as liquidated damages, depending on state laws and practices.

easement. A legal right of way or use of the property given to someone other than the owner. A utility company, for example, may have an easement across a property to run power lines. Another example is a neighbor who has access to his or her property across a shared driveway that is partially on another property owner's lane.

equity. In real estate, equity refers to the difference between the sales price, or antiquated sales price, and the amount owed on the mortgage.

escrow. Money that is held on behalf of the buyer or seller, often by a third party. Deposit money from a buyer is often placed in an escrow account. If the sale of the property reaches closing, this money is used by the buyer towards his or her down payment or closing costs. If the sale falls through because a condition or contingency of the sale is not met, this money or deposit is generally given back to the buyer.

exclusion to a listing contract. A term in a listing contract that allows the seller to sell his or her property directly to a party without paying the Realtor®. This clause is often used if the home seller had attempted to sell the home for sale by owner prior to listing and does not want to pay the Realtor® if one of the buyers that the seller introduced the property to comes back and purchases after the listing goes into effect.

exclusive listing. Also called an *exclusive listing contract*. This contract gives a specific real estate broker exclusive right to sell a property for a specified period of time.

expired listing. A home that was on the market for a period of time with a real estate agent or broker and is taken off the market when it fails to sell.

F

fair market value. The price a typical buyer would pay for a particular property during a normal marketing period, as negotiated with a typical seller.

Fannie Mae. The Federal National Mortgage Association (FNMA) is a congressionally-chartered, shareholder-owned company and the nation's largest supplier of home mortgage funding. Because Fannie Mae I the largest supplier of mortgage funding, its standards and requirements for determining a borrower's acceptability for lending are used as the rules by most mortgage companies and banks in writing mortgages.

fee simple. The highest form of ownership of real property. A fee simple deed includes rights and use of the property and anything attached to the property.

FHA loans. Mortgages that are insured by the Federal Housing Administration which is an agency of the United States Department of Housing and Urban Development (HUD). The Federal Housing Administration sets standards for loaning money that is loaned by private lenders but insured by FHA.

fixed rate mortgage. A mortgage where the interest rate paid by the borrower does not change during the life of the loan.

fixture. When a piece of personal property is physically attached to a home, it becomes a fixture and generally stays as part of the home. For example, a chandelier is a personal item, but when affixed to the ceiling in the dining room, it becomes a part of the home.

H

home inspection: A complete inspection of the structure and systems of a property.

home insurance or hazard insurance. Insurance to cover repairs to a property in the event of fire, vandalism, or other damage. Insurance is generally required of buyers by mortgage lenders when purchasing a home. Hazard insurance often has stipulations that do not cover natural disasters such as floods, earthquakes, or sink holes.

home warranty. A type of insurance purchased in order to cover repairs in a home. Most common home warranties insure against the breakdown in systems such as heating, hot water, plumbing, electric, and appliances. Some home warranties also include warranties of the roof and basement. A buyer can purchase coverage for themselves or they can request that the homeowner provide a home warranty as part of the agreement of sale.

HUD-1. Also known as a *settlement statement* or a *closing statement.* The document that outlines the final accounting of all fees paid by the buyer and the net amount paid to the seller.

L

lien. A legal debt against the property that must be paid off when the property is sold. A mortgage is a specific type of lien.

loan to value. The ratio between the amount a buyer or borrower is mortgaging and the purchase price or appraised value of the home. For example, if a buyer mortgages $80,000 on a $100,000 home purchase, the loan to value ratio is 80%.

M

material defect. In a real estate sale, a physical defect in the property, such as a foundation crack or roof leak. Material defects can affect the property's use or property value.

mortgage. A legal document that pledges a property to a lender in return for money borrowed from a lender. Some states use *first trust deeds* instead of mortgages.

move-up buyer. A home purchaser who is moving or stepping up from one home to another home that is either larger than the original home or in a more preferred location for the buyer.

O

owner financing. In a real estate transaction, owner financing refers to the property seller financing part or all of the sale for the buyers. For example, a buyer paying $200,000 for a home may put $25,000 down, finance $150,000 through bank loans, and ask the seller to hold an additional loan for the remaining $25,000.

P

personal property. Any furniture, clothing, or other items in a home that are not part of the real estate and not attached to the real estate.

preapproval. A written statement from a lender starting the buyer has been preapproved for a mortgage of a certain amount. The written statement lays out the terms of the approval and any requirements to receive a final approval, including an appraisal of the home.

prequalification. A written statement from a lender or mortgage broker sating the buyer's qualifications for purchasing a home. These statements are generally based on a review by the lender of the buyer's assets, income, and debts. The review may or may not include a credit report. A prequalification is generally not as strong as a preapproval, because for a prequalification the lender typically relies on the buyer's verbal testimony of his or her assets, income, and debts. Verifications are done prior to a full preapproval.

Purchase contract. The sales contract or agreement of sale for the sale of real estate.

Q

qualifying rations. One of the primary lenders use to determine a buyer's qualifications for obtaining a mortgage and paying back the lender. There are two ratios used to determine the buyer's maximum mortgage payment. The *front ratio* is the calculation of the buyer's mortgage payment, including taxes and insurance, as a percentage of total monthly income. For example, if the mortgage payment, including taxes and insurance, is $1000 and the buyer's monthly income, before taxes, is $4000, his or her front ratio is 25%. The *back ratio* is a calculation of the buyer's entire recurring monthly debt as a percentage of income. A buyer must fall within the acceptable range of a particular mortgage on both the front and back ends in order to qualify.

R

real estate agent. A licensed professional whose job it is to list, market, and sell real property.

Real Estate Settlement Procedures Act (RESPA). A consumer protection law that requires mortgage lenders to give borrowers advanced notice of closing costs.

Realtor®. A real estate broker or agent who holds a membership in the National Association of Realtors®.

S

second mortgage A mortgage that has a second position to the first or primary mortgage on a house.

settlement statement. Also known as a closing statement or an *HUD-1*. The document outlining the final accounting of all fees paid by the buyer and seller and the net amount due from the buyer and the net amount paid to the seller.

T

title insurance. Insurance that protects the buyer or lender depending on the type of policy, against the losses from disputes over liens or ownership of a property.

title insurance company. A company that examines and insures titles to real estate.

title search. An examination of the deeds and the mortgages against the property. A *full title search* also includes examination of any county and municipal records to determine if there are any liens against the property.

transfer tax. Taxes paid to a government body, such as the state, county, or local municipality when a property is sold or transferred to another person.

townhouse. A home attached to other homes in a row.

U

URAR. Uniform Residential Appraisal Report. The most commonly accepted appraisal form by lenders.

Interview Checklist
for Agents

☐ Are you a full-time agent?

_____

_____

☐ What kind of real estate experience do you have?

_____

_____

☐ How many properties have you sold in the last year, or in your career?

_____

_____

☐ What is your average list price to sales price ratio?

_____

_____

☐ Have you sold other homes in my neighborhood or area?

_____

_____

☐ Do you have any assistants or support staff?

_____

_____

☐ Do you have any references?

_____

_____

☐ Can you provide me with samples of marketing you've done on other properties?

_____

_____

☐ How often will you be in contact with me during the term of the listing?

_____

_____

☐ Do you offer any guarantees?

_____

_____

☐ Am I locked into this listing for six months?

_____

_____

☐ Will you send me copies of all advertising?

_____

_____

☐ What do you believe sets your marketing and service apart from other Realtors®
?

_____

_____

☐ At what point in time would we need to sit back down and re-evaluate the marketing?

_____

_____

appendix b:

Useful Websites

Home Marketing Websites

- **Craigslist.org**
  A free classified advertising site

- **Zillow.com**
  Real estate valuation site that allows owners and Realtors® to add listings for free.

- **Realtor.com**
  The most-visited real estate site on the Internet. This is a good place to start looking for property values, but a home may only be added to the database by a licensed Realtor®.

- **Century21.com**
  A wealth of information on the process of selling a home, and another great source of listings for comparable property values.

- **ZapHomeSearch.com**
  My personal favorite!

- **Forsalebyowner.com**
  A pay website that allows owners to market a home on his or her own.

Assistance for For Sale By Owners

- **RealFlyer.com**
  Flyers and brochures printed for your home

Index

www.ingramcontent.com/pod-product-compliance
Lightning Source LLC
Chambersburg PA
CBHW031953190326
41520CB00007B/234